THE **CURSE** OF THE **MOGUL**

What's Wrong with the World's Leading Media Companies

JONATHAN A. KNEE

BRUCE C. GREENWALD

AND

AVA SEAVE

PORTFOLIO/PENGUIN

To the great teachers in our past
Jonathan A. Knee: Sigmund Koch, Alasdair MacIntyre, Judith Sadowsky
Bruce C. Greenwald: Dave Bradford, Bill Branson, Bob Solow
Ava Seave: Michael Harper, Jim McLaughlin, Leonard Murphy

PORTFOLIO/PENGUIN
Published by the Penguin Group
Penguin Group (USA) Inc., 375 Hudson Street, New York, New York 10014, U.S.A. • Penguin Group (Canada), 90 Eglinton Avenue East, Suite 700, Toronto, Ontario, Canada M4P 2Y3 (a division of Pearson Penguin Canada Inc.) • Penguin Books Ltd, 80 Strand, London WC2R 0RL, England • Penguin Ireland, 25 St. Stephen's Green, Dublin 2, Ireland (a division of Penguin Books Ltd) • Penguin Books Australia Ltd, 250 Camberwell Road, Camberwell, Victoria 3124, Australia (a division of Pearson Australia Group Pty Ltd) • Penguin Books India Pvt Ltd, 11 Community Centre, Panchsheel Park, New Delhi–110 017, India • Penguin Group (NZ), 67 Apollo Drive, Rosedale, North Shore 0632, New Zealand (a division of Pearson New Zealand Ltd) • Penguin Books (South Africa) (Pty) Ltd, 24 Sturdee Avenue, Rosebank, Johannesburg 2196, South Africa

Penguin Books Ltd, Registered Offices: 80 Strand, London WC2R 0RL, England

First published in the United States of America by Portfolio,
a member of Penguin Group (USA) Inc. 2009
This paperback edition with a new postscript published 2011

10 9 8 7 6 5 4 3 2 1

THE LIBRARY OF CONGRESS HAS CATALOGED THE HARDCOVER EDITION AS FOLLOWS:

Knee, Jonathan A.
 The curse of the mogul : what's wrong with the world's leading media companies / Jonathan A. Knee, Bruce C. Greenwald, and Ava Seave.
 p. cm.
Includes bibliographical references and index.
ISBN 978-1-59184-264-4 (hc.)
ISBN 978-1-59184-390-0 (pbk.)
 1. Mass media—Management. I. Greenwald, Bruce C. N., 1946– II. Seave, Ava. III. Title.
P96.M34K62 2009
302.23068—dc22   2009019954

Printed in the United States of America
Set in Goudy Old Style • Designed by Jennifer Wasson

THE CURSE OF THE MOGUL

Jonathan A. Knee is a longtime investment banker and the author of *The Accidental Investment Banker*. He is also an adjunct professor and director of the Media Program at Columbia Business School.

Bruce C. Greenwald, an economist, is the Robert Heilbrunn Professor of Finance and Asset Management at Columbia Business School. His books include *Competition Demystified*.

Ava Seave is principal and cofounder of the consulting firm Quantum Media. She is also an associate adjunct professor at both Columbia Business School and Columbia Journalism School.

———

Praise for *Curse of the Mogul*

"The authors argue lucidly that the cadre of media moguls who dominated headlines for much of the past two or three decades have been deal junkies chasing rivals out of misguided notions about how to achieve long-term success. . . . It's hard to argue with these folks." —*Fortune*

"The results of twenty years of obsessive-compulsive media combinations—something like a thousand companies reduced to five—are succinctly outlined in the best media book of the season: *The Curse of the Mogul*, by Jonathan Knee, Bruce Greenwald, and Ava Seave."
—Michael Wolff, author of *The Man Who Owns the News*

"The moguls have justified deal making with platitudes: the importance of globalization, the necessity of convergence, and the slogan that content is king. Mr. Knee and colleagues demolish the business arguments derived from these banalities." —John Kay, *Financial Times*

"Knee, Greenwald, and Seave have written a must-read book for students of the media industry and strategy. Stressing the quest for margins over mogul status and a drive for efficiency over the best table at Michael's, they weave strong economic advice for those who would try to understand—or even make money in—the media business."
—Glenn Hubbard, dean and Russell L. Carson Professor of Finance and Economics, Columbia Business School

"*The Curse of the Mogul* is a true blessing for anyone with a stake in the future of news, books, movies, music, TV, or any other branch of the entertainment-information complex. The authors' diagnosis of the malaise afflicting media companies is brilliant, and their conclusion that bad management decisions rather than inexorable economic trends are mostly to blame is compelling."

—Sylvia Nasar, author of *A Beautiful Mind* and Knight Professor of Business Journalism, Columbia University

"Worthy of a juicy TV drama." —*Star*

"[*The Curse of the Mogul*] delivers by separating real from imagined aspects of the competitive landscape." —*The Deal*

"Any media executive who doesn't 'get' *The Curse of the Mogul*—or anyone who doesn't think it will be a long-term bestseller—proves the point that authors Jonathan A. Knee, Bruce C. Greenwald, and Ava Seave are making throughout the book: most media companies . . . have their proverbial heads in the sand, operate on an outmoded business model that was probably always destined to fail, and stick with their old ways out of fear, inertia, and, yes, vanity." —*Asset International*

"This thoughtful analysis of the media business appears to be also a textbook for consulting seminars and required reading for business students." —*Booklist*

"The media business has long been the home of outsized egos and shrunken returns on investment. Three media experts . . . explain why this gap exists in this meticulously detailed and documented study. This book is unusually fine-grained in its arguments and detail, reflecting the deep experience of the authors and the extensive research they conducted. . . . Their arguments have to be taken seriously." —*Strategy+Business*

"It is a rare and and welcome analysis that brings these numbers out into daylight, measuring media companies by the drab metrics of shareholder value and not, say, by the number of weekend wins at the box office or the number of photo ops with Johnny Depp. . . . Their critique is especially worth considering as media companies face a brutal and fast-changing landscape." —The Warp

Contents

Acknowledgments

This book grew out of the Strategic Management of Media course we offer at Columbia Business School, and so our greatest debt is to the hundreds of students and dozens of visiting media executives who have contributed to the discussions that have filled that classroom and shaped our thinking. In this regard, Phyllis Grann and Erin Bellissimo played a unique role in formulating and teaching the course since we began in 2003.

Over the course of this project we have had a number of diligent and resourceful research assistants—Elizabeth Milonopoulos, Justin Katz, Charles Murphy, Andrew Welch, Jane Edell—who helped gather the data on which the book is based. Karen Entwistle and Linda Neithardt helped keep us organized, if such a thing is possible. A long list of friends and colleagues have given feedback on the manuscript, provided some key pieces of data, or offered much-needed moral support. These include Judi Allen, Alison Anthoine, Christine Arrington, Alan Axelrod, Soren Bech, Beatrice Cassou, Anne Chen, Margaret Downs, Mark Gerson, Carla Graubard, Diana Greenwald, Nick Greenwald, Erica Gruen, Jean Hellering, Ruth Jarmul, Judd Kahn, Anne Kinard, David Knee, Elizabeth Koe, Myra Kogan, Melody Koh, Andrew Lipsher, Lisa McGahan, Chaille Maddox, John Edward Murphy, Lawrence M. Nagin, David Ow, Scott Patrick, Eric Rosen, Jason M. Sobol, Patrick Tierney, Gayle Turk, Hal Vogel, Paul Wojcik, and Almahdi Yousif. We are also lucky to have understanding and thoughtful agents in Elaine Markson and John Wright, who were wise enough to direct us to Adrian Zackheim at Portfolio as the right editor for this project. Our experience has confirmed their excellent judgment. Many others at Portfolio have provided great support, but Courtney Young in particular has helped make the book far more accessible to a general audience than any of us thought possible.

The authors, in addition to teaching and writing, have served as consultants and advisers to a variety of media companies, including some of those covered in this book. Although these experiences cannot have helped but inform our general perspective, this book is based exclusively on public information and selected interviews undertaken for that explicit purpose. The views expressed here should not be attributed to any organization or individual other than the ornery authors themselves. Although everyone knows that no good deed does go unpunished, it would be cruel and unusual to ascribe our idiosyncratic perspective to anyone kind enough to help us out on this project or generous enough to employ us. The buck stops with us.

Introduction:

The Curse of the Mogul

Hooray for Hollywood! Or maybe not.

The media industry is facing multiple financial and operational crises on an unprecedented scale. Just since 2000, the largest media conglomerates have written down well over $200 billion in assets from their collective balance sheets. These write-downs represent the real destruction of value from relentlessly overpaying for acquisitions, "strategic" investments, and contracts for content and talent. The magnitude of these losses also reflects the level of desperation among media moguls faced with new competitors, new technologies, and new customer demands.

As new as many of these challenges are, one aspect of the media business has remained unchanged for a generation: The performance of the leading companies has been lousy. Although things are getting worse, this has as much to do with the inability of the moguls to effectively adapt as with the underlying conditions. The basic approaches to confronting these challenges articulated by the leading executives will only exacerbate the problems. This book explains why these companies are following such self-destructive paths and proposes a radically different way to think about media businesses and their strategies. Understanding media and the historically fraught relationship with their moguls is essential to successfully navigating the changing landscape. The urgent issues we raise should matter to anyone who cares about the fate of the media sector—whether as a manager, as an investor, or as a consumer.

Our task is complicated by the aura of mystery that perennially cloaks the business of media. Today, even the biggest celebrity cannot escape the watchful eye of YouTube, TMZ.com, or smokinggun.com, but the same level of transparency doesn't apply to the operations of the media industry itself. This general lack of understanding about the media business derives in part from the nature of the unusually intense interest in the sector.

The media industry is a vast, heterogeneous web of enterprises representing hundreds of billions of dollars of value. Yet those segments that attract public and press attention do so based largely on their celebrity value, without regard to their relative size or profitability. The public is far more likely to pay attention to the replacement of an executive at a small, unprofitable hip-hop label than to the combination of two multibillion-dollar, high-margin yellow page companies. This disconnect between interest and actual economic value is not due just to our involvement in the media we use and experience on a regular basis. If that were the case, yellow pages would attract far more attention, as would consumer products companies in general. But how many people know the name of the CEO of Procter & Gamble as compared with Rupert Murdoch, despite the fact that P&G has many times the market value of News Corporation? Tide detergent, however, is better known than either Murdoch or the head of P&G—who happens to be Robert McDonald, a twenty-nine-year company veteran who became CEO in July 2009. What other consumer products' sales figures draw such broad public notice as weekend films' opening box-office receipts?

A second, subtler but equally powerful explanation for the level of both interest and confusion is a peculiarly American paranoia about the media industry's ability and inclination to mold the national psyche. This suspicion is reflected most prominently in articulated fears about the diversity and independence of news but extends to broader fears about potential cultural indoctrination by massive malevolent media conglomerates. These fears seem largely impervious to the dramatic and accelerating trends toward increased media fragmentation. In 2008, the top-twenty circulation newspapers in the United States had fifteen different owners, and only one of the half-dozen major media conglomerates owned any of them. Furthermore, these conglomerates—and indeed all traditional media outlets—have been rapidly losing share of both mind and revenue to relatively new and fiercely independent market entrants like Google.

The extent of these fears is reflected in a bizarre and incoherent labyrinth of regulations governing the ownership of media in the United States.

Cable operators in a market can own local newspapers, TV or radio stations, but the broadcasters and newspaper publishers generally can't own each other; a foreigner can own a newspaper, cable franchise, or movie studio but not a radio station; satellite TV operators or cable channel owners have no preset limit on how much of the country they can reach but broadcasters can only own stations reaching 38 percent of the country; and on and on.[1] There appears to be no limit to the public appetite for more and increasingly restrictive rules on what media companies can buy or do. When the Federal Communications Commission tried to relax some of these rules in 2003, the public outcry was so great that the Republican Senate voted overwhelmingly to reverse key parts of the commission's efforts.[2]

The great irony is that, because the First Amendment limits how much the government can restrict who owns what media and what they say, these regulations almost all hinge on the granting of broadcasting licenses. The airwaves are government property, so the government is generally free to place conditions on granting private individuals the right to use them. Broadcast media, however, are among those that are losing share of mind the fastest, as consumers spend more time online, on wireless devices, on cable, and on satellite. As broadcasters represent a smaller and smaller part of the media that the public consumes, these regulations become more and more irrelevant and the massive regulatory infrastructure that supports them becomes more and more anachronistic. The fact that these rules persist and new ones continue to be proposed is a reflection of just how deep-seated and irrational these fears about the media are.

A final explanation for the intense public interest in and deep inscruta-bility of the business side of the media industry is the person at the helm of many media conglomerates—the media mogul. To the extent that we have cast the proverbial "media mogul" as the villain of our story, we should clarify precisely what we mean by the term. In the title and throughout the book, media moguls are used as a metaphor for how the industry has been consis-tently operated and the results it has produced. Not all media CEOs always behave like "media moguls" in the sense we mean, but enough often do so that their presence represents a unique and defining attribute of the overall sector. As such, we use the term broadly to apply to any media company executive or owner with significant influence over significant operations. Nonetheless, because the term is pejorative, we consistently take pains to distinguish good "mogul" behavior from bad "mogul" behavior—and devote the entire last section of the book to providing examples of each. As a practical matter, all media CEOs have both some good and some bad mogul in them. To the extent that there is a "mogul's curse," as the title of this book provocatively suggests, it is that with disturbing consistency over time the bad begins to overwhelm the good.

For our purposes, there are three key characteristics of moguldom that together represent the primary warning signs that a mogul is turning toward the dark side:

1. Actual or perceived absolute power over the operations and governance of their business. This is sometimes achieved structurally through special classes of shares reserved for the mogul and his intimates, but sometimes through less formal means.

2. A variety of mythic attributes ranging from the ability to manage creative talent and select ultimately successful creative properties to uncanny prophetic skills with respect to the future shape and direction of the industry specifically and media consumption trends generally. All of these attributed talents somehow elude traditional description, explanation, or evaluation but explain why terms like *visionary*, *brilliant*, and *genius* are applied with some regularity.

3. An unhealthy but relentless interest in expanding the scope of their domains, usually with other people's money, but with no corresponding reduction in control over the business. Acquisition is the preferred growth vehicle of the mogul.

Well before the wave of superstar CEOs who became all the fashion in the late 1970s,[3] the public knew the names of many of those who ran media companies. Louis B. Mayer ran a company, Metro-Goldwyn-Mayer, that was a tiny fraction of the size of Standard Oil, but his name was probably as well known as that of Rockefeller, and maybe still is. We will examine the question of whether the industry draws attention to the moguls or the other way around, but there are clearly factors intrinsic to the moguls that have accentuated their profiles.

At least historically, the mogul's own "voice" was very much reflected in the product. This was not just true of, say, a Pulitzer newspaper versus a Hearst newspaper, where the style of journalism—not just the substance of editorials—clearly manifested the owner/operator's aesthetic and political sensibility. It was also true of most forms of broad-based consumer media. As the great director Billy Wilder described the early days of the movie industry:

"Studios had faces then. They had their own style. They could bring you blindfolded into a movie house and you looked up and you knew. 'Hey, this is an RKO picture. This is a Paramount picture. This is an MGM picture.' They had a certain handwriting, like publishing houses."[4] That handwriting belonged to the particular media mogul with which each studio was associated. Today the notion that a viewer could guess which studio produced a particular film seems laughable.[5]

Media companies now typically eschew any notion of promoting a particular company-wide corporate aesthetic or political agenda in favor of a more "fair and balanced" approach. Given the diversity of audiences being targeted by the portfolio of brands housed by even modestly sized media companies, more controlling approaches are simply less practical. But what does remain of this early legacy of entrepreneurial firms dominated by an opinionated patriarch is an industry overwhelmingly controlled by families or other closely held private groups. Even among public media companies, most are still controlled under so-called dual-class share structures. These structures provide "super shares" to founding shareholders that ensure their continued control even as their economic ownership is diluted to, in some cases, a tiny minority.

Of the fifteen largest U.S. media companies by revenue in 2005, only four are broadly held public companies without absolute control or disproportionate influence by a mogul.[6] If Comcast consummates its acquisition of NBC Universal, that number will be reduced to three. Although excessive debt has loosened the grip of some moguls on these media companies, their likely replacement is a small group of banks, private equity investors, and distressed debt hedge funds who are emerging as a new breed of mogul.

The ability of the controlling holders to do as they will, for better or for worse, without fear of at least immediate repercussions gives media moguls a certain swagger not as readily found in other industries. And that swagger reinforces the public fascination with the sector.

Media moguls are also the source of the most damaging disinformation about the nature of media businesses. This book examines in some detail a number of oft-repeated myths that have become entrenched conventional wisdom in the industry and demonstrates that each is demonstrably wrong. But the core media myth that allows all the others to flourish is this: The media industry involves managing creative talent and artistic product and as such is not subject to appraisal using traditional strategic, financial, or management metrics.

TABLE I.1 Largest U.S. Media Companies ($ in millions)

Company	Controlling Mogul/CEO	2005 Net U.S. Revenue	2005 Parent Global Revenue
Time Warner	**/Jeffrey Bewkes**	**$33,728**	**$43,652**
Comcast	Roberts Family/Brian Roberts	22,078	22,255
Walt Disney	**/Robert Iger**	**17,154**	**31,944**
News Corp.	Rupert Murdoch/ Rupert Murdoch	12,563	23,859
NBC Universal	**/Jeff Zucker**	**12,437**	**14,689**
Liberty Group	John Malone/Greg Maffei	12,343	N/A
CBS Corp.	Sumner Redstone/ Les Moonves	11,797	14,536
Cox Enterprises	Cox Family/James Kennedy	9,087	12,000
Viacom	Sumner Redstone/ Philippe Dauman	8,249	9,610
EchoStar	Charlie Ergen/Charlie Ergen	8,048	8,426
Advance	Newhouse Family/ Newhouse Family	7,536	N/A
Gannett Co.	**/Craig Dubow**	**6,399**	**7,599**
Tribune Co.	Sam Zell's Creditors/Randy Michaels	5,392	5,596
Charter Communications	Paul Allen & Former Creditors/ Michael Lovett	5,254	5,254
Clear Channel Communications	Bain, TH Lee & Mays Family/ Mark Mays	5,018	6,610

Note: Boldface represents broadly held public companies.

Sources: Advertising Age Data Center. Pro forma for Liberty's acquisition of News Corp.'s DirecTV stake.

All great myths have two things in common: They have a grain of truth and they serve to protect some entrenched interest. The grain of truth here is not hard to identify: Managing Jennifer Lopez does involve radically different skills from managing the efficient manufacture of widgets. Nor is the entrenched interest that needs protection difficult to discern: With no real metrics to be judged against, a media mogul can always come up with some basis to justify his performance.

Media moguls and industry analysts who should know better actually do come close to claiming that media management should not be subjected to the same performance standards as other businesses. And when they don't say it directly, the incoherent media-speak that is used as justification for the latest acquisition, strategic initiative, or restructuring strongly implies a lack of interest in these more economically grounded criteria.

How else could one explain the Weinstein brothers' ability to raise over $1 billion to finance a new company under their control in 2005? With few hard assets and based essentially on their supposed talent-spotting and management skills, the Weinsteins' checkered past proved no hindrance to attracting investors and lenders—no matter that Disney, their previous employer, complained that the business the Weinsteins ran there had made money in only two of the last five years[7] or that a recently published book documented allegations of highly aggressive behavior, both financial and, in the case of Harvey, physical.[8] The Weinsteins' success at fund-raising also makes clear that it is not simply a gullible public that has fallen under the spell of the mogul myths, but sophisticated investors. The Weinstein Company got its money exclusively from institutional investors and wealthy individuals in a private transaction. The largest equity holders could hardly be accused of naïveté: They are Fidelity and Wellington, two leading global money management firms, and Goldman Sachs, still the leading global investment bank.

But the most damning evidence supporting our claim can be found in the one place that this book focuses on with the same intensity that media moguls and their chroniclers avoid like the plague: the data. The shocking, evident, persistent, and oddly ignored fact is that the financial returns of media companies significantly and relentlessly fall below those of the stock market as a whole. Media moguls have had remarkable success in shifting the conversation to whether content is king or if distribution is still relevant or how to manage convergence. The press and industry analysts seem more interested in what the moguls are having for breakfast at the latest mogul retreat rather than asking the one screamingly obvious question: For all the excitement, glamour, drama, and publicity releases they produce, why can't these companies manage to come close to delivering the kind of returns available from closing your eyes and throwing a dart?

On average, over the ten-year period ending in 2005, the media conglomerates achieved less than a third of the returns available from the S&P and none of them came closer than four hundred basis points (or 4 percent)

TABLE I.2 Largest Media Conglomerate Total Shareholder Ten-Year Returns

Last 10 Years—as of 12/31/05	
News Corp.	5.0%
Viacom	3.3%
Disney	2.6%
Time Warner	(0.7%)
Media Conglom. Average	2.5%
S&P	9.0%

of this benchmark. This data is available to anyone who cares to look and has access to the Internet. But many don't look and that, for obvious reasons, is in the interest of the moguls who are responsible for this performance.[9]

We performed the same analysis for every possible ten-year period from the most recent going back twelve years. For the ten years ending near the peak of the Internet boom on December 31, 2000, the conglomerate index did manage to approximate the overall S&P returns, but for every other ten-year period, the conglomerates meaningfully underperformed the S&P as a group.

Only a very careful selection of dates can make any of the individual media conglomerates look good, and some of these occasional periods of outperformance are a bit of a fluke. For instance, Time Warner outperformed between 1990 and 2000, but this end point represents a moment in time when AOL's takeover at a 71 percent premium was pending—and the true value of AOL's shares was not yet fully appreciated. That said, we will examine in great detail in the book's final section the most striking examples of extended periods of successful conglomerate performance for clues as to how to best maneuver in the current environment.

For now, what is most relevant is the huge gulf between the actual drivers of the rare periods of superior media company performance and the reasons given by the media moguls at their respective helms at the time. If we were to believe the moguls, their success was the result of strategic foresight, visionary acquisitions, harnessing synergies between divisions, and a supernatural ability to predict the outcome of the creative process. Our analysis will demonstrate, however, that in fact these superior returns were overwhelmingly the result of far more pedestrian, but far more effective approaches—raising prices, using low-cost production techniques, and employing cooperative capacity rationalization strategies.

The moguls' tendency to attribute their brief periods of actual success to fantastical factors seems designed in part to make them seem indispensable to the business rather than the distractions they often are. Rather than harmless puffery, this systematic misdiagnosis of the causes of success in media makes it highly unlikely that the moguls will be able to repeat this achievement. And at no time has the industry been in such dire need of a repeat performance.

The most cynical explanation of mogul obfuscation is that their objective is wealth creation among the moguls themselves, their lieutenants, the "talent," and others who benefit from company largesse rather than among the shareholders. Come to think of it, the last time you heard a media mogul referred to as a genius was probably the fawning of a famous artist or producer who just signed a multimillion-dollar multipicture deal. And given how many moguls absolutely control a majority of their companies' governance while holding a minority stake in their economics, maybe their genius is in their ability to continue to attract investors who have little to show for their trouble and even less to say about it.

At some level, it doesn't matter whether moguls' misguided strategic approaches represent genuine beliefs or are an elaborate put-on to justify pay and perks unrelated to performance. Either way, without drastic action, there is little reason to think that performance during the next ten years will be any better—and it could get much worse. The drastic action required here entails going back to basics: understanding the key characteristics of various media segments and applying generally applicable business strategy principles to determine the best way forward. This book simply attempts to strip away the mogul-orchestrated noise around the media industry and examine the individual businesses on their own terms.

Although hardly revolutionary on its face, the stark contrast between the management strategies that follow from this approach and those that are regularly articulated by the moguls suggests how much work needs to be done. A huge disparity exists between the media's conventional wisdom and our economically grounded framework for thinking about the media industry. This fundamental disconnect will become blaringly obvious as we define the media landscape and our approach in the first few chapters.

A recurring theme is that most media moguls started by running focused and efficient operations. These moguls originally had little recourse to the jargon that has since come to characterize their justifications for otherwise incomprehensible strategic initiatives or just plain poor performance. The curse of the mogul is that even the very best media executives eventually fall prey to these tendencies. Our objective is no less than to break the curse by shining the light of historic performance and traditional economic theory on this critical sector.

PART I | **The Framework**

1 | The Media Landscape

Defining the media industry is complicated by the moguls who have clogged the media vernacular with content-free catchphrases on the one hand and diverted attention to the celebrity-driven aspects of the business on the other. Both of these phenomena are perfectly captured by a full-page *New York Times* advertisement taken out on July 5, 2001, by Vivendi Universal announcing its almost $2 billion acquisition of Houghton Mifflin. Vivendi Universal has since been largely dismantled and Houghton Mifflin has changed hands twice more. At the time, however, Vivendi Universal was a company on the move under the leadership of a former banker turned media mogul named Jean-Marie Messier.

Messier had become the leader of a French water utility in 1996 and quickly infused it with his grand vision of becoming "the world's preferred creator and provider of personalized information, entertainment, and services to consumers anywhere, at any time, across all distribution platforms and devices."[1] Messier wanted his company to own it all. The title of Messier's first book captures his mogul ambitions: *J6M.com* is a reference to Messier's nickname from a French comedy show.[2] The appellation stood for *Jean-Marie Messier Moi-Même Maître du Monde*, which translates as "Jean-Marie Messier, Myself, Master of the World."

In the broad scheme of the overall frenzy of investments that occupied Messier's half-dozen years at the helm—a collection of "strategic" stakes, joint ventures, and acquisitions that included areas as diverse as a Moroccan telephone company, U.S. and U.K. satellite broadcasting, European Internet portal and French mobile phone licenses—the Houghton Mifflin deal does not really stand out in either absolute size or strangeness. By the end, the number and quantum of transactions exceeded one hundred and $100 billion, respectively.[3] Still, the "selling" of the strategic relevance of the Houghton Mifflin transaction to shareholders and the public is reflective of an important phenomenon that drives the need for this book in the first place—the lengths to which moguls will go to disguise the nature of what they do and the businesses they own.

Houghton was a struggling publisher of elementary-school textbooks. The company was a distant fourth among the four major players who competed intensely to have their textbooks "adopted" by states and localities as part of their official curriculum. Houghton's smallest and least profitable business was a tiny consumer book publisher (this is known as "trade publishing" in the industry) with a list of children's books making up less than half[4] of that division's sales. In broad terms, Houghton was expected to have $1.1 billion in 2001 revenues, of which less than 10 percent represented the entirety of the trade publishing arm.

Under the headline "Curious George Goes to Vivendi Universal," produced in the immediately recognizable typeface of the perennially popular children's books first published by Houghton in 1941, appeared a letter to shareholders from Monsieur Messier.

"Soon," wrote Messier in the letter surrounded by a half-dozen precious images of the charming title character of the series, "George will be able to feed his curiosity by tapping into Vivendi Universal's incredible content and distribution network."

The advertisement is disingenuous in two important ways. First, and most obviously, it is misleading about the very nature of the business being purchased, which is overwhelmingly an educational publisher rather than a children's trade book publisher. Showing a fourth-grade math textbook would be less compelling even if more truthful than showing adorable pictures of Curious George. More subtly but more substantively, the image of George is clearly meant to imply some kind of synergy emerging from the combination of the textbook publisher and the entertainment conglomerate. But even if the trade book publishing were a more significant part of the overall Houghton business, it would not make this false implication any more true: Houghton did not own the movie, television, audio, or merchandising rights to *Curious George*. Authors, in this case Margret and Hans Rey, the remarkable German couple who escaped Paris on bicycles with the original *Curious George* manuscript as the Nazis invaded, typically retain these and

FIGURE 1.1 Universal Vivendi Shareholder Letter

all other ancillary rights for themselves. These are then auctioned separately to the highest bidder, who should turn out to be the party in the best position to fully exploit the character in the particular medium up for grabs. For their part, executives at Universal Studios were surprised by the purchase. As far as they were concerned, Universal already had the relevant rights and they had been actively developing a *Curious George* project for some time. Vivendi Universal's acquisition of the company that happens to publish *Curious George* books gave it no significant advantage in securing rights in media other than books. There may be some marketing efficiencies from combining the book publisher with the movie studio that had separately already obtained some film rights. But major studios like Fox and Paramount with larger sister trade publishing operations (News and Viacom have owned HarperCollins and Simon & Schuster, respectively) are usually not the high bidders for the film rights of their authors, so any such benefits are marginal at best. When Viacom spun off CBS in 2005 it expressed no strategic regret in including Simon & Schuster with the separated broadcasting assets. Indeed, Universal itself had been the long-time owner of a larger trade publisher, Putnam, with a highly respected children's list. Seagram divested Putnam in 1996 barely a year after buying Universal precisely because of the lack of any apparent synergistic benefit from joint ownership.

The great irony is that by the time Universal got around to making a Curious George movie, it had already sold Houghton Mifflin to a consortium of private equity buyers. All of which makes the crescendo of Messier's missive to his hapless shareholders all the more comical in retrospect:

> With Houghton Mifflin, we will further reinforce our goal of becoming the world's preferred creator and provider of personalized information, education and entertainment across all distribution platforms and devices.
>
> Welcome George. Here's to your insatiable curiosity.

Presumably Messier was hoping that his investors did not share George's curiosity, at least with respect to what rights Houghton owned, what the real nature of the other 90+ percent of Houghton was, and whether any of it meaningfully promoted Vivendi Universal's breathtakingly broad strategic objective.

Our point here is simply to emphasize how much of the information media moguls present about their businesses is designed to obscure rather than enlighten. Given the performance of the big media conglomerates, this is not surprising. The mere existence of a group of companies called "the media conglomerates" is suggestive of the issues faced by the industry. It is as if the media industry did not get the memo the rest of the business community got back in the 1980s that conglomerates do not create value.[5] The usual retort is that because these "conglomerates" are within the magical realm of media, they offer valuable interdivisional synergies not available to other mere "industrial" conglomerates. Even when moguls seek to distance themselves from the term *synergy*, they claim that "breadth" of businesses gives management an understanding of key issues that are unique to media and its shifting technology.[6]

The tables on the following pages demonstrate that there is no consistency and barely any correlation among the twenty starkly different business segments operated by the different media conglomerates. Table 1.1 looks at the six major conglomerates that include a movie studio and Table 1.2 includes eight other multibillion-dollar consumer-oriented media conglomerates that operate in at least three different lines of business.[7] Some studios have TV networks, some TV networks have TV stations, some TV stations have cable channels, some cable channels have cable systems, and so on. But in every case, some don't. And in general there is no evidence that those that do operate more profitably than those that do not.

The one consistency that jumps out is that all of the studios seem to have some interest in cable channels. On closer inspection, however, there is less to this than meets the eye. Sony, Columbia Pictures' parent company, for instance, owns insignificant channel operations predominantly in the form of partial stakes in international channels. Even some of the larger channels associated with the studios, like Disney's ownership of ESPN, represent only partial stakes, making operational synergies highly unlikely. In addition, the fact that almost all of the conglomerates without studios also own cable channels suggests that they do not view their lack of movie production as a competitive disadvantage to participating in the segment. Finally, Discovery Communications, one of the most successful cable channel operators, achieves this performance with no significant presence in any other media segment.

The stunning diversity of businesses with little apparent operating connection housed within these conglomerates suggests the potential impossibility of constructing a straightforward general definition of media. Mercifully, despite the moguls' best efforts at obfuscation, capturing what all these media enterprises and others have in common is much less difficult than understanding what makes them different. All of the businesses under the media umbrella share one essential trait: They are engaged in the production and distribution of information and entertainment.

TABLE 1.1 Overview of Media Landscape: Studio Conglomerates

		News Corp.	Time Warner	Sony	Comcast/NBC Universal	Disney	Viacom
Content	Movie/TV Studios	●	●	●	●	●	●
	Sports	◐			●		
	Music			●		◐	
	Book Publishing	●				◐	
	Business Information	●					
	Video Games			●		◐	◔
	Magazine Publishing	◐	●			◔	
	Online Content/Social Network	●	◔	◔	◔	◐	◐
	e-Commerce			◐	◐	◐	
	Direct Marketing	●					
	Newspapers	●					
Distribution	TV Networks	●	◐		●	●	
	Cable Channels	●	●	◐	●	●	●
	Theme Parks				●	●	
	Outdoor	◐					
	Radio Broadcasting					◐	
	TV Broadcasting	●			●	●	
	Satellite Broadcasting	●					
	Cable Systems		*		●		

Studio Conglomerates

● Signifies a strong presence. No circle implies no (or minimal) presence.

TABLE 1.2 Overview of Media Landscape: Other Conglomerates

	Vivendi	Cox Enterprises	Bertelsmann	Hearst	Advance	Liberty Media	CBS
Content							
Movie/TV Studios	◐		◐			◔	◐
Sports						◐	
Music	●						
Book Publishing			●			◔	●
Business Information					●		
Video Games	●						
Magazine Publishing		◕	●	●	●		
Online Content/Social Network		◔	◔	●	◔	◕	◐
e-Commerce		◐	◔	◐		◕	
Direct Marketing		◐	●	◐			
Newspapers		●	●	●	●		
Distribution							
TV Networks							●
Cable Channels	●	◔		◕	◐	●	◐
Theme Parks							
Outdoor							●
Radio Broadcasting		●	◔	◔			●
TV Broadcasting		●	●	●		◔	●
Satellite Broadcasting						◔	
Cable Systems		●			◕		

Studio Conglomerates

● Signifies a strong presence. No circle implies no (or minimal) presence.

TABLE 1.3   Total Media Spending (2002–2007) ($ in billions)

	2002	2003	2004	2005	2006	2007	
Institutional Spending	145	155	171	188	207	226	25%
Consumer Spending	161	171	181	186	195	206	24%
Subtotal Direct Spending	307	326	352	374	401	432	49%
All Advertising and Market Spending	345	357	383	404	428	444	51%
TOTAL Media Spending	652	683	734	778	830	876	100%

Source: 2008 Veronis Suhler Stevenson Communications Industry Forecast (22nd edition).

This definition covers a wide range of businesses beyond even the scope of activities pursued by some media conglomerate or other. The media we actually experience directly—music, books, TV, movies, and, increasingly, the Internet—mostly targets consumers. Media, though, extends to business and professional markets as well. In fact, more media is sold to institutions than to individuals, even if the multibillion-dollar global businesses that do so—with decidedly unsexy monikers like Wolters Kluwer and Reed Elsevier—are not exactly household names. A respected survey of the U.S. media market estimates the total size to be $885 billion, with just under half of this coming from direct spending on media by individuals and institutions. Just over half comes from spending by companies to reach those individuals and institutions through advertising and other marketing tools. It is worth highlighting some of the differences between the different media markets.

CONSUMER MARKETS

By *consumer markets* we mean any product sold to or otherwise targeting individuals in their personal rather than professional lives. These should be most familiar to all readers and represent the bread-and-butter businesses of the conglomerates profiled: the latest movie, CD, TV show, or bestseller; a social networking Web site, an amusement park, a football game, or a celebrity magazine.

Think about consumer markets as either general interest or special interest. General interest media (or "mass" media) seeks the broadest audience possible: a general entertainment cable channel, *People* magazine, Yahoo, or any media in pursuit of a "blockbuster." Special interest media (sometimes called "niche" media) targets some shared demographic, psychographic, or geographic characteristic of the user group. Among many other implications of the emergence of the Internet as a major new force in the media industry is the ability to cost-effectively reach increasingly narrowly defined special interest groups with their very own media properties. This "Long Tail" phenomenon has been the subject of books and articles of varying levels of quality,[8] some of which seem to suggest that niche media was "invented" by the Internet. It was not. Consumer media will always represent some mixture of mass and specialized media.

The line between general and special interest is not a scientific one. But what distinguishes true "niche media" is that the product itself is designed around the shared interest or activity. The Food Channel vs. USA Network; *Fly Fisherman vs. Newsweek;* dailycandy.com vs. MSN.com. Certain media properties are structurally hybrids—for instance, a daily newspaper seeks to attract the broadest mass audience within a niche geography.

In addition, one generation's general interest media can become another's special interest media and vice versa. For instance, in the early 1900s farming magazines were quite mainstream, but today they are more of a niche. For decades in the early part of the century, *Successful Farming* was the publisher Meredith's largest-circulation publication, although today it is dwarfed by many of its other titles such as *Better Homes & Gardens.* And *Progressive Farmer,* owned by Time Inc. through its Southern Progress subsidiary until only a couple of years ago, once boasted a circulation of 1.4 million, although it is now much less than half that level.[9]

Niche media business models offer several clear advantages. On the one hand, an advertiser of a product used exclusively or predominantly by the intended audience of a niche media property will pay substantially more for every audience member it reaches. On a per reader basis, Nike will certainly pay more for access to the audience of *Runner's World* magazine than for the audience of even a high-end general interest magazine like *Vanity Fair.* Because niche products are by definition more personalized, they foster both greater user engagement and a tighter sense of community among users, increasing customer captivity. Accordingly, the advertising rates charged for niche media are far higher than for general interest media, yielding correspondingly higher profit margins overall.

Despite these advantages and others we will explore later, media moguls have a clear preference for general interest media. Size seems to matter for moguls, and general interest media tends to be bigger. Unfortunately, this is true on the top line (revenues) but usually not on the bottom line (profits). And let's face it—the Christmas party for *Runner's World* probably does not have quite the pizzazz of the *Vanity Fair* Oscar party.

BUSINESS AND PROFESSIONAL MARKETS

If niche consumer media often lack the sex appeal of general interest media, media serving institutional markets are even less likely to draw the attention of traditional media moguls. Given that spending on media by institutions surpasses that by individuals, size can't explain this phenomenon. As the story of Messier's committed efforts to obfuscate the true nature of the Houghton Mifflin acquisition reflects, however, there seems to be something deeper about the inherently unsexy nature of institutional markets with which these moguls would rather not be associated. Although school textbooks are ultimately used by individual students, the sale is an institutional one: The marketing of the product is to the state education administrators who make the key buying decisions. Below is a breakdown of the largest categories of media within the pool of $226.1 billion purchased by institutions in 2007.

The largest category of institutional sales is Business and Professional Information Services. Business Information Services encompasses marketing, credit, risk, financial, human resources, and corporate information. These products include data, software, and services to help businesses operate efficiently and ensure that they are incorporating the most up-to-date information into critical corporate strategic and operating decisions. Professional

TABLE 1.4   2007 Institutional Media Spending ($ in billions)

	$	%
Business Information Services	94.3	42%
Professional Information	34.0	15%
Educational & Training Media and Services	34.1	15%
Business-to-Business Media	11.0	5%
Other	52.8	23%
TOTAL	226.1	100%

Source: 2008 Veronis Suhler Stevenson Communications Industry Forecast (22nd edition).

Information Services are primarily used in legal and regulatory markets and in the so-called STM industry (scientific, technical, and medical). Here the information provided is central to the specific professional function being performed—whether searching for a relevant case precedent, the proper drug dosage, or the right engineering part on a construction project.

In addition to the various Educational and Training Media and Services, of which the K–12 publishing sector we have already discussed represents barely a quarter, another major category is Business-to-Business (B2B) media. B2B media are used by one company trying to sell its products to another and the primary tools used are industry-focused magazines (known as trade rags in the vernacular), face-to-face events called trade shows, and various online information, directories, and marketplaces that have sprung up in recent years that target business markets.[10]

Given the lack of glamour of business and professional markets, one might expect the companies that engage in these businesses to look nothing like the massive consumer media conglomerates. And to be sure, there are hundreds of small businesses that operate in a single business or professional segment. There are even some larger segments that are dominated by relatively focused players: The consumer and business credit information segments, for instance, are the primary purview of Experian, Equifax, TransUnion, and Dun & Bradstreet. Overwhelmingly, however, the largest businesses in the largest segments are housed in enormous conglomerates whose composition does not appear to make any more or less sense than that of the consumer conglomerates.

Table 1.5 notes the key operating segments of a half dozen of the largest multibillion-dollar business and professional conglomerates. As in the case of their consumer counterparts, there is little consistency in the mix of business lines. And where patterns seem to emerge, they are more apparent than real. For instance, both Pearson and McGraw-Hill operate in both the K–12 and Higher Education markets, which on their face sound as if they could be "synergistic." But until recently, when they divested the segments, Thomson operated exclusively in Higher Education and Reed Elsevier exclusively in K–12. Both achieved profitability at or above the levels seen at McGraw-Hill or Pearson. Similarly, Scientific and Medical segments were often housed together. But Wolters Kluwer divested its Scientific segment with no apparent adverse impact on its Medical segment and both Reed and Thomson operate these segments quite separately. This is not to say that there is never any benefit from operating in these arguably adjacent sectors, only that there is much less there than meets the eye.

TABLE 1.5 Overview of Media Landscape: Business/Professional Conglomerates

		McGraw-Hill	Thomson Reuters	Reed Elsevier	Wolters Kluwer	Pearson	Bloomberg
Business Newspapers Magazines						●	●
Trade Shows				●			
B2B Magazines		◐		●		◔	
Consumer Books		◔				●	
Ratings		●					
Business/Professional Information	Other	●		◐	◔		
	Financial	●	●		◔	◔	●
	Medical		●	●	●		
	Scientific		●	●			
	Legal		●	●	●	◔	
K–12		●				●	
Higher Ed.		●				●	

The granddaddy of the Business and Professional group is Dun & Bradstreet. Over the previous decades, the company had built up the largest collection of business and professional media assets covering a wide range of research, ratings, business information, and even yellow page businesses. In 1996, in response to a persistently anemic stock price, the company began a process of deconstructing itself into almost a dozen constituent parts. A number of the pieces themselves are still major independent public companies today—Moody's, IMS Health, RH Donnelly, Gartner, and even the original Dun & Bradstreet asset are all leaders in their respective market segments.

The result of the radical restructuring of Dun & Bradstreet was to deliver to their long-suffering shareholders returns over the subsequent decade of around double what was available from the overall stock market.

One might have expected the remarkable success of the D&B experiment in corporate restructuring to have attracted followers. But although there has been striking consistency in the paths taken by the other public business and professional conglomerates during the decade spanning the mid-1990s to the mid-2000s, it has been in a very different direction. And it has yielded very different results.

The case of the Dutch conglomerate VNU is representative of this alternative path. VNU is an abbreviation of the Dutch words *Verenigde Nederlandse Uitgeversbedrijven,* and translates to "United Dutch Publishing Companies." Although not very exciting as a name in English or Dutch, it did accurately reflect the genesis of the company—it was formed through the merging of two old-line Dutch publishing companies in 1964.

VNU serves as a particularly useful counterpoint to Dun & Bradstreet because the company literally sought to put much of the old D&B conglomerate back together again. In the early 1990s, VNU was a predominantly local media company with leading positions in Dutch newspapers (both national and regional) and magazines (both consumer and B2B). The company spent the subsequent decade selling out the vast majority of its existing predominantly consumer asset base and replacing it with entirely new assets in a variety of business and professional markets. The major purchases and divestitures (sometimes of the same assets) over this period are detailed below. The former D&B businesses it purchased were AC Nielsen and Nielsen Media, the leading market data providers in the consumer product and television audience measurement industries, respectively.

On July 11, 2005, VNU announced it had reached an agreement to purchase a third major business that had been spun off from D&B: IMS Health,

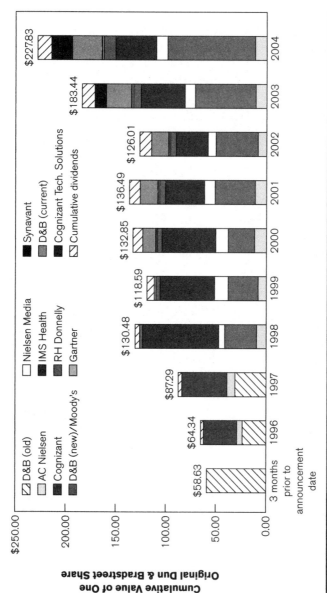

FIGURE 1.2 Dun & Bradstreet: Total Returns

Sources: FactSet and Bloomberg.

TABLE 1.6 VNU Purchases and Divestitures (1994–2004) ($ in millions)

Purchases			Divestitures		
Year	Asset	Price	Year	Asset	Price
1994	BPI Communications	$220			
1994	Bill Communications	125			
1995	SRDS	70			
1998	World Directories	2,100	1998	Broadcasting assets	NA
1999	**Nielsen Media Research**	**2,700**			
1999	**Nielsen NetRatings**	**246**			
2000	Miller Freeman	650	2000	VNU Newspapers	$867
2001	**ACNielsen**	**2,300**	2001	Consumer Information Group	1,091
			2001	Educational Information Group	172
			2003	Claritas Europe	41
			2004	World Directories	2,075

Note: Previous D&B businesses are **boldface.**

the leading provider of market data to the pharmaceutical industry. Despite the fact that an all-stock IMS deal was struck at a relatively modest premium to its then share price and was a friendly transaction, VNU's shareholders had had enough. The failure of VNU to deliver on the promised benefits of recombining the two former multibillion-dollar D&B companies it had purchased led the public shareholders to communicate an unwillingness to support the transaction, almost at any price.[11]

This dramatic and unprecedented repudiation of VNU management effectively put the company in play and resulted in its purchase in June 2006 by a consortium of some of the largest LBO buyers, including KKR, Blackstone, and Carlyle. Even with the premium the buyout group paid to the previous share price, the returns to shareholders since the aggressive portfolio realignment driven by large diversifying acquisitions (starting with the $2.1 billion World Directories purchase in 1998) were well below those available from the overall market. The level of underperformance had accelerated in more recent years.[12]

TABLE 1.7 Business and Professional Conglomerates—Product Portfolio Mix Overview

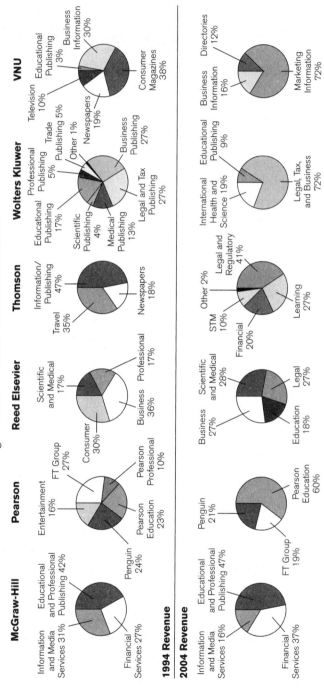

McGraw-Hill

1994 Revenue

- Information and Media Services 31%
- Educational and Professional Publishing 42%
- Financial Services 27%

2004 Revenue

- Information and Media Services 16%
- Educational and Professional Publishing 47%
- Financial Services 37%

Pearson

1994 Revenue

- Entertainment 16%
- FT Group 27%
- Pearson Professional 10%
- Pearson Education 23%
- Penguin 24%

2004 Revenue

- Penguin 21%
- FT Group 19%
- Pearson Education 60%

Reed Elsevier

- Scientific and Medical 17%
- Professional 17%
- Business 36%
- Consumer 30%

- Business 27%
- Scientific and Medical 28%
- Legal 27%
- Education 18%

Thomson

- Information/Publishing 47%
- Newspapers 18%
- Travel 35%

- Legal and Regulatory 41%
- Learning 27%
- Financial 20%
- STM 10%
- Other 2%

Wolters Kluwer

- Professional Publishing 5%
- Trade Publishing 5%
- Other 1%
- Newspapers 19%
- Business Publishing 27%
- Legal and Tax Publishing 27%
- Medical Publishing 13%
- Scientific Publishing 4%
- Educational Publishing 17%

- International Health and Science 19%
- Educational Publishing 9%
- Legal, Tax, and Business 72%

VNU

- Television 10%
- Educational Publishing 3%
- Business Information 30%
- Consumer Magazines 38%

- Business Information 16%
- Directories 12%
- Marketing Information 72%

The parallels between the VNU case and the other major public business and professional conglomerates, save one, are quite striking.

Each conglomerate was a mix of business and consumer media properties in the early 1990s, but with the exception of McGraw-Hill, none was apparently happy with what it owned. All of the others spent the subsequent decade essentially replacing, through an aggressive acquisition and divestiture program, their starting asset mix with an entirely different collection of assets. Each pursued a portfolio realignment that involved exiting most, if not all, of their consumer assets and redeploying the proceeds in some existing business and professional segments but also in a wide variety of entirely new ones. And, as the table below demonstrates, this highly proactive group has significantly underperformed the market as a whole during the ten-year periods most closely corresponding to these radical shifts in asset mix.

Although Thomson modestly outperformed the market for most years, the one consistent outlier in terms of both strategy and performance is McGraw-Hill. Ironically, despite this record, McGraw is often ridiculed by its peers and industry observers for a variety of perceived sins—refusal to exit obviously unconnected consumer businesses like *BusinessWeek* magazine and a group of ABC-affiliated TV stations; maintenance of excessive corporate overhead; a lack of aggressiveness and resolve in pursuing "strategic" acquisitions; and a revolving door of senior executives under longtime CEO Harold W. ("Terry") McGraw III.[13]

But, once again, it is the numbers that really tell the tale. This is not to conclude that there is no basis for the various criticisms of the stewardship of Terry McGraw, only that the impact of what he has done right has apparently more than compensated for any sins. What he has done right appears to be not spending his time trading assets like so many pieces on a Monopoly board but rather running the businesses with which he began. The response to this line of reasoning is to say that McGraw was lucky enough to start with great assets, whereas these other companies had no choice but to engage in aggressive portfolio management. And the collapse of the McGraw stock price in the summer of 2007 as the impact of the credit crisis on their debt ratings business became apparent provided another excuse for the asset traders to dismiss the previous performance of McGraw.

It is a little premature to definitively resolve these debates. If this book serves any purpose, a reader, when finished, will have acquired the tools to distinguish between "great" media assets and "lousy" media assets. It is still possible to observe that the terms *great* and *lousy* are not the exclusive

TABLE 1.8 Selected Ten-Year Total Returns: Business and Professional Conglomerates

12/31/96–12/31/06		12/31/95–12/31/05		12/31/94–12/31/04		12/31/93–12/31/03	
McGraw-Hill	18.5%	McGraw-Hill	16.3%	McGraw-Hill	17.8%	McGraw-Hill	15.2%
Thomson	7.9%	Thomson	10.4%	Thomson	11.9%	Thomson	12.4%
Pearson	5.3%	Pearson	5.5%	Pearson	6.8%	Pearson	5.8%
Reed Elsevier	3.6%	Reed Elsevier	4.1%	Reed Elsevier	5.8%	Reed Elsevier	4.5%
Wolters Kluwer	1.5%	Wolters Kluwer	2.4%	Wolters Kluwer	4.0%	Wolters Kluwer	2.1%
Average	7.4%	Average	7.7%	Average	9.2%	Average	8.0%
S&P	8.2%	S&P	9.0%	S&P	11.8%	S&P	10.8%
Average ex-McGraw-Hill	4.6%	Average ex-McGraw-Hill	5.6%	Average ex-McGraw-Hill	7.1%	Average ex-McGraw-Hill	6.2%

province of either consumer media assets on the one hand or business and professional media assets on the other. So the uniform decision by these other companies to sell their consumer media properties and reinvest the proceeds in business and professional media properties—and not always ones related to their existing business and professional media assets—cannot credibly be justified based on an asset quality criterion.

No good economic explanation exists for the decision of these companies to broadly follow the same path—sell consumer, buy business and professional, in lockstep. This leaves little alternative but to search for psychological explanations. Although we do not suspect mass hysteria, the intensity and aggressiveness of the drive to reinvent themselves through a veritable orgy of merger and acquisition activity within a relatively short time frame is striking.

All of these global business and professional media companies are based outside of the United States. The relevance of this observation is not—as our discussion of the largely U.S.-based consumer media conglomerates should have made clear—that we believe Americans have a lock on superior strategic management techniques. Rather it is simply that the companies' home countries—in these cases, Canada, Great Britain, and, most notably, Holland—are a small fraction of the size of the U.S. market. Consumer markets, unlike many business and professional markets, tend to be intensely local. Of the hundreds of major newspaper publishers globally, only a handful have tried to publish outside of their home market for obvious reasons: The potential advertisers are local, the tastes and culture are local, the distribution infrastructure is local, and very often there is a political overlay that could place additional burdens on a foreign owner. Markets for scientific research or financial data on the other hand are increasingly global in nature. Putting aside the question of whether this globalization is good or bad for these businesses, what is unambiguous is that these markets are indeed bigger.

If you are already the CEO of the largest consumer magazine or newspaper publisher in, say, Holland, what do you do for your next act? Local antitrust laws probably prohibit further consolidation at home. You have no expertise for operating such businesses in other markets and history has shown that buying such businesses in other markets—particularly in the giant U.S. market—is either prohibitively expensive, likely to end badly, or both. You could simply focus on operating these businesses well, growing them organically, and returning the extra cash to shareholders. But what fun is that? Owning a Dutch weekly women's magazine like *Margriet* or *Vrouw Vandaag* is unlikely to get you a good table at Michael's or frankly even give you a good excuse for a trip to New York. On the other hand, becoming one of the world's leading scientific or financial publishers could do both. And there are still plenty of businesses around the world that could be bought, albeit not inexpensively, without pushing up against the antitrust constraints applicable to these huge global markets.

Whether these kinds of considerations played a major or any role in the remarkably similar paths followed by today's business and professional media giants is pure speculation. What is not open to debate, however, is that the path chosen has not been a happy one for the companies' shareholders. If we are right about the cause of the decisions made by the leaders of these organizations that led to these results, it suggests that the disease of moguldom is an insidious strain liable to infect those at the helm of even less sexy varieties of media enterprises. But then, sexy is in the eyes of the beholder and size seems to matter disproportionately.

The next chapter deals with the question of what makes a media business attractive as an investment and what strategies to pursue to make it stay that way. One of our core conclusions is that it is often precisely the kinds of intensely local media franchises sold by the businesses and professional publishers to finance their global acquisitions binges that are best able to defend against competitive encroachments and achieve consistently superior results. The point of this chapter was to outline the range of markets and segments that are the subject matter of this book. The moral, however, may be that media moguls can manifest themselves in as many different forms and guises as there are media businesses to support them and shareholders who let them.

2 | The Landscape of Competitive Advantage

What makes a business great? A good place to start in answering this question is to look at a great business and identify the qualities that make it that way. In media, no one has created more value than Michael Bloomberg. Starting with a few million dollars from his severance in 1981, Bloomberg built a leading news and financial information franchise that was valued at over $20 billion in 2008. We will have much more to say later in the book about this business and the industry in which it operates. For now, the example of Bloomberg's unique achievement will be used to guide us in thinking about what makes businesses great generally—and why most of those qualities promoted by media moguls as central to success actually have little to do with it.

The basic insight of this book should be familiar to anyone who has struggled through an introductory microeconomics course. In business, barriers to entry are required to generate superior returns. Without any barriers, the moment a business begins to produce better financial returns than are available elsewhere, others will enter. The process of entry will push up costs, drive down prices, or both, quickly bringing returns back to earth. Accordingly, by definition, only sustainable barriers to entry can support sustainably outstanding performance.

This simple yet powerful observation has dramatic implications for how we think about strategy generally and media specifically. If we use the term *strategic* to describe an activity that is designed to enhance the long-term value of a business, then strategy is exclusively about establishing or reinforcing barriers to entry. This is in stark contrast, as we have already described, to the term's profligate use in the media context, where acquisitions and investments are often described as strategic even when they relate to the addition of entirely new and unconnected business lines.

Businesses that have no barriers to entry, of which there are many within the media firmament, have no business talking about strategy in the sense that we mean it. Managers of such enterprises have a single imperative—operating as efficiently as humanly possible. *Efficiency* refers to extracting the greatest possible profit that can be generated from the operations of a given collection of assets. Efficiency deals with operating issues relating to the business itself and its relationship to customers and suppliers over the short to medium term. Strategy requires additional consideration of the broader environment and the likely reaction to strategic decisions from actual and potential competitors over a longer time horizon. Efficiency matters to all businesses, whether barriers to entry are present or not. But strategy is frankly a waste of time in a market without barriers because strategy is ultimately concerned with managing competitive entry and behavior. Where there are no barriers to entry, it is pure delusion to believe that either competitive entry or behavior can be managed.

For some reason, media managers sometimes seem to think that talk of efficient operations is beneath them and have a tendency to mischaracterize all manner of operating issues as "strategic." Or even worse, managers of media businesses with absolutely no barriers to entry actually spend time thinking "strategically" when no amount of strategic thought can make any difference given the structural reality of the industry. This devaluing of efficiency is unfortunate given the dramatic differences in results achieved between the best and worst in class in many high-profile media segments.

Even though *efficiency* doesn't sound as sexy as *strategy*, efficiently operating a media company can be plenty sexy. Just as strategy looks different when applied in the media context, efficient operations can have an entirely different cast. Using management tools for getting an artist to stay committed to a label when a competitor is offering a better revenue split on her next album is much different from implementing a just-in-time production system in an auto parts plant. But both are all about efficient operations, not strategy. We devote the entirety of Chapter 7 to efficient operations in media.

In the media industry, what we call things seems to have an unnatural influence, so let's revisit the phrase *barriers to entry*. There is a sexier-sounding although identically meaning phrase: *competitive advantage*. What is a competitive advantage but a structural benefit enjoyed by a business that allows it to attain better results than others? For the reasons outlined, only barriers to entry can enable a business to enhance performance in such a fashion. Competitive advantage and barriers to entry are the same thing, and the terms are used interchangeably here.

Businesses with competitive advantages come in two flavors: those that have that advantage all to themselves and those that share an advantage with one or more industry peers.

When a business has a unique barrier, strategy is all about reinforcing that competitive advantage. This is what Warren Buffett describes as continuously digging the moat around the business.[1] How to dig that moat in a specific case depends entirely on the source of competitive advantage that is being protected. In media, particularly since the advent of the Internet, misunderstanding the source of competitive advantage often leads managers to inadvertently construct bridges for competitors when they think they are actually strengthening the moat.

Where multiple competitors share identical or similar competitive advantages, strategy is all about ensuring peaceful coexistence. Beneficiaries of these shared advantages have two choices: They can either cooperate and share the competitive advantage or they can compete intensively to collectively negate whatever advantage they shared. There are multiple examples of media sectors where the cooperative path was followed, such as the television broadcasters. Sadly, there are far more examples of the competitive path being followed, as in music and film production. The key to successful cooperation is to find mechanisms that divide the benefits fairly among industry participants without running afoul of the antitrust laws. In Chapter 9 we will explore some of the media sectors that have found perfectly legal ways to cooperate.

Figure 2.1 on the following page broadly describes this analytical framework for thinking about strategy depending on the structure of a particular industry segment.

We will now consider the full range of potential competitive advantages in the media context. It is equally important to debunk the putative competitive advantages frequently cited by media moguls that do not stand up to close scrutiny.

The list of genuine competitive advantages is surprisingly short and falls into four broad categories: scale, customer captivity, cost, and government protection. These categories are the same for all types of companies, although the specific advantages may vary. However, certain categories of media companies share common manifestations of these advantages and

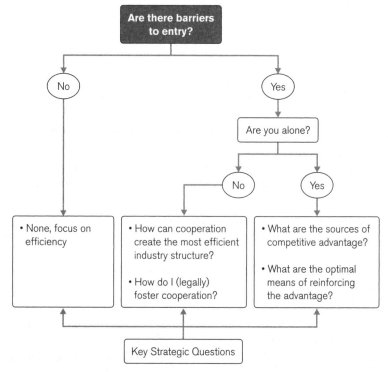

FIGURE 2.1 Analytical framework

effective methods for utilizing them. In part, this book aims to show readers how to identify the relevant categories of competitive advantage for any media enterprise.

REAL COMPETITIVE ADVANTAGES

Scale

Economies of scale are the most common source of competitive advantage, and the most often misapplied. There are two causes for this pervasive confusion.

First, it is not merely being big that endows a company with economies of scale. Unless the business has specific characteristics that allow it to operate better than its smaller competitors, size may be a disadvantage. And even when size does help, the relative rather than absolute size is what matters. If there are large numbers of competitors operating at the same scale—regardless

TABLE 2.1 Competitive Advantages: Real and Imagined

Real Sources of Advantage	Sham Sources of Competitive Advantage
Economies of scale	Deep pockets
• Fixed cost	Brands
• Network effects	Talent
Customer captivity	• Creative
• Habit	• Managerial
• Switching costs	First mover
• Search costs	
Cost	
• Proprietary technology	
• Learning	
• Access to resources	
Government protection	

of how massive that absolute scale is—it is unlikely to be of any particular benefit. Bloomberg quietly built relative scale by focusing on a niche of fixed-income traders within the broader financial market. Over time he was able to achieve greater penetration within this important market segment than his much-larger broad-based competitors and serve it more profitably.

Second, there are two very different structural characteristics that can be the source of true economies of scale, and these are often confounded. Most typically, economies of scale stem from a business having *high fixed costs*. In such cases, the largest player can spread its fixed costs over greater volumes and operate more profitably than competitors. The smartest strategy for a company with this kind of advantage is to continually invest in capital improvements that raise the ante on the required fixed cost base. This tactic, if pursued aggressively enough, can help ensure that any upstart that seeks to achieve a comparable scale will remain at a relative disadvantage—always one step behind.

With the advent of the Internet, a second kind of scale economy that is not a function of high fixed costs has emerged as increasingly relevant in the media context. The term *network effects* refers to businesses where the number of customers in itself increases the value of the service provided. The iconic example of a network effects business is eBay. The more users, the more attractive eBay is as a destination to list items for sale; the more items for sale, the more attractive eBay is as a place to go shopping. Before the Internet, classified sections of dominant newspapers exhibited the same characteristics. Bloomberg, too, was able to benefit from this aspect of scale by establishing the go-to place for fixed-income market participants to meet—and used instant messaging well before AOL popularized it in the consumer market to quickly build a viral network of traders.

This virtuous circle of "liquidity" provided by the number of buyers and sellers is frequently referenced in the context of "exchanges"—whether real financial exchanges, like stock, bond, or commodity exchanges, or other types of exchanges, like dating services or job boards. Network effects do not require a literal "exchange," but can be observed in any online community where the depth, or "liquidity," of the client base improves the quality of the user experience. This would apply to business models as diverse as social networks like facebook.com or simple customer ratings sites like tripadvisor.com. Network effects businesses benefit from scale, but do not typically require significant fixed costs. The smartest strategy here is obvious: Continually increase the size of the network. The player with the largest incumbent network is typically best placed to do this: Liquidity begets liquidity.

Customer Captivity

The characteristics that can give a business a leg up on the demand, or customer, side of the equation all fall under the rubric of "customer captivity." The extent of the advantage is a function of the extent to which the particular business attribute ties the customer to its product or service. There are three sources of customer captivity: *habit, switching costs,* and *search costs.*

Habit is a nice way to say "addiction." An addict will go back to the same brand of cigarette or soda or video game in the face of potentially significant enticements from competitors along the dimensions of either price or quality. As every good pusher knows, the best way to keep addicts coming back for more, and not trying alternative sources of product, is to encourage high frequency of use and fiercely enforce product consistency.

Habit is instilled and reinforced over time, and the more frequent and regular the usage, the more automatic the purchasing behavior, the more ingrained the habit becomes. Examples of this in the media world are daily soap operas, a personalized Web home page, or newspaper subscriptions. Bloomberg's famously idiosyncratic terminal is notoriously difficult to give up once a user has incorporated it into the daily work flow. Any change in the nature or quality of the product must be carefully monitored for the potential opening it gives to the otherwise committed user to try different purveyors of similar product.

Switching costs and search costs, for different but similar reasons, make the customer think twice before changing product horses midstream. The burdens on the customers in the case of switching costs are the direct costs of ending the relationship. Software businesses are an example of high switching costs businesses. In an institutional context, to the extent that a company's records and processes are integrated into a particular software program, there are both significant financial costs to placing them on a new system but also a real risk of ongoing business disruption. Many professional information businesses have added software elements to their offerings—recharacterizing themselves as "solutions" rather than mere data providers—in order to increase these kinds of customer switching costs. In a consumer context, shifting your personal data from one home tax or financial software package to another imposes similar burdens on a smaller scale. And the psychic investment a software game user makes in the perfection of her technique on a particular system or game series is also not lightly discarded.

The burden on customers in high search cost businesses is not the pain of giving up the old relationship as in switching costs, but in identifying satisfactory new ones. Search costs are expensive in situations where quality is of paramount importance and where minor service variations—think drug dosage databases used in critical care units at hospitals—can have potentially catastrophic implications. In the case of both switching and search costs, the greater the complexity of the product or service, the greater the competitive advantage.

Bloomberg's slavish devotion to customer needs has ensured a steady stream of new data and software products that are tightly integrated into its core service. The net impact is to both impose high costs on a customer for leaving it behind and entail significant lifting to be able to cobble together a satisfactory alternative.

Cost

There are fewer instances in which businesses can achieve an enduring leg up on the supply, or cost, side of the equation than on the demand side. Markets are less sentimental and more ingenious than customers, and the ability to achieve a cost structure that simply cannot be duplicated by rivals is challenging indeed. But it does happen, even in media. There are three sources of structurally superior cost structures: *proprietary technology, learning,* and *special resources.*

What makes a technology truly proprietary in the sense that we mean it? It is not enough that someone has developed a piece of code or a business process that no one else can discern or use. It must actually bestow a sustainable nonreplicable cost benefit in providing a valuable product or service. The most typical manifestation of this is a patent. Although there are over 1.5 million patents filed annually worldwide, of which around 350,000 are filed in the United States,[2] very few outside of the pharmaceutical industry meet this definition. In media there are occasional high-profile disputes over patents—TiVo vs. Echostar on TV time-shifting devices, Gemstar vs. everyone on electronic program guides—but these tend to be both rare, related to relatively marginal businesses, and in areas where competitive products have managed to proliferate around the so-called proprietary technology.

Within the media landscape the most frequent claims of proprietary technology relate to software enhancements to a core product. Unfortunately, as often as not, before the claim is even uttered, a newer, better, faster, more elegant alternative has been developed elsewhere—whether by an established competitor or in a basement with venture capital backing. Even Bloomberg, which has developed plenty of unique and clever software, cannot really hope to perform financial functions that cannot be readily imitated by competitors. For them, the key is that once a customer is hooked, he is unlikely to leave even if the competitor comes up with a marginally better product, given the switching costs and advantages of being part of the network. The elephant exception to the rule here is Google, which will be explored in great detail in Chapter 5. Although still a relatively rare phenomenon, the number of instances of proprietary technology being present in media companies has grown with the increasing importance of the Internet as a medium of distribution.

Technology aside, in businesses with highly complex processes, learning and experience by themselves can be a source of structural cost advantage. By hurtling down the so-called learning curve ahead of competitors, making myriad minor process and input adjustments to improve efficiency based on experience as they go, select manufacturers in industries like chemicals and semiconductors have delivered superior performance over extended periods. The lack of complex manufacturing businesses with media, however, makes it difficult to identify examples—other than Google—where learning and experience are significant differentiators.

Some businesses, simply by virtue of their proximity to a valuable asset, can have a cost advantage relative to their peers. Those valuable assets can be natural resources like an oil or mineral deposit or just geography—say, if your resort is the only one near a newly hot tourist destination with no alternative development opportunities or if your historic position as the hometown carrier is enhanced by a suddenly booming or critical hub city.

In media, an individual's special "talent" is often confused with being a kind of "special resource" of the type discussed here. It is not, for reasons discussed in detail shortly. More analogous is when a media company ends up owning a "franchise" property—whether James Bond production rights in film, the Goodson-Todman game-show format library in TV, or Madden sports in entertainment software—that has demonstrated a predictable ability to generate supernormal profits across time and even geographies.

Such windfalls do occasionally drop into the lap of a company. More often, the well-represented owner of the original intellectual property manages to ensure that the profits do not become supernormal at their expense. And over time, even the great franchises like Bond must compete with Jason Bourne and Jack Ryan and whoever else comes along. Not to mention that although Daniel Craig seems like a great replacement for the latest aging Bond, some of us remember George Lazenby. Even if you've never heard of him, take our word for it: Bond is not bulletproof. More important, these idiosyncratic examples of popular franchises are not only few and far between, they tend to resonate with particular audiences so that they cannot really translate to sustained broad market dominance.

Government Protection

The number of ways in which government can interfere with the normal operations of the market is limited only by the imagination of legislators and bureaucrats. Most of these rules do not bestow sustainable competitive advantages, but some of them do. Industry subsidies and preferential purchase policies on the one hand and import tariffs and quotas on the other are direct efforts to establish governmental barriers to entry in favor of domestic industries. Although some countries, like Canada, do provide these kinds of benefits and protections to their media industries, in the United States this is relatively rare. There are a number of media-specific rules on foreign ownership, particularly related to broadcast licenses, but these have not had a meaningful impact on competition. The movie business in the 1970s did benefit from limited partnership tax rules that allowed investors in films to take full deductions greater than the amount actually invested for the losses incurred by a film. This resulted in the creation of a number of partnerships—Silver Screen Partners was the most famous of these—that provided the studios with an effective government subsidy to the capital cost of producing films. These rules were significantly reformed in 1976 and completely repealed in 1986.[3]

Governments sometimes establish an officially authorized monopoly or oligopoly. Although in the United States there is no official state-run or designated oil company, other rules, some applying to the media world, operate in similar ways. Patents can be seen as monopolies giving the owner the exclusive use of that technology for seventeen to twenty years. The control of broadcast licenses has been a source of such enormous competitive advantage to television and radio operators that they have continued to achieve astounding profits even in the face of proliferating competition from new media channels. The granting of exclusive local cable franchises has created dozens of millionaires. Similarly, the Securities and Exchange Commission's designation of a handful of "Nationally Recognized Statistical Rating Organizations" allowed Moody's, S&P, and Fitch to generate remarkable shareholder returns over an extended period through many credit cycles, even when the recent credit market turmoil is considered.

More subtly, and sometimes perversely, whenever the government establishes business regulations ostensibly to protect consumers or the public at large, it often serves to reinforce or even establish a competitive advantage to the existing market leaders. Such regulations, whether environmental, safety-related, procedural, or otherwise, typically impose an incrementally larger fixed financial burden on anyone wishing to operate a business. To the extent that scale economies are driven by the existence of fixed costs, these consumer protections also provide additional competitive protection to the industry incumbent with the greatest customer base across which to spread these burdens. The structural tension between the government's predilection for micromanaging businesses through regulation and encouraging new competitive entrants is obvious in the current debate over the regulatory response, if any, to the role of the Nationally Recognized Statistical Rating Organizations in the recent mortgage credit crisis.

Each of the competitive advantages described here is potentially sustainable, but each has its own Achilles' heel. Relentless vigilance is required to maintain this precious leg up on competitors. With scale, at least of the high fixed cost variety, growth is ironically the biggest enemy of competitive advantage. By definition, as the business grows, the fixed costs become a relatively less important part of the overall cost structure. Similarly growth, whatever its other attractive characteristics, threatens customer captivity by relentlessly introducing new customers into the system who have yet to be addicted.

The structural fragility of competitive advantages is such that they are much more likely to be sustainable when found operating in concert. The most typical and powerful combination of advantages is that of scale and customer captivity. It is precisely this mutually reinforcing combination of advantages that is the source of the durability of the Bloomberg franchise.

More generally, imagine a scale leader confronted with an attack from a well-financed new entrant where the newbie matches his price in the hopes that it will be able to split the market and gain comparable relative scale. The additional advantage of captivity would ensure that unless the new entrant's price were meaningfully below the leader's, few customers would be likely to switch. To maintain his position, the leader simply need announce a policy of matching any competitor's price. In the absence of customer captivity, the struggle to maintain relative scale would become much more complex and difficult. Conversely, businesses with customer captivity have no advantages with respect to "virgin" customers. This is the most likely ground on which a competitor will seek to attack. Scale, however, ensures that the fixed marketing costs needed to reach these prospective users will be spread over a larger existing customer base, making it relatively far more costly for a new player to develop similar captivity advantages.

Table 2.2 summarizes these potential sources of competitive advantage, highlights media examples of businesses with the qualities described, and identifies both the optimal strategies for reinforcing each particular flavor of competitive advantage and the key respective threats to maintaining it.

No one likes to admit they don't have a competitive advantage. Even if there is agreement on the four categories of advantage, it can be painful watching otherwise serious media executives explain why their business has one of these advantages when it clearly doesn't. The spin that ensues has the flavor of Cinderella's sisters trying to get on that glass slipper that just won't fit. Luckily, the simplicity of our concept of competitive advantage—sustainable barriers to entry—lends itself to straightforward empirical testing. The most obvious manifestation is superior returns over an extended period of time. If a company has high profit margins or returns on capital that can't be achieved elsewhere, it will attract competitors that will naturally depress these over time. Unless, of course, there are barriers that impede these prospective

TABLE 2.2 Sources of Competitive Advantage

	Scale		Customer Captivity			Cost			Government Protection
	Fixed Cost	Network Effects	Habit	Switching Cost	Search Costs	Proprietary Technology	Learning	Special Resources	Various
Optimal Reinforcing Strategies	Reinvest in fixed cost base	Broaden network	Enforce product consistency, encourage usage frequency	Focus on complexity and embedding into core processes	Invest in quality, complexity, and comprehensiveness	Invest in rapidly changing environment and get a patent	Generate relentless production improvements	Location, location, location	Hire a good lobbyist
Key Threat	Growth, patient well-financed new entrants, adjacent niche players		Battle for new customers, execution failure in quality or consistency			New better technology	More relevant lessons elsewhere	Environmental disaster, development of alternate location	A better lobbyist
Media Examples	Cable	eBay	Newspaper	Personal Finance Portal	Nielsen	Qualcomm[4]	Google	Broadway	TV broadcasters, rating agencies

competitors from entering. Similarly, if entry is difficult, we would expect that relative market shares would remain quite stable over time.

These two rules of thumb—high returns and stable market shares— are remarkably effective tests for the existence of competitive advantage. It is hard to claim there are meaningful barriers to entry in the face of huge jumps in share among new and existing players from year to year. And a mogul who wants to convince you that his business has competitive advantages may become less emphatic when confronted with the firm's rather pedestrian returns. After all, what kind of executive can deliver only average returns from a business with competitive advantages? Although Bloomberg's financials are private and market share estimates are highly contested, there is little question that the company has consistently met these two criteria for well over a decade.

Of course, moguls have a tendency to reject implicitly or explicitly all easily measurable metrics of success and tend to focus instead on various forms of industry recognition. Although these are undoubtedly satisfying to the mogul, there is no empirical evidence that any of them translate into corresponding satisfaction for shareholders.

SHAM COMPETITIVE ADVANTAGES

If the universe of genuine competitive advantages is mercifully brief (and the tests for identifying their existence, remarkably simple), the catalog of false gods worshipped by some misguided executive or investor is startlingly long. Within the media world, there are, however, four golden idols that are clung to with particular vehemence and consistency to justify all manner of madness, and it is to these that we turn now. Notably, none of these putative advantages played any role in assisting Bloomberg achieve its remarkable success.

TABLE 2.3 Alternative Tests to Assess Competitive Advantage

Economic Tests to Assess	Media Mogul Tests to Assess
• Consistently superior profitability Earning returns on capital in excess of cost of capital • Market share stability	• Good table at Spago • Invited to Sun Valley • Number of Oscar, Grammy, Emmy, Golden Globe, Tony, Pulitzer, People's Choice, MTV VMA, "lifetime achievement," "humanitarian of the year," etc., awards • CEO compensation levels

Deep Pockets

Ask any mini–media mogul who runs a major division of a large entertainment conglomerate about the benefits of being a part of the broader empire. With shocking consistency, the answer comes back the same: "deep pockets." This justification most often emerges in the context of high-risk, creatively based, hit-driven businesses where significant up-front investment, often in talent, is required well before any evidence of success or failure becomes available. What is most shocking is not how rarely anyone even attempts to talk of creative synergies, cross-promotion, scale, or any of the other qualities that were typically touted at the time the conglomerate acquired the division in the first place. Equally shocking is the lack of self-consciousness in admitting deep pockets as the only real "advantage" that comes from the combination.

Who gets the advantage of deep pockets, and is it a competitive advantage? It may be an advantage to the manager of a business that would otherwise go bankrupt if it did not have a corporate parent to finance his or her mistakes. But is it an advantage to the shareholders of the company doing the financing?

The only possible argument that deep pockets are a sustainable competitive advantage rests on the assumption either that the capital markets are persistently inefficient or that media conglomerate owners have systematically superior abilities to assess the viability of media projects. If the capital markets are inefficient around media projects, it is because they are not too tight, but too loose. There never seems to be a shortage of individuals and institutions happy to take a lower return than would otherwise be appropriate to the level of risk for the opportunity to attend a movie premiere or party backstage with the band. Similarly, the claim that conglomerate executives have special skills at quantifying and managing creative risk is inconsistent with both the overall company returns already presented and the business-specific returns we will present shortly.

Even if both these conditions were fulfilled, deep pockets would still be unlikely to represent a significant competitive advantage. Remember competitive advantages must be measured against an enterprise's strongest, best-financed competitors, not its weakest ones. It is the former who threaten future profitability, not the latter. And, in the world of media conglomerates, there are large numbers of deep-pocketed competitors and large numbers of putatively efficient capital allocators, so in this environment in particular, deep pockets do not confer any relative advantage. The fact that Michael Bloomberg was able to initially finance his enterprise with his modest severance payment should give anyone pause before opening up their deep pockets as a supposed advantage to a media business.

Businesses that provide deep pockets as the source of their competitive advantage have a predictable tendency to empty those pockets over time, so whatever kind of advantage it represents is certainly not a sustainable one. This lesson was learned the hard way by the succession of large Japanese conglomerates that were bamboozled into investing in the movie and music businesses in the late 1980s.[5] It is not only unsuspecting foreigners who have fallen prey to this dangerous line of reasoning—America's own Coca-Cola had an equally unfortunate experience in having its pockets emptied by Columbia Pictures.[6]

Some may argue that there is a general social value to arrangements that provide a financial safety net to those who take difficult-to-measure creative risks. The implicit suggestion is that shareholders in media conglomerates should just suck it up in the name of the greater good. As a policy matter, those who believe creativity requires subsidization should lobby for taxpayer funding or seek the kind of wealthy patron that has historically served this role for selected artists. There is no good policy basis for imposing this burden on unsuspecting shareholders who expect boards and managements to fulfill their fiduciary obligations. As a practical matter, regardless of where the subsidy comes from, there is reason to question the societal benefits from providing unlimited funds to pursue creative endeavors. We have all known enough trust fund babies to be skeptical about the value of making deep pockets available. Indeed, our anecdotal evidence suggests that such an approach is as harmful to the "protected" children's character and development as it is to the parents' financial well-being.

Brands

Great brands are forever touted as competitive advantages. Media companies are chock-full of them, some of which have been built and nurtured over many decades. The performance of these companies suggests that if brands represent competitive advantages in themselves, the management has done a remarkable job in squandering their supposed benefits. Brands can in fact support and reinforce one or more of the "real" competitive advantages discussed, but more often they do not. And whether they do or don't is less related to how "great" or "strong" the brand itself is than it is to the structure of the industry in which the brand operates. The case of Mercedes-Benz is instructive.

Mercedes is one of the premier high-end global consumer brands. Mercedes operates in the luxury car market. Does the Mercedes brand strength create barriers to competitors entering or remaining in this market? Certainly establishing and maintaining a successful global luxury brand requires scale to meet the fixed cost associated with everything from product development and marketing to distribution and service. But does Mercedes enjoy scale relative to the U.S., Japanese, and other European automobile companies equally committed to playing in this market? And how captive are the customers—are there meaningful switching or search costs to getting a different luxury car next time around, and how "addictive" is it really to own a Mercedes? Does Mercedes or anyone else have proprietary technologies that provide a sustainable cost advantage over competitors?

Given the relentless stream of new entrants to the luxury car market since the 1970s, it is hard to believe that the answer to any of these questions is other than no. And Mercedes' unexceptional returns to shareholders during this period reflect that structural reality. The broader point is that brands are not by themselves a competitive advantage. Some brand-related consumer behavior may lead to competitive advantage, but this would be unusual in cases where the product itself is not naturally habit-forming, the purchasing frequency is not high, or the switching costs are not considerable. Table 2.4 applies the two financial indicia of competitive advantage— share stability and profitability—to some of the best-known brands across industries to demonstrate the lack of clear correlation between the existence of "brand" and competitive advantage.

These differences among brands apply equally in media. Some branded products—women's service magazines like *Better Homes & Gardens*—have dominated their markets for a century or more. Others like the *Saturday Evening Post*, *Life*, or *Look* magazines have experienced sudden deaths. Some high-profile brands—the *New York Times* and the *Wall Street Journal*—have been consistently less profitable than their less celebrated local brethren: the dozens of small market newspapers published by companies such as Gannett or Lee Enterprises.

Bloomberg became a brand *after* he had built a business with the real competitive advantages discussed above. Before, Bloomberg was just the name of some guy who got fired at Salomon Brothers. Indeed, the business started off with the distinctly unexciting name Innovative Market Systems. Once a business with competitive advantages is established, a strong brand can help reinforce customer captivity, as it does with Bloomberg today. But it is a dangerous misunderstanding to confuse the brand with the advantage itself.

TABLE 2.4 Brands as Competitive Advantage

	Superior Profitability and Share Stability?	
	Yes	No
Automotive		
Harley-Davidson	Mixed	
Cadillac		✔
Mercedes-Benz		✔
Consumer Products		
Budweiser	Mixed	
Coca-Cola	✔	
Colgate	✔	
Tide	✔	
Marlboro	✔	
Financial Services		
Wells Fargo	✔	
JPMorgan Chase		✔
Citibank		✔
Retail		
Wal-Mart	✔	
Gap		✔
Liz Claiborne		✔
Technology/Electronics		
Intel	✔	
Dell		✔
HP		✔
Motorola		✔
Sony (RCA)		✔
Telecom		
AT&T		✔
Cingular	✔	
Sprint		✔
Verizon	✔	
Other Industries		
Insurance	✔	
Cosmetics		✔

Talent

In the consumer entertainment side of media in particular, extraordinary talent is often treated as creating value analogous to brands in the consumer product side. Genuine talent, particularly creative talent, is a rare and mysterious thing. Behind many successful media properties lies some inspired mastermind, whose talent is both unique and unreplicable. Is it not obvious, then, that the company with the most talent under its hood will drive that much faster than the rest? The answer is probably yes, assuming the talent is appropriate to the tasks required and that it is managed effectively. But that does not make talent a competitive advantage, and certainly not a sustainable one.

There are two types of creative "talent" spoken of in the media context. Successful performers and producers are often viewed as being central to the success of particular institutions and sometimes are even shareholders. Steven Spielberg at DreamWorks, the Beatles at EMI, Howard Stern at Sirius, J. K. Rowling at Scholastic (in the United States), and Bloomsbury (in the U.K.) are celebrity examples, but these are not the only kinds. Within less glamorous sectors, or at least playing more behind-the-scenes roles, there are "superstar" performers who become legendary within their own narrow domains: the K–12 editorial director who consistently developed wildly successful math and reading programs, the game geek whose code lies behind several consumer software franchises, the screenwriter whose every word seems to turn to gold for the lucky studio.

The other type of creative talent is managerial. These are the individuals who have shown an uncanny ability to identify performing talent or select "hits" before they become prohibitively expensive. A related but distinct talent is that of managing the creators of this content to ensure that they continue not only to produce it but to produce it for them, preferably without first bidding it out. Here it is harder to provide concrete examples with any confidence. Media executives are shameless self-promoters and every successful project has many fathers, while the bombs always appear to have been approved by no one at all. That said, Clive Davis, Jimmy Iovine, and "L.A." Reid between them seem to have "discovered" an awful lot of productive recording artists. And at various points in their careers Jeffrey Katzenberg and one or other of the Weinstein brothers at a minimum have had impressive filmmaking hot streaks.

The question remains whether a company that employs more or better talent of either kind has a sustainable competitive advantage relative to its peers. To the extent "competitive advantage" and "barriers to entry" are the same, given that this kind of talent is by definition unique, the barrier would seem insurmountable. But even if one subscribes to the strongest version of this "uniqueness" theory of talent and refuses to believe that Cate Blanchett is a perfectly good, or even preferable, substitute for Gwyneth Paltrow, this does not make it a competitive advantage. Like love, talent may not be available for purchase, but it can be rented. Indeed, even before the Internet, the market for talent of all kinds has always been remarkably liquid.

If particular kinds of talent put to particular kinds of uses can yield particular levels of profit with any predictability, it is safe to say that the well-represented owners of that talent will ensure that it accrues to their own benefit. The Thirteenth Amendment to the Constitution, banning slavery, does not have an exception for media companies hopeful of retaining the low-cost services of their star performers. Once a nobody becomes a somebody, even on a relatively small scale, they will get an agent or a lawyer or both and ensure that whatever media company values their talent most has the opportunity to pay for it. For example, this is the second book for one of its authors, whose first book was a modest success. The advance paid on this book was more than five times that paid on the first, largely on the strength of that performance—even though the topic is not one for which any of the authors has any publishing track record.

Even if slavery is illegal, contracts are not. This may be so, but the laws involving personal service contracts are complex and subject to stringent restrictions. These restrictions are particularly onerous under California law and they do not favor the employer. Every subindustry of the media business has its own contracting conventions. In the movie business, standard on-screen talent deals are on a one-off basis, although provision is sometimes made for sequels. In the book business, authors typically give their publisher an option on their next book, but that is just an option to match whatever is offered by another publisher. The music business alone has a standard practice of multirecord deals. So, it could be argued, if an unknown breaks out after the first recording, the music company can reap its just rewards for having discovered this previously unknown talent by getting the benefits of the original deal on the subsequent output. It never works that way. If the recording company doesn't want the second CD to be called *Sounds I Made in the Bathroom This Morning*, it will renegotiate the deal. Every once in a while a music company will try to enforce a contract as written, but this is generally viewed as bad for business, and talent usually figures some way around it—just ask the artist once again known as Prince. On the other hand, if a hot act negotiates an expensive long-term deal and suddenly goes cold, you can be sure they will enforce the deal and come out fine—just ask Mariah Carey. No amount of creative lawyering will change the basic economics of talent-based businesses—heads, talent wins; tails, the corporate sponsor loses.

Talented managers are as loyal as talented artists. The best time to sell is at the top of the market: when the last season or movie, TV, or record slate you "produced" makes it appear that you have a Midas touch. Jamie Tarses was widely credited with developing hits like *Friends* and other "must-see" TV that catapulted NBC into the number one network position for several years in the late 1990s. She quickly parlayed that reputation to become the head of the entertainment division at rival ABC, the first woman ever to secure such a role at a Big Three network. The point is not that she was unable to reproduce that success at ABC, although she was not,[7] only that managers are also very good at monetizing for themselves the value of their actual or perceived talent.

More broadly, however, having great management is no more a sustainable competitive advantage in the media business than it is anywhere else. Good managers are also rare and mysterious things and boards of directors are happy to pay up for them. But boards operating in competitive industries should beware. If their terrific new manager comes from a company that enjoys a barrier to entry and they throw him into a competitive industry, someone is going to cry. As Warren Buffett has said, when a manager with a reputation for brilliance meets a business with a reputation for poor fundamental economics, it is invariably "the reputation of the business that remains intact."[8]

The final argument in favor of talent constituting a competitive advantage is the special case in which the talent owns the company, and its interests are thus aligned. Obviously talent typically "owns" the fruits of its labor. What is not typical is that this is in corporate form or that others share in that ownership. This is not a new idea. From Charlie Chaplin, Douglas Fairbanks, D. W. Griffith, and Mary Pickford creating United Artists in 1919 to Martha Stewart Omnimedia going public in 1999, there have been financial and creative drivers behind various attempts of this kind to bridge the often divergent perspectives of the suits and the artists. These have not ended well, for two reasons.

First, the data on employee ownership is mixed at best. As romantic as the notion of employee owners working collectively in pursuit of the common good is, the reality on the ground has been less idyllic. Generally both very small and very large amounts of employee ownership do appear to be a benefit. Unfortunately, there is evidence of a vast middle ground where the employees have enough ownership to affect corporate decision making but experience enough dilution from outside investors so that their economic interests significantly diverge from that of the other shareholders.[9] So, for example, when the unions took over control of United Airlines, some of the sentimental employee-ownership acolytes were undoubtedly horrified to discover that the unions continued to press to shift value from the company overall to their members directly—and now were in a better position to succeed since they controlled the company.[10] Given the math, it should not have been surprising: If the unions owned 55 percent of the company and they could shift a dollar of value from the shareholders into the members' pockets, whether through benefit, wage, or work rule changes, they would still be forty-five cents ahead.

Second, even if the calculus of aligning ownership interests were perfected, the nature of talent is that sustainability is unattainable. Even with advances in plastic surgery and medical care, all evidence is that both the nature of the talent itself and the tastes of users are highly variable and unpredictable. When Martha Stewart was on her IPO road show, she was continually asked about the risk that she would be "hit by a bus." Little did the investors know that they would have been better off if she had been, rather than subject to a scandal that would permanently undermine consumer perception. Even the most resilient talent cannot sustain the same level of productivity beyond a relatively brief period of megasuccess.

Now that Michael Bloomberg himself has left the company to run the city of New York, the average person would be hard-pressed to name a single employee of Bloomberg. When he started the business, Bloomberg brought along three partners—one to focus on product, one to focus on customer needs, and one to focus on technology infrastructure.[11] Each built world-class organizations that were designed to thrive past both their respective tenures and that of the founder. The secret of Bloomberg's success is that the strength of the franchise did not rely on his talent.

First Mover

Who can turn down a once-in-a-lifetime opportunity? Being the first to do anything is by definition a unique opportunity. Whether or not it represents a worthwhile opportunity is a separate question. Just as in the case of brands, being a first mover can in certain instances support the establishment of a competitive advantage. And just as in brands, this turns out to be the case in a small minority of instances. Indeed, based on the data, one might be tempted to conclude that the more widespread phenomenon is the existence of a first mover disadvantage.

TABLE 2.5   Strategic Approaches—First Mover Advantages?

	First Mover	Dominant Competitor
Mainframes	UNIVAC	IBM
PC	Apple	Dell, Compaq
Operating Systems	CP/M	Microsoft
Spreadsheets	Visicalc	Microsoft
Portals	Prodigy	Yahoo
Search Engines	Inktomi, AltaVista	Google
TV Networks	NBC	CBS, NBC, ABC, CBS, Fox
Airlines	Pan Am, TWA	none
Cell Phones	Motorola	Nokia
Automobiles	Ford	none
Online Auctions	eBay	eBay
VCRs	Betamax	VHS

When is going first a good thing? When the market is of a nature that facilitates establishing sustainable scale, customer captivity, or cost advantages. In media, in particular, the markets are now often changing so fast that companies are quite unsure of the depth and price sensitivity of the arena they are seeking to enter. In many cases these new markets are in their infancy and projected to grow rapidly. But where there are few initial customers, how likely is it that a company can establish a sustainable scale differentiation compared to competitors who seek to enter later? Similarly, how would any captivity achieved with the few early adopters translate into corresponding benefits with those who will come later? And why won't those who wait to see what shape market demand actually takes be able to produce a more streamlined, cost-effective product that avoids the legacy effects of the trial and error inherent in developing a new market?

In short, where there is a large preexisting customer base that could be locked in with the new product or service, being a first mover can help establish potentially sustainable advantages. But where the market is still largely undefined, there is a potentially massive free-rider problem. The first mover does free market research for the industry at large and has no way to recoup that investment. Time Warner's massive Orlando broadband trial in the early 1990s is a perfect example of this danger. By the time Time Warner aborted the scaled-back version of the trial less than three years after it had begun in 1994, it had expended hundreds of millions and had little to show for it beyond a sense of potential consumer interest in video on demand.[12] Other cable operators were reportedly thrilled "to let Time Warner get the glory right now in exchange for taking a lot of the knocks" in the form of investments whose results they could all piggyback on once a real market for these products developed.[13]

Even where there is a large preexisting customer base, there are dangers to being the first mover. Where there are significant barriers to entry in an existing business and that position is used to establish a similar position in an adjacent business, being a first mover makes eminent sense. But when the new business is competitive with the existing business but has fewer barriers to entry, being the first mover is not necessarily wise. This is precisely the difference discussed between digging a moat around a core franchise and building a bridge to facilitate competitor attacks. The most striking example of this was the IBM personal computer, which accelerated the development of the PC market, ultimately undermining major parts of IBM's core mainframe business. In return, IBM failed to benefit from the exploding PC markets, as the absence of barriers to entry led to its displacement by Compaq and Dell and ultimately its absorption by Lenovo.

Returning to the case of Bloomberg, in the financial information world he wasn't the first mover—he was about a hundred years late! Even within the niche of fixed-income data and software, another competitor called Telerate had already established itself in the industry. In Chapter 8 we dive more deeply into the sector and see how Bloomberg overcame Reuters' century-long head start. The point here is simply that Bloomberg had a lot of things going for it, but a first mover it certainly was not.

First mover strategies, like brand, deep pockets, and talent-based strategies, are a sham competitive advantage. Such strategies can give the impression of leading to sustainable superior returns only when they happen to coincide with one or more of the four actual sources of competitive advantages—economies of scale, customer captivity, proprietary technology, and government support. Strategic mogul initiatives based exclusively on these putative competitive advantages, however, go far to explain the poor, unstable returns the moguls have actually produced.

3 | The Structure of Media Industries

Ted Turner, like his media mogul nemesis Rupert Murdoch, is a complicated guy. His career has spanned over fifty years and cut a wide swath of very different media businesses with very different characteristics. During the course of this journey, Turner experienced extraordinary highs and breathtaking lows. These extremes reflect the underlying quality of the businesses he was pursuing at the time.

From the age of twelve, Turner worked at his family's Savannah-based billboard company, the largest in the southeastern United States.[1] When Ted took over, he continued to fill in the regional footprint of Turner Advertising Company and complemented it with other local media—first radio, then television stations, and then the Atlanta Braves.

Turner got his first taste of the broader media world when he cleverly figured out how to turn his once money-losing Atlanta UHF station, TCG, into the TBS Superstation, one of the first channels to be distributed nationally through the still-young cable industry. He leveraged those early relationships with the cable industry and his national distribution infrastructure to launch CNN and Headline News.

Now, no longer satisfied with being a large regional player or even one of the larger national cable programmers, Turner turned his attention to becoming a full-fledged media mogul, which, in his mind, entailed owning a movie studio. Turner is so enamored with *Gone With the Wind* that he named a son Rhett and fashioned his own mustache on the character, so of course the preferred studio had to own the rights to that film. Turner paid $1.6 billion to Kirk Kerkorian for the studio, almost bankrupting his company in the process. With each film release losing the company another $15 million on average, Turner was forced to sell much of MGM back to Kerkorian for $300 million in under a year and take on new shareholders who restricted his operating flexibility going forward.[2]

Having barely escaped disaster, Turner returned to the business of expanding his collection of cable channels. He built on the lessons of TBS and CNN by focusing on repurposing inexpensive content that does not rely on stars to build franchises that meet an underserved aspect of the market. Old movies and cartoons provided the backbone of TNT, Turner Classic Movies, and the Cartoon Channel. Through its acquisition of his company, Time Warner made Turner a multibillionaire and its largest shareholder in 1996. The subsequent acquisition of Time Warner by AOL, as part of an effort Turner supported to embrace the digital future, reduced his personal worth from $10 billion to $2 billion in thirty months.[3]

So far, we have laid the groundwork for understanding the basic parameters of the media industry and the sources of true competitive advantage. The arc of Turner's career provides a convenient template against which we can discuss the key structural attributes of media businesses that tend to support or undermine the existence of competitive advantage. Once we overlay our strategic approach to the particulars of the media industry, one fact quickly becomes apparent: The businesses that attract the greatest mogul interest seem to have the fewest competitive advantages.

Conventional wisdom suggests that media enterprises are best grouped into either "content" or "distribution" businesses. Content refers to the businesses that create the media that is ultimately consumed and distribution encompasses those that deliver the final product to the consumer. Much of the debate over the strength of particular media businesses is framed in terms of whether or not "content is king." But this content-distribution dichotomy ignores some critical distinctions that actually drive the underlying media business dynamics. We get a much more useful and apt general framework by expanding the content-distribution paradigm along two dimensions.

First, content remains a central attribute, but distribution is divided into two categories: those businesses involved in the local or retail area of distribution and those directed toward the aggregation, marketing, or wholesale area of distribution. Retail distribution is concerned with delivering the so-called last mile of connectivity to the customer. Wholesale distribution is concerned with packaging and preparing content for broad dissemination. Many media businesses operate in more than one of these three categories, but most businesses are concentrated in one of them. Within this framework,

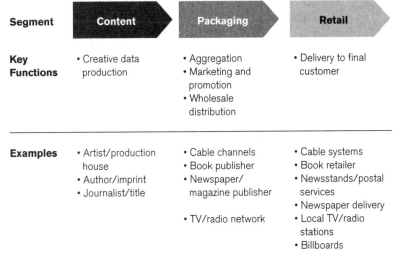

Segment	Content	Packaging	Retail
Key Functions	• Creative data production	• Aggregation • Marketing and promotion • Wholesale distribution	• Delivery to final customer
Examples	• Artist/production house • Author/imprint • Journalist/title	• Cable channels • Book publisher • Newspaper/ magazine publisher • TV/radio network	• Cable systems • Book retailer • Newsstands/postal services • Newspaper delivery • Local TV/radio stations • Billboards

FIGURE 3.1   Basic Industry Structure

a film production studio is still a content business that might sell a program to a cable channel, which packages this and other programming for redistribution by cable and satellite companies that provide the last mile.

For each of these three types of enterprises—content, packaging, and retail—we consider one additional operating characteristic. The idea is to identify an attribute that has such an overwhelming impact on the economics of these businesses that it justifies being added as a separate dimension of analysis. For content, the distinguishing feature is whether the content is discrete or continuous. By *discrete* we mean content that is onetime in nature, like a movie, book, or record, which does not entail an ongoing relationship with the customer. For packaging, it is whether the delivery is physical or electronic. And for retail, it is whether the ultimate distribution is local or national (or even global). Many media businesses have some mix of the characteristics highlighted, but understanding the nature of this mix is critical to understanding the business dynamics.

Considering all these factors, we have replaced the content-distribution distinction with the matrix below. As we examine individual media businesses and segments, we will use this framework to get a snapshot of the environment in which each operates. These industry maps are our primary tool, in conjunction with the analysis of returns and market share stability over time, for assessing competitive advantage.

Let's apply this framework to the basic business of cable channels, which was ultimately the largest part of Turner's independent company. Cable channels' core function is to package on an ongoing basis largely discrete content into a continuous themed stream to attract viewers, advertisers, and cable systems. The actual packaging has always been a mostly electronic affair—both in terms of aggregating the entertainment content and delivering it by satellite to the various retail distribution outlets. A variety of technological advances made the business relatively more electronic, however, facilitating the ease of putting a channel together, finding outlets to which it might be profitably delivered, and transmitting the programming. When Turner began in this business, relatively few homes received cable, and he needed to scramble around to find satellite capacity and contract to build the equipment that would allow his signal to reach the satellite.

Interestingly, as the channel capacity has grown and the number of channels has proliferated, channel ownership has not dispersed quite as fast. Part of the reason for this is that much of the additional capacity is being taken up by time-shifted or high-definition versions of preexisting channels or various video-on-demand or other services offered by the cable companies. Accordingly, the large absolute number of channels still corresponds to a much smaller number of owners and, among those owners, the largest capture a disproportionate amount of viewership. Nine of the top ten and twenty-three of the top thirty cable channels are owned or partially owned by the studio conglomerates.

If these channels are primarily in the packaging business, they also typically produce at least some of the content themselves in the form of original programming. But the list of companies that provide content for the

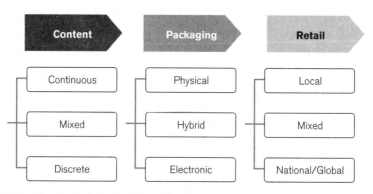

FIGURE 3.2 Basic Industry Map—Mapping to Assess Competitive Advantage

cable channels also includes the large film studios, television networks, and dozens of small independent production houses. Although most entertainment content production is discrete in nature, cable channels like television broadcasters deliver content continuously. From the perspective of a production house, when it is lucky enough to have a successful series in-house, that portion of content creation is continuous. Yet since even the most successful franchises don't last forever, the overall mix of the activity in most content creation businesses is still more properly characterized as discrete. The fact that Turner owned some cable channels did not change the inherent nature of MGM as primarily a maker of discrete content once he purchased it.

Cable channels are distributed to the "retail" end consumer primarily through cable, satellite, and, increasingly, telephone companies. The number of companies that could be included under "retail" in this industry map overstates how crowded the field really is. These markets are local, and cable companies do not compete with one another nor do telephone companies, as each serves different geographies. The two major satellite companies, DirecTV and Echostar, however, do compete on a national basis. But at the end of the day, an individual consumer in a particular market probably has only two or three practical options for receiving access to his or her favorite cable channel.

Later chapters more closely examine the operating characteristics of the particular segments composing this overall industry map, but one key broad observation should be made. As we move from content to packaging to retail, the absolute number of competitors goes down. Since almost all of the cable channels produce at least some of their own content, by definition the number of players producing content is dramatically greater than the number

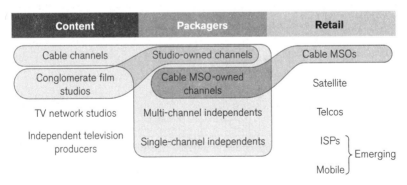

FIGURE 3.3 U.S. Cable Channel Map

Note: Circled categories represent common ownership.

FIGURE 3.4   Competitive Advantage by Segment

of channels. Although the channels owned by the five studio conglomerates are responsible for a majority of cable channel viewership, there is no such concentration among the producers of actual content shown. At the retail end of the industry, by contrast, the concentration among outlets for the channel operators to reach consumers is even more intense. As we move from industry map to industry map throughout this book, we will see a remarkable consistency in this tendency for the industries involved in content creation to be relatively fragmented, while those involved in actual delivery to the customer are relatively concentrated.

If we apply the competitive advantage analysis of the last chapter to the media industry structure of this one, it would not be unreasonable to suspect that large numbers of competitors suggest a lack of barriers to entry. As we move from content toward retail distribution, the sustainability of competitive advantage is generally enhanced.

Content may be king in snagging you seats to the latest red carpet premiere, but content creation by its nature does not entail significant fixed costs and is, accordingly, not a scale business. This is not to say that one could not spend a lot on a particular film by paying for stars and fancy costumes and exotic locales and special effects. It is saying that there are no scale advantages from doing so—these are largely variable costs that anyone can fund as well as anyone else. If one looks at how multimillion-dollar megaproject films are financed and funded—through a complex web of third-party financing and presales and distribution and talent deals—it is clear that there are no particular barriers to putting together such deals beyond creativity, initiative, and hubris.

Where the content produced is of a continuous nature—whether for a daily television show, newspaper, or financial information business—there is a greater need for fixed cost infrastructure in order to produce it on an ongoing basis. Furthermore, the continuous nature of the content lends itself to greater customer captivity, whether through habit or actual switching costs depending on how that content is embedded in the user's daily life. Almost by definition, customer captivity is unlikely to be established from discrete one-shot content, no matter how popular or what a "hit" it may ultimately be.

It is not a coincidence that Ted Turner's decision to bet his entire business on the acquisition of MGM—a discrete content business with no barriers to entry—represented one of the lowest points of his career. In his autobiography, Turner describes his elation in capturing the storied studio even as he realized both that there were few opportunities for cost synergies, as "we didn't have overlapping operations between our companies," and that "given the unpredictable nature of the movie business, [a studio's] profits were usually low during good years and nonexistent in bad ones."[4] Turner would justify the deal based on his ability to ultimately use the MGM film library assets he managed to keep to help build some of his later cable channels. This could have been achieved, however, by simply buying or renting the required film library rights for hundreds of millions of dollars less than he effectively paid. Bizarrely, even after his near-death experience at MGM, Turner would continue to pursue ownership of a working studio.

Unlike content creation, the business of packaging and marketing content requires some fixed infrastructure. Once that infrastructure is set up, there are scale benefits of pushing as much product through it as possible. And once a creator of content has developed a relationship with an effective packager and marketer of his product, there is likely to be at least some level of customer captivity. Turner's early entry into the cable channel business gave him a sales force, relationships with content producers and distributors, and a technological architecture that allowed him to efficiently develop, market, and distribute new channels. This content was generally continuous, themed to target a particular audience, and largely a mix of low-cost, non-star-driven original programming and relatively inexpensive repackaged (or colorized) older fare. Although not as glamorous as his disastrous foray into the movie studio business, Turner's bouquet of cable channels created the bulk of the value that made him a billionaire.

The packaging and marketing of content can be done electronically or physically, with electronic being by far the more efficient method. If a product can be marketed to local distributors without a national field sales force, for instance, the fixed costs required to perform that function will be reduced dramatically. But it is precisely the size of the required fixed cost base that creates the economies of scale. So while the replacement of physical with electronic means—or, as in the case of cable channels, as electronic means become relatively more sophisticated—will reduce expenses, it will also reduce barriers to entry. Chapter 5 is dedicated to demonstrating how digital distribution more generally destroys rather than creates value for shareholders. Ted Turner will not need to read Chapter 5 to understand this point—the dramatic impact of his decision to support Time Warner's combination with AOL on his net worth provided him with a much more memorable lesson in this regard.

The business of getting the content into the actual hands of the consumer is the most capital intensive of all. Whether building movie theaters to show the films or digging up streets to lay cable or driving around in trucks to deliver newspapers, the last mile is in many ways the toughest row to hoe. But it is precisely because of this quality that media farmers who intensely focus on these fields can benefit from significant economies of scale that are often paired with powerful customer captivity. As the size of the field being served gets larger and larger, it becomes harder and harder to enforce barriers and stop interlopers from gaining a foothold in one small corner or another.

Most observers forget that the initial successful franchises upon which the Turner family built its media empire were of an intensively local nature. Billboard advertising in Savannah, Georgia, is as local as you get, and the Turners understood the power of local and regional scale in creating barriers to entry. The critical transaction that allowed the Turner Advertising Company to become an industry leader reflects this appreciation. When Turner's father, Ed, bought General Outdoor in 1962, he did so with a partner who had billboards in the northern states. By splitting the assets, Turner became the dominant player in the Southeast—precisely the kind of relative scale that translates into competitive advantage.[5]

When Ted took over the business from Ed, he continued to reinforce this regional strength by buying more billboards in existing and adjacent markets. Turner then complemented these assets with other local media: first radio and later television and the Atlanta Braves, which he bought for $10 million on a layaway plan.[6] He was ultimately able to leverage this combination of local assets to build first a regional and then a national cable channel, the TBS Superstation. TBS became the basis of the collection of channels that are the source of his wider fame. But it should not be forgotten that none of what followed would have been possible without the success and profitability of the dominant local businesses upon which Turner built.

The local-global distinction is really just one example of the broader distinction between special interest or niche businesses on the one hand and general interest or broad-based businesses on the other. If the targeted area is a location, the predominant relevance is to the retail segment. If the niche targeted, however, is technology professionals or teenage girls, it will be more relevant to the content and packaging segments. But the basic point remains

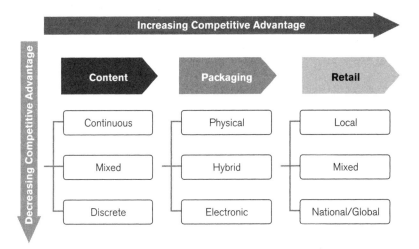

FIGURE 3.5   Media Industry Structure: Competitive Advantage

the same: As a practical matter, it is easier to enforce barriers to entry within a targeted arena, whether that arena is a clearly defined special need, shared activity, physical geography, or demographic or psychographic niche.

Taken together, these overarching perspectives broadly define our approach to the media industry, one segment at a time. At this point, we have provided neither convincing theoretical arguments nor compelling empirical data for these assertions. But taken together, they offer a kind of simple answer key that will facilitate efforts to do just that in the chapters that follow.

These preliminary directional observations may not seem earth-shattering in themselves. But the framework they represent is completely at odds with the conventional wisdom that pervades the broader media environment: that investors should bet on the media "franchise" most likely to develop the next successful blockbuster, that content is in any sense king, that the Internet is a wonderful new development that has provided a potential lifeline to otherwise slowly degenerating media franchises, that globalization will provide a critical media growth engine, and so on.

To understand this fundamental disconnect between the reality of the media business and the conventional wisdom, we take on the key myths propagated by moguls and internalized by the broader media intelligentsia. The next chapter targets the four core myths that challenge our approach to understanding the media business. We then end this section with an entire chapter devoted to the latest development used by media moguls to justify all manner of madness and underperformance: the Internet.

4 | Debunking Media Myths

Every media mogul has his or her own style and way of talking about the media industry. But if you listen closely, a handful of common themes emerges. All of these, while sounding eminently reasonable, are in fact profoundly misguided and go a long way toward explaining the chronic underperformance of these companies. Before turning to a detailed analysis of the specific key media industry segments, it is worth examining a few of the most prevalent of these ubiquitous media myths.

Earlier we highlighted four "sham" competitive advantages repeatedly cited by media moguls as representing structural barriers to competition: deep pockets, brands, talent, and first mover. Here we attack four core myths about the nature of the media businesses that have been used to justify a variety of misguided strategies.

1. GROWTH IS GOOD

The ultimate truism in the media industry is that all manner of growth is intrinsically attractive. Every media mogul is relentlessly focused on communicating his or her commitment to driving growth, whether internally or through acquisitions. This preoccupation is perhaps best captured in Edgar Bronfman Sr.'s explanation justifying the fateful decision to allow his son to buy media conglomerate Universal. This ultimately disastrous transaction required divesting their family business, Seagram, along with their 25 percent stake in DuPont. "The whisky business is not a growth business and you can't ask a forty-year-old chief executive to run a stagnant company," said

Bronfman père. "We could have taken over DuPont," he added, "but what fun would it have been to go to Wilmington, Delaware, and run that business."[1]

The media growth fetish is as misguided as it is ubiquitous. Let's start with the obvious: There is no such thing as a free lunch. All "good" things, including growth, come at a cost. In the case of growth, that cost comes in the form of whatever investment is required to generate the growth. The relevant question then is not whether the growth being sought is a good thing in the abstract. The relevant question is whether the investment required to generate that growth provides an adequate return. In the language of finance, the basic issue is whether your return on capital (ROIC, or Return on Invested Capital) is greater than your cost of capital (WACC, or Weighted Average Cost of Capital). When the return is greater, investing in growth creates value. When the cost is greater than the return, however, every incremental dollar of growth actually destroys value.

Returning to our basic analytic framework, only a business with barriers to entry can support investments in growth that yield excess returns. When a business without barriers invests in growth, it either does so on unattractive terms or attracts new entrants that soon depress returns to normal levels. The fallacy of the growth myth is that it fails to distinguish good growth from bad growth. Unfortunately for the media industry, this fallacy is embedded in its very being.

Furthermore, the two key sources of reinforcing competitive advantage—scale and customer captivity—are both put under pressure by high growth.

Because scale is a relative concept, operating in a high growth environment is particularly challenging. Small or new competitors can grow more quickly than the market with relatively modest absolute revenue increases, while the leader can lose relative share even as its growth in absolute terms dwarfs the rest of the industry. The law of large numbers is such that the faster the industry growth, the harder and harder it becomes to maintain relative scale.

To the extent that customer captivity relates to existing customers, the faster an industry is growing, the more it is likely to be relying on new customers to fuel that growth. And new customers, unlike existing ones, have no habits or switching costs—so new entrants in a market have a level playing field when competing with incumbents for customers in virgin territory.

All this sounds very theoretical, and it is. But the numbers confirm the validity of this perspective. Let's return to the large media conglomerates. Although we have yet to examine in detail which businesses benefit from competitive advantage and which do not, it is safe to say that large media conglomerates are made up of some combination of both types of media businesses. An analysis of the relationship between these companies' return on invested capital and their cost of capital over time demonstrates that the cost of their capital has been consistently greater than the return generated by the capital.[2] This is quite consistent with the stock performance already discussed.

Next, we dive deeper and focus on how fast the revenue grew in these companies. If we compare the revenue growth to the stock performance of the media conglomerates, there is an important relationship. Unfortunately for the owners of stock in these companies, the correlation is decidedly negative: The faster the revenue grew, the worse the stock performed. This is exactly what you would expect from companies whose return on capital is stubbornly and significantly below their cost of capital. And it is what you would expect from an industry that worships growth in itself, regardless of its source.

A skeptic might argue that we have stacked the deck against the media companies in these analyses. Each of these companies undertook at least one expensive and misguided acquisition during the period covered, which, it could be argued, explains both the connection between revenue growth and poor stock performance and the gap between ROIC and WACC. But our skeptic is misguided: The analysis of whether growth was worth the cost of achieving it is the same whether the investment was made internally or through acquisition. Not counting the bad acquisitions is like the student

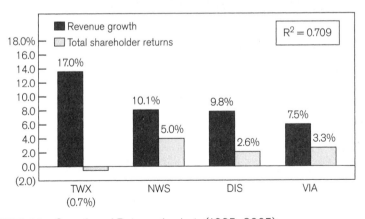

FIGURE 4.1 Growth and Returns Analysis (1995–2005)

Note: Total shareholder returns include capital gains and dividends. Shareholder returns represent the time period of 12/31/95–12/31/05; revenue growth represents the period between calendar year 1995 and 2005.

who says he has a 3.5 GPA if only you don't count the C's. But the fact is, even if we went to the trouble of distinguishing between returns from internal investment and returns from external investment, it seems highly unlikely that the results would be any different. To demonstrate this point, let's take a closer look at the business that all of these media conglomerates have in common: film production.

The business of making movies when looked at over an extended period of time has precisely that quality that media moguls claim they desire: It has grown significantly faster on an organic basis than most other media businesses and faster than the economy as a whole. This may seem surprising given the proliferation of forms of competition for consumers' time and attention and the increasing problem of piracy. To be sure, the movie business has benefited from occasional revenue windfalls corresponding to the introduction of a new distribution platform like DVDs. But the observation regarding growth is true over a much longer period of time than could be explained from these kinds of occasional revenue spikes.

In addition to high growth, the film production business has another quality relevant to our analysis: It unfortunately has no significant competitive advantages. High revenue growth in the absence of barriers to entry is bad news, not good: It represents throwing good money after bad to generate

TABLE 4.1 Film Revenue ($ in millions)

Source	1980	2000	% Change
Theatrical			
Domestic	$1,183	$3,100	4.9%
Foreign	$911	$2,900	6.0%
Home Video	$280	$7,800	18.1%
Pay Cable	$240	$1,600	10.0%
Network TV	$430	$300	−1.8%
Syndication	$150	$800	8.7%
Other TV	$800	$3,900	8.2%
Total	**$3,994**	**$20,400**	**8.5%**
Domestic Gross %	29.6%	15.2%	
Theatrical %	52.4%	29.4%	

Source: Harold L. Vogel, *Entertainment Industry Economics* (New York: Cambridge University Press, 2001), 5th edition.

TABLE 4.2 Film Costs (Percent Per Annum Growth) 1980–1999

	Average Cost/Film
Production	9.4%
Advertising	9.9%
Prints	7.5%
Total Releasing	9.4%
Growth in Number of Films	1.6%
Overall Cost Growth	**11.1%**
Overall Revenue Growth	**8.5%**

Source: Harold L. Vogel, *Entertainment Industry Economics* (New York: Cambridge University Press, 2001), 5th edition.

revenue growth without any hope of achieving superior returns. In the case of the movie business, this would suggest making more and more movies that generate less and less incremental revenue all the while bidding up the cost of talent to fill these increasingly unprofitable vehicles.

Although we have yet to fully explain why the movie business is intrinsically one that does not have competitive advantages, the data is wholly consistent with this hypothesis. For as fast as revenues have grown in the film business, costs have grown even faster. An 8.5 percent long-term revenue growth rate is impressive as compared not only to other media businesses but to the broader economy. But when this is associated with an 11.1 percent long-term growth in costs, impressive does not translate into good, from a shareholder perspective. And despite the occasional blockbuster or successful franchise that is touted as the savior of the industry in one season or another, the revenue generated per dollar of cost put into each film has been on a steady downward trajectory. More recent data confirms the continuing validity of this observation.[3]

The view that growth is not necessarily good and that, in the absence of competitive advantages, it is unquestionably bad, conflicts with deep-seated beliefs in the media industry. The decisions made by media moguls based on these beliefs explain media underperformance more than any other single factor. Those decisions come broadly in two varieties. First, as in the case of the film business, media moguls evince a consistent and unhealthy urge to invest for growth in businesses that they are better off not growing. Second, unsatisfied with the lack of growth in a business that may actually have competitive advantages, media moguls seem congenitally unable to give the cash thrown off by these enterprises back to shareholders. Instead, the desire for growth is so overwhelming that they insist on entering new, faster-growing businesses that may or may not have barriers to entry and that they may or may not even have any expertise in operating.

The notion of just giving the cash back is anathema to the media companies precisely because it represents an acknowledgment that they are not growth businesses. Stocks tend to be viewed either as "yield" plays, without much growth but with significant dividends, or "growth" stories, from which value is expected from the equity appreciation that comes from reinvesting the cash. The split of Viacom in 2005 into two separate entities was justified on the grounds that CBS was the former type of stock and that the resulting "new" Viacom was the latter type. This theoretical framework is fine as far as it goes, but reinvesting in growth where there is no competitive advantage will not result in equity appreciation—quite the opposite. The stock performance of Viacom since the split, which to the surprise of many was inferior to that of CBS for the first two years that the companies traded as independent companies even before taking into account CBS's significant dividend, suggests that something like that occurred.

Certainly the most public and dramatic form of investing in growth is through acquisitions. We examine the disastrous track record of the largest media acquisitions in some detail in Chapter 12, but it is worth making a few preliminary observations with respect to some of the more recent high-profile growth acquisitions, particularly in the form of Internet acquisitions. Many point to the apparent financial success of News Corp. in acquiring MySpace for $580 million in 2005.[4] Just a year later, News announced that Google had agreed to pay News a minimum of $900 million over three and a half years just for the right to provide search and advertising to MySpace.[5] What's not to like?

Hopefully we are not so committed to our general thesis that we are unable to give credit where credit is due. News Corp. and Rupert Murdoch over time have shown genuine flashes of brilliance in identifying untapped market and profit opportunities. There are a number of highly successful businesses that have exploited the inefficiencies in the relatively nascent Internet advertising market. In different ways, these businesses have been able to profit from an arbitrage between the prices at which the thousands of small independent Internet sites would be willing to sell their unused advertising inventory and the value of this inventory—particularly when packaged with other sites that deliver similar demographic characteristics—to advertisers. Google has a unique ability to monetize Web traffic in this way through search and was willing to pay handsomely for the right to do so.

There has been much speculation over whether Google significantly over-paid—fueled primarily by the statements of Google itself.[6] This does not detract from News Corp.'s success in paying for its MySpace acquisition by exploiting this perceived inefficiency, and Google's apparently misguided belief that it could monetize it, on a grand scale.

While that makes the MySpace transaction a potentially financially attractive one, arbitrage opportunities by their nature are not sustainable sources of value over time. In addition, it is important not to overstate the benefits or understate the costs of the transaction. When you get back one and a half times what you paid for a property in under four years, it is understandable that the focus is on taking victory laps and not on competitive advantage and barriers to entry. The future returns News is able to achieve from its investment are unclear, however, given that the division is currently losing money even after the revenue from Google.

There can be powerful network effects from successful social networking businesses like MySpace and in the next chapter we highlight the explosive growth of user-generated content in general. That said, as Google has learned both from the MySpace operating deal and its expensive acquisition of YouTube, the ability to effectively monetize this kind of content has yet to be proven.[7] The subsequent loss of share to Facebook in just the few years since the transaction highlights how fragile competitive advantage is on the Internet.

The question of how financially attractive the investment in MySpace was is entirely separate from whether News Corp.'s ownership of the asset is "strategic" in the sense that we use the term. Are there any meaningful cost savings from combining MySpace with News? Would forcing News Corp. content on MySpace users make the site more or less attractive? Does cross-promotion of MySpace and other News properties achieve anything not available to third-party advertisers? There is no evidence to date that suggests any significant benefits in these regards.

Finally, media moguls do a fine job of trumpeting their successes but an even better job of sweeping their failures under the rug. If one counts only the wins, it's easy to look like a genius. When was the last time you heard about a company called IGN Entertainment? Less than two months after the MySpace deal, News announced it was paying even more for the acquisition of the online gaming site.[8] News's last-minute willingness to pay top dollar with few questions asked snared the prize, with Rupert Murdoch himself intervening to get the deal done.[9] This dramatic turn of events may have even played a role in the firing of Tom Freston as CEO at Viacom, whom owner Sumner Redstone apparently faulted for not being more decisive at closing Internet deals.[10]

That was pretty much the last anyone has heard of IGN. Since then, the CEO, who was briefly made COO of Fox's entire interactive division, left the company, and IGN has performed poorly. Our point is not that there can never be a smart growth acquisition, only that shareholders bear the impact of all of these taken together, not just the highlighted few.

Murdoch was quoted shortly after the MySpace and IGN deals as saying: "Both are either $500 million dollar mistakes, or they are going to look very, very smart."[11] He was wrong. One is clearly a mistake and the other could still turn out to be smart, but not very, very smart. The jury is out, as far as the net impact for shareholders is concerned. For the fiscal year that ended in August 2007, the entire renamed Fox Interactive Media (FIM) group, which included the nearly $1.5 billion spent on Internet acquisitions as well as all of the company's homegrown efforts, managed to generate just $10 million in profit.[12] By fiscal year 2009 this had become a loss and has remained so.

2. THE GOSPEL OF GOING GLOBAL

The virtues of operating internationally are asserted as dogmatically as the virtues of growth. And the God of globalization is worshipped with the same lack of nuance. Targets are proposed for achieving an optimal mix of "global" revenue within a set period of time without any discussions of which businesses and which markets would justify such a diversification. Claiming the intention to achieve a target of 50 percent of revenues coming from international markets in five years is particularly popular.[13] Part of the fascination with global markets may in fact simply be a by-product of the fascination with growth. To the extent that some non-U.S. markets are less media-saturated on the one hand and generally faster growing on the other, there would appear to be a kind of growth multiplier effect available to exploit. Why wouldn't a media mogul want to shift more operations in that direction?

There are three reasons why blind pursuit of a global footprint is a dangerous strategy.

First, as a structural matter, the ability to enforce barriers to entry on a global rather than local scale is significantly diminished.[14] Just as high growth threatens the market leader's advantages, large markets do the same. Big markets by definition can support many competitors even where fixed costs are large in an absolute sense. Scale advantages come from the size of the fixed cost base relative to the overall cost base, and in a vast global market it is likely that more players can justify the fixed cost "nut" required to operate competitively. Furthermore, the ability to defend barriers is always more manageable within narrowly defined frontiers. A niche operator or one within narrow geographic limits can much more effectively reinforce the barricades of competitive advantage. As proponents of building a fence along the entire length of the U.S.-Mexico border have learned the hard way, enforcing hegemony on a national, much less international, basis may be an inspirational goal, but it is a practical impossibility. The broader the mandate the more likely the business will be subject to successful incursions by smaller, focused niche players.

Second, and consistent with these observations, the track record of great nonmedia franchises in pursuing global strategies should give anyone pause. Wal-Mart may be invincible in the United States, but elsewhere their results have been anemic. McDonald's, the poster child for consumer globalization, has historically been markedly more profitable in North America than elsewhere. Nestlé, the original global corporation, is far less profitable in particular product areas like chocolate confectionary than in more nationally focused rivals like Hershey and Cadbury. Banks, too, including HSBC, earn higher returns in their core markets than they do in their global ventures, which, like their disastrous foray into U.S. mortgages (in which they were joined by Deutsche Bank, UBS, RBS, Barclays, and CSFB, among others) are characterized by an unusually high incidence of shipwrecks. To this, add the fact that because of the highly sensitive nature of media to many emerging governments, there are severe restrictions on the ability of foreigners to own significant media assets.

Third, the trends have been decidedly toward greater consumption of intensely local content. The movement to replace the American series that had long dominated international television markets with local fare, for example, has been evident for over a decade. There is great irony, as *Fortune* reported, in the fact that just "as the studios morphed into global entertainment conglomerates" to tap into what they viewed as the increasingly crucial international markets, "they started to discover something no one ever expected: a limit to the appeal of American pop culture."[15]

Among major consumer media conglomerates, only News Corporation is meaningfully global today, with almost half of its revenue coming from outside the United States. To its credit, however, News has achieved this over an extended period of time by pursuing a multilocal rather than a "global" strategy as such.[16] Even Viacom, whose modest international operations are predominantly from syndicating its MTV brands, has a policy of programming those networks with at least 70 percent local content.[17]

3. CONTENT IS KING

Although Sumner Redstone likes to claim that he coined the phrase *content is king*,[18] former Time Warner CEO Gerald Levin had been saying it since the early 1990s[19] and it was Michael Eisner's mantra at Disney and continues to be in connection with his new Internet ventures.[20] Ironically, the phrase was actually originally popularized in the late eighties in connection with the series of ill-considered and now widely repudiated media deals undertaken by large Japanese consumer hardware makers.[21] This undistinguished history has not dissuaded moguls from continuing to parrot the slogan, including the Japanese media moguls who should really know better.[22]

In addition to the alliterative allure of the notion that content is king, there is great intuitive appeal to the fundamental idea that it is in the substance of the media where the greatest value lies. I consume media content based on what I enjoy or find useful—surely the best company is the one that has the best content. This simple observation is reinforced by the intense emotional response the most powerful media can elicit. We all associate critical turning points in our lives or our understanding of the world with our exposure to a particular film, song, or book. The owners of this kind of precious intellectual property have dominion over our most sacred memories and are at this very moment producing the sacred memories of future generations. Regardless of any developments in technology or distribution, the argument goes, at the end of the day they will own the keys to the media kingdom.

To understand why this is not true we must return to first principles of competitive advantage. In debunking the content-is-king myth, it is worth distinguishing the creative content that is the core material for consumer media from the more data-driven business and professional media. Although the conclusions are not different, the processes for creating these kinds of content are quite distinct, as are the cultures of the organizations that produce them.

On the consumer side, the reasons why content is not king echo the reasons why talent is not a sustainable competitive advantage. Even if the ability to produce compelling content stemmed from qualities inherent in certain individuals or groups, there is simply no efficient way to monetize this skill for the benefit of shareholders rather than the producers themselves. This observation may seem inconsistent with the conventional wisdom about creative artists being perennially exploited by big media companies. Our point is not that artists aren't exploited, only that any exploitation does not over time result in superior value creation in media companies. First, much of the exploitation comes from the lawyers, managers, agents, family members, and other hangers-on rather than from the media companies.

Second, where the media companies have executives clever enough to consistently exploit the talent, these executives are typically clever enough to ensure that they are paid enough to reflect that skill. Either way, shareholders shouldn't expect much left over.

Media moguls are very adept at describing the tools at their disposal to mitigate risk in apparently hit-driven businesses. In the film businesses, a combination of preselling foreign rights, creating complex cofinancing arrangements, and leveraging proven brands or formats is presented as limiting downside on the one hand and improving the "hit" ratio on the other. There is no question that content businesses can be run more or less efficiently and this can have a dramatic impact on the results of operations.

The problem is that the tools of efficient operations are generally available to everyone and by definition cannot be a source of sustainable competitive advantage. Furthermore, when particular brands seem like a sure thing, as in the case of a popular film franchise, more often than not there is a well-represented creative artist critical to that level of certainty who is in a position to appropriate much of that value.

These observations most obviously apply to what we have called discrete rather than continuous content businesses. Content businesses that are delivered continuously are less reliant on hits. These businesses, producing daily newspapers or weekly magazines for instance, or the soap operas or game shows that fill daytime TV schedules, generally have less sex appeal and are not usually what media moguls have in mind when they spout on about content being king. And although continuous content businesses lend themselves to competitive advantage far more readily than discrete content businesses, they, too, have challenges that would suggest that they fall far short of being "king."

A much higher proportion of content delivered to business and professional markets is continuous in nature, typically sold through costly subscriptions. These businesses try to distinguish themselves in the minds of investors by explaining that they provide "must-have" rather than "nice-to-have" content. A lawyer needs the latest case precedent and a trader needs the most current prices, so providing this critical content to them on a continuous basis, the argument goes, creates inherently better businesses than providing content meant merely to amuse or divert.

The must-have appellation by itself is no more illuminating than the general assertion that content is king. Oxygen is the ultimate must-have product, but it is neither costly nor likely in the near term to support any entrepreneurial efforts to commercialize its sale. The relevant question is not just whether the content is mission critical, but whether it is generally available.

Where does the content used in business and professional media businesses come from and just how widely available is it? There is no single answer to this question, but two examples from the financial and legal sectors will suggest the complexity of the question. These examples highlight that to the extent that these businesses have competitive advantages, it is not necessarily the content (continuous or otherwise) that provides it.

Financial prices reviewed by a trader usually report a transaction between two parties. This transaction occurred either on an exchange, through a dealer, or directly between the buyer and seller. The financial information provider typically needs to buy this information, and it is rarely sold on an exclusive basis. There was a time when obtaining continuous data from stock exchanges around the world required a high level of relative technological sophistication. Today exchanges provide their real-time data feeds to anyone who wants them, whether a financial information provider or the trader directly.

To support barriers to entry, a media company must do more than simply retransmit the continuous content available to anyone who wants to buy it directly. Instead the company must integrate this data with pricing information on more obscure financial instruments and apply software and analytics to make the total package more valuable and switching more costly. It is the sophisticated packaging of content largely owned and created by others that is the core business of financial information providers.

Similarly, legal case "content" is produced by judges. There was a time when these were disseminated under exclusive contracts with a particular lucky publisher. Today most courts simply post the decisions on their own Web site for anyone to review or use. To provide a product that professionals will pay for, a legal publisher needs to aggregate this content and provide

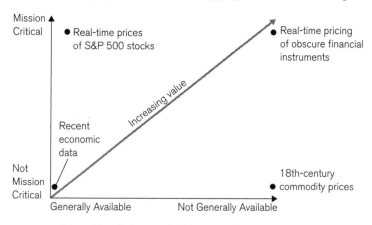

FIGURE 4.2 "Must-Have" Content?: Financial Information

software and tools that allow a lawyer to easily search, analyze, and compare it to other relevant cases.

Most professional database businesses, like those in the financial and legal information segments, sell continuous content. But in doing so, they are typically integrating largely third-party content with additional proprietary information and analytics. We examine the economics and barriers to entry available in database businesses in Chapter 8. The general point is that the core of any competitive advantage is more often than not from the manner of aggregation rather than the creation of content, continuous or otherwise.

4. THE CULT OF CONVERGENCE

As it emerged from the devastating recession of the early 1990s, the media industry latched onto a new concept that represented a ray of hope in the face of the coming new century. Most of the largest sectors were quite mature, and those that were not could see signs of maturation creeping into their previously relentless growth trajectory. The opportunity on the horizon for each of these very different businesses came in the form of a digital revolution that would break down the walls between previously distinct and unrelated business lines. The new source of growth would come from the ability to get into these new businesses that had been beyond their reach. It was the ultimate win-win: everybody is able to use everybody else's business as a source of growth!

If this idea of convergence sounds like a huge pyramid scheme to you, that is a sign that you read all the previous chapters. Whenever someone suggests that breaking down barriers to entry is good news, it is time to grab your wallet and hold on very tight. Convergence may sound sexy, but anything that facilitates others' ability to enter your business is terrible news by definition. Your ability to enter anyone else's business on a reciprocal basis cannot possibly make up for the loss, as this very ability indicates their business is worse as well. It is a classic case of one plus one being substantially less than two.

Contrary to popular belief, the cult of convergence did not emerge in conjunction with the Internet explosion, but predates it quite substantially. In 1992, a group of eight equity research analysts across a wide range of industry sectors from Goldman Sachs produced a hugely influential report that coined a term that entered the media vernacular: *communicopia*.[23] Although the report never formally defined the term, its opening sentences captured the breadth and the urgency of the issues raised: "As a result of rapid technological developments in the computer software and hardware, consumer electronic, cable and telecommunications industries, we believe a true revolution in the delivery of entertainment, information, transactional and telecommunications services may be at hand. Through a confluence of interests, this revolution could bring together a broad cross-section of industries that heretofore have considered themselves unrelated."

Goldman Sachs successfully leveraged this newly established "brand" into an annual conference that still attracts the biggest media moguls from all the converging sectors to trumpet to investors how they would benefit from these revolutionary changes. By the time the Internet boom did come, the Goldman analysts looked even more prophetic. As the *New York Times* breathlessly reported during the height of the boom:

> One week it is a white-hot debut for a new business on the Internet. The next it's a telephone company breaking a taboo by buying a cable network. Last week, a spirited bidding war broke out over a major wireless phone company. Like pixels lighting up one by one on a flat-screen display, these seemingly disjointed events add new clarity and detail to a developing picture of what analysts at Goldman, Sachs seven years ago called "Communicopia": an intertwined landscape of data and voice communications, entertainment programming and electronic commerce. But for all its complexity, this world is rapidly converging. More and more of the companies in these industries are doing more and more of the same sorts of things.[24]

Many of the Goldman analysts' predictions, even if they took many more years to unfold than originally envisaged, were largely correct. But, as the subtitle of the original report, "A Digital Communications Bounty," suggested, they missed, or at least did not wish to highlight, the fundamental economic implication of these observations. Sure, the report acknowledged, as in every revolution there will be winners and losers.[25] But in the case of the communicopia revolution, their view was that the former would dwarf the latter. Music companies, production studios, and any owner of copyright, according to "Communicopia," would be big winners: "The litany of potential new business opportunities is practically endless."[26] Even an obvious loser like Blockbuster, according to the authors, should not be overly concerned about the negative impact of communicopia. In their view, "the beauty" of the emerging products and business models is that they would not cannibalize Blockbuster's core franchise but instead entail "enough distinguishing features to allow [them] to be largely incremental to the videocassette industry."[27]

Unfortunately, if there was bounty to be had, it would not be for the investors who were Goldman's audience. Instead, it would be for the consumers who would benefit from the frenetic competition among these converging sectors. And the introduction of the Internet into this mix has only further accelerated this trend of value destruction among incumbent media players.

5 | The Internet Is Not Your Friend

If you ever have a hankering to get under a media mogul's skin, suggest that he is in the "old media" business and that the future lies in new media, as epitomized by the Internet. It is poignant to hear the desperation in media moguls' protestations that they are not yesterday's news. "Clearly the new media businesses seem to have more sex appeal than the old media businesses," observed Robert Iger shortly after taking the helm as CEO of Disney in 2005. "My goal is not to be treated like an old media company."[1] There is something cringe inducing—like when one's grandparent uses modestly contemporary slang in order to establish "street cred"—in these forceful assertions of continuing relevance.

Given our focus on whether a particular business has barriers to entry, it will not be surprising that we are not quite as preoccupied with whether media is old or new. But because of the overwhelming focus of moguls, investors, and the public on this topic, in this chapter we examine in more detail both the impact of the Internet and digital distribution on other media businesses and the strength of various Internet businesses themselves.

It is worth noting at the outset that there is something increasingly artificial in the new-media versus old-media distinction. If the birth of the commercial Internet era is dated from the 1995 IPO of Netscape, the medium is now well into middle age or at least past puberty. Although new, unproven Internet businesses continue to emerge whose aim is to undermine some existing established media franchise, today it is not unusual for that targeted established franchise to itself be an Internet company.

Let's look at Monster.com. Established in 1994, and employing essentially the same employer-advertising business model as the newspapers from which it has taken market share, the company quickly became the largest online destination for job search and employment classified advertising.[2] But, over the last decade, Monster understandably has attracted dozens of competitors. Other broad-based online employment sites like careerbuilder .com, owned by a consortium of affiliated newspapers, and hotjobs, a venture-backed competitor that was purchased by Yahoo in 2002, go head-to-head with Monster for the same customers. In addition, niche businesses like Dice .com, a recruitment destination for technology professionals, have been able to establish leadership positions in those narrower areas of focus. Finally, dozens of emerging companies employing a variety of different business models and technologies—ranging from a subscription service for high-end job seekers in the case of TheLadders.com, a referral service among like-minded colleagues in the case of LinkedIn, and a Web crawler that aggregates the listings of all the other services in the case of SimplyHired—have collectively begun to have a meaningful impact on the marketplace.

At this point, is Monster new media or old media? More important, is this even the relevant question?

The concept of competitive advantage applies only to *incumbent* businesses. How could a new entrant have a barrier to entry if it hasn't entered yet? "The existence of barriers to entry means that incumbent firms are able to do what potential rivals cannot. Being able to do what rivals cannot is the definition of a competitive advantage."[3] Monster, then, was a new entrant but became, as all successful new entrants do, an incumbent. As we turn to examine the impact of the Internet on the media environment, we would propose to dispense with the unhelpful new-media/old-media distinction and focus instead on the more germane entrant/incumbent distinction in conjunction with our framework for analyzing competitive advantage.

One objection to this approach may be that it discounts any number of potential entrant advantages frequently found in the new-media environment. The old-media incumbent may be saddled with an expensive physical infrastructure or labor costs and it may need to support a line of decaying legacy products and services. Furthermore, the entrant is likely not to be encumbered with the cultural baggage of the lumbering old media giants. More concretely, the nimble entrant may have developed exciting new technology, product design, or marketing materials to exploit the inability of the incumbent to react quickly.

One of the lessons of the original Internet boom is that the ability to harm an incumbent business does not in itself suggest an ability to sustain an attractive alternative model. Of the thousands of new media businesses that did some damage to the established media franchises, remarkably few have survived. Where there are incumbent disadvantages, there will certainly be new entrants. But if all potential new entrants share exactly the same advantages vis-à-vis the incumbent but no such advantages vis-à-vis one another, none really has any sustainable advantages at all. The entrant will barely have had time to savor its "success" at outmaneuvering the old-media barons before realizing that it must contend with all newcomers who want to get in on the act. Once a firm manages to enter the market, it has become an incumbent and will thrive or flounder based on the same laws of competitive advantage.

A company's perspective on the impact of the Internet depends significantly on whether it is an incumbent or a potential new entrant. In examining the Internet, then, we will consider separately the impact on incumbents on the one hand and the ability of new Internet businesses to actually establish their own defensible barriers to entry on the other.

THE INTERNET AND THE INCUMBENTS

To hear media moguls explain it, the advent of the Internet was the best thing for them. Their arguments have come in three related flavors.

First, the Internet is growing, and since all of their existing businesses have some digital manifestation or other, the net impact on their overall business will be to hasten growth. To the extent that there are new, independent, growing Internet businesses, these will likely be new customers who need the incumbent's content or expertise to support their growth, which will in turn further accelerate the incumbent's own growth. "As far as we are concerned," asserted Rupert Murdoch confidently, "the Internet is broadening our opportunity, as well as for other big media companies with huge resources in sports, entertainment and news. There's just more opportunity."[4] CEO Robert Iger similarly sees only upside from the emergence of Google, a company with many times the market capitalization of Disney. "I'm not worried about Google cannibalizing our advertising," he said. "Google's search capabilities are more important to us because they will drive consumers to our companies."[5]

Second, incumbent competitive advantage is transferable to the new medium. The brands, customer relationships, and content that support their existing businesses will create a barrier to others online as well. "The days of old media and new media are over," CBS CEO Les Moonves said confidently. "Now, it's just media."[6] The idea is that distinctions between old and new are artificial, the latter simply representing a seamless transition from the former, and that the basic rules of the game have not changed.

Third, the Internet will allow media companies to do what they were doing before but at much higher profitability levels. By reducing the cost of production and delivery, the theory goes, incumbent media companies will be able to grow margins as they shift product from the off-line environment to the online. Rupert Murdoch has been quite specific about the net impact on profits: "We are going to be seeing more [profits] in newspapers coming out of electronic delivery. The film industry may find that . . . the way it distributes films change[s]. It's going to force a lot of change in the business models. But the absolute demand for content won't change. We believe that puts us on the eve of a new era of opportunity."[7]

As reasonable sounding as these platitudes may be, they do not stand up to close scrutiny. Even if the Internet were a source of overall net top-line growth to the incumbent media companies—and all evidence is quite to the contrary—this begs the fundamental question of whether this would represent profitable growth. There is also little evidence that the incumbent media companies are the major source of the content consumed on the Internet. Indeed, user-generated content rather than mogul-generated content continues to be the fastest-growing category in the medium.[8] Take a look at YouTube's "most viewed" videos screen on any given day and you are likely to see that well over half of them represent user-generated content—and even that minority contributed by Google "partners" is not predominantly from the large media conglomerates. Only 4 percent of the clips on YouTube have been posted or approved by media companies.[9] More broadly, two-thirds of Internet users are spending their time on social networking sites.[10]

This perspective is consistent with the lopsided nature and modest scale of the revenue-sharing agreements that have been negotiated between digital media companies and the incumbent media conglomerates. iTunes may be very successful for Apple, but Apple manages the business to maximize sales of hardware, not revenue to media companies. So although the revenue split of 70/30 in favor of content providers sounds generous, Apple will not take videos unless providers agree to the very low and simple pricing policy they enforce.

With all of YouTube expected to generate barely $200 million of advertising revenues for Google in 2008,[11] it's safe to assume that the revenue available to media companies that together make up a small portion of YouTube's video inventory and usage is insignificant. Celebrity gossip columnist Perez Hilton, one of YouTube's original content "partners," reportedly received $5,000 in ad-sharing revenues during a three-month period in which his popular videos were viewed 25 million times. "Fuck you, YouTube. Fuck you," Hilton proclaimed in his farewell video.[12] Although media companies have belatedly rallied around Hulu as their official Internet venue of choice for video, the jury is very much out as to the potential size and profitability of this venture.[13]

Furthermore, the preexisting assets of incumbent media companies may be central to their homegrown Web properties, but there is no indication that this has served as a meaningful barrier to entry for competing Web businesses. And although the incumbents benefit from the cost reductions made possible by the Internet, on a relative basis, potential new entrants benefit even more. The source of economies of scale in media as elsewhere is the fixed cost nature of the business, which is reduced by precisely the cost phenomenon touted as a "benefit" by incumbents. In vertical after vertical we see the owners of the leading off-line brands unable to dominate the online medium and often they do not even have the leading position—for example, The Knot owns the online bridal category, while Condé Nast dominates the off-line world with *Bride's, Modern Bride,* and *Elegant Bride* magazines. The conglomerates certainly have the cash to buy the successful upstarts—as Disney did with Club Penguin, an online virtual world for kids—but then they have to wonder: Who will come next?

When one stands back and considers the impact of digital distribution on each of the specific sources of competitive advantage, not just economies of scale, the conclusion is the same: The Internet may be somebody's friend—most notably, the consumers of media—but it is not the friend of incumbent media companies. For the incumbent, any benefits from the Internet on either the cost or new revenue opportunity side are overwhelmed by the damage done by the lowering of barriers to entry.

We can identify no incumbent media businesses for which the introduction of the Internet strengthened a preexisting competitive advantage[14]— much less one in which the Internet, like a talisman, established an advantage where none previously existed. The case of the impact of the Internet on the newspaper industry is instructive in this regard. Newspaper executives initially claimed that the Internet would serve as a boon to them. "It's wonderful,"[15] exulted *New York Times* chairman Arthur Sulzberger when asked in an interview how the Internet would transform the economics of the business.

TABLE 5.1 Impact of Digital Distribution on Competitive Advantage

	Sources of Competitive Advantage			
	Scale	Customer Captivity	Cost (Proprietary Technology)	Government Protection
Impact of Digital Distribution	Available to more, sooner and cheaper	Lowers switching costs	More ephemeral than ever	You can still hire a lobbyist

All the basic arguments proffered in favor of the supposed benefits of the Internet should have applied to newspapers in spades. Daily newspaper circulation had been in decline since the late 1980s, while readership had been falling at least since the early 1960s,[16] so this sexy new medium seemed to provide a powerful tool to reverse these trends. The newspaper local advertising sales force or content collection could not be easily replicated, so Internet sites would need to either buy from or otherwise rely on the newspaper for its content and infrastructure. The newspaper itself would keep the best of this for itself, however, becoming the leading online source not only of news and information but of the fast-growing Internet classified businesses and a wide variety of potential transactional business that was previously out of the question. Best of all, over time, this industry, weighed down by the cumbersome business of actually printing a daily paper and driving the copies around in trucks for delivery—activities that were overwhelmingly in the grip of powerful unions and, on occasion, less savory elements of commerce—would free itself of these costly and inherently inefficient activities.

It didn't turn out that way.

The dawn of the modern newspaper industry in a sense coincides with the birth of the television industry. In earlier times, a major urban market could support literally dozens of newspapers, each with its own voice targeting its own demographic, political, or social-economic niche. With the adoption of television as a ubiquitous mass medium through which advertisers efficiently achieved coverage of an entire locality, there was simply not enough revenue left to support a multitude of newspapers.

Newspaper production has relatively high fixed costs. Because of the high volumes produced daily and the importance of timely arrival, the newspaper industry is one of the last publishing businesses to own and operate its own massive printing operations, rather than outsourcing this function. A state-of-the-art, color printing facility capable of producing a major market daily requires hundreds of millions in up-front investment. Furthermore, the infrastructure required to physically deliver the newspaper each day to subscribers and newsstands is substantial, as is the critical mass of salespeople needed to cover all the categories of potential advertisers in a locality.

As the economic realities of the new local news order took hold, it became clear that the surviving newspaper in each jurisdiction would be the one with the greatest reach across which to spread these fixed costs. The key to achieving a mass audience is to offend as few constituencies as possible. The result was a massive rush to the middle, with newspapers confining their viewpoint to a few slim editorial pages and the balance of the paper devoted to more anodyne "objective" reporting of the day's events. Journalists who cling to the notion of this style of reporting—which is a peculiarly American phenomenon—as stemming exclusively from high-minded professional values rather than economic realities generally have no sense of this historical context.[17]

When the smoke cleared, the last newspaper left standing in each market was an awesome business. Well-managed newspapers in small or midsize markets could achieve profit margins well in excess of 30 percent. In major metropolitan markets, even with higher labor and associated costs, on the one hand, and a variety of free or targeted local niche competitors, on the other, profit margins were comfortably and consistently above 20 percent. To understand what brought this happy state of affairs to an abrupt end we need to follow the money.

Newspaper revenues come overwhelmingly from advertising. On average less than 20 percent of newspapers' top line comes from readers actually buying copies of the paper. Most of the rest is represented by various forms of advertising: Local retail advertising is the largest single category, classified advertising (made up predominantly of help-wanted, auto, and real-estate classifieds) follows, and national brand advertising rounds out the picture. But from a profit perspective, all advertising is not created equal. Although classified advertising, even at its pinnacle during the dot-com boom, represented less than a third of newspaper revenue, it has long been responsible for well over half of the profit.

What made classified advertising so different? If you were looking to sell your house or your car, how else could you get the word out effectively? Other kinds of advertisers might use direct mail, TV, or radio, maybe put up a billboard or take out space in the yellow pages. But for an individual with a single item to sell quickly, none of these came close to the impact of a tiny classified advertisement in a daily newspaper. Newspapers, as a result, could charge extraordinarily high rates for a few well-chosen words buried in the classifieds. In addition, unlike other advertising, no sales force is needed. Just someone to take the call and jot down what you want to say—along with your credit-card number. Think they are charging too much or annoyed that the person who answered the phone was rude or misspelled words in your ad? Get over it. You had no practical alternative. And at those prices and that cost structure, the publishers were laughing all the way to the bank.

There is something counterintuitive about the notion that these oft-ignored small-print pages at the back of the paper constitute the financial heart of the great newspaper franchises. Surely it is great journalism that is the lifeblood of great newspapers. And at some level this is true: Without readers, there will be no advertisers of any kind. But the scale nature of the business was such that, as a practical matter, no serious competitor could profitably launch an alternative, so publishers had a huge amount of discretion as to what stories to run in the paper without posing a risk to the franchise. With plenty of money to go around, editors and journalists were largely left to their own devices. They have written many fine articles that may or may not have been of great interest to their core audience—studies have consistently shown readers are overwhelmingly focused on more mundane topics like local community events[18] than those favored by graduates of journalism schools—even as readership has been in consistent decline since the 1960s. Such was the power of the core business engine fueled by classified advertising, however, that circulation declines were easily more than compensated for by advertising rate increases. Why rock the boat?

Then came the Internet. The first killer moneymaking application of the net was classified advertising. Although there are certainly Internet content businesses, the core power of the medium relates to its extraordinary packaging capabilities. The online environment lends itself to easily searching a database for products and services with the specifications desired. And with none of the fixed cost infrastructure requirements of a newspaper, Web sites dedicated to every conceivable category of classified advertising emerged.

The cost of placing an online listing was a fraction of the print version (or actually free in the case of craigslist). Newspapers were well positioned to compete in this world, but in their own world they hadn't really had to compete at all. And the last thing they wanted to do was trade in high-priced print advertisements for low-priced online ones. So many newspapers set up a Web site and either gave away an online ad "free" with a print ad or up-sold a low-priced online ad with the high-priced off-line one. Very few initially offered an "Internet-only" option.

In the off-line world, newspapers had well over 90 percent of the classified advertising pie, with a smattering of free apartment, home, or automotive "shoppers" representing most of the balance. In the online world, the newspaper might be the leader in some categories and not in others, but the competitive landscape and relative shares were both constantly shifting and difficult to track. The huge price differential between online and off-line classified advertising ensured that it would take time before online would take a significant share of the overall revenue pie, even as it undermined the pricing flexibility of print classified advertising. But in the last decade the share impact has been dramatic in all the key classified categories.

If the newspapers had been less reactive and more aggressive in pursuing the online opportunity, it might have had an impact on their ultimate share, but it would not have altered the structural dynamics of the industry. There are some network scale economies of online classified businesses, but because

Help Wanted Online Classified Advertising Revenue Market Share Analysis, 1998–2011E

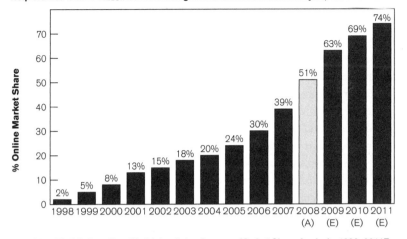

Auto Classified Online Classified Advertising Revenue Market Share Analysis, 1998–2011E

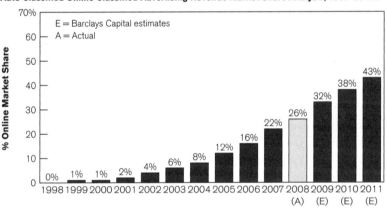

Real Estate Online Classified Advertising Revenue Market Share Analysis, 1998–2011E

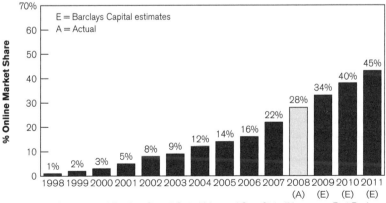

Sources: NAA, Forrester, and Barclays Capital. Craig Huber and Greg Stein, "Newspaper Fact Book, April 2009," Barclays Capital.

FIGURE 5.1   Online Classified Advertising Revenue Market Share

of the minimal switching costs and low cost relative to print, the competitive landscape in each category usually supports several scale players (of which newspapers are usually one) and a variety of niche players—as reflected in the earlier example of Monster.com and the online employment classified market. It is still a good business, but smaller and less profitable than the previous one. And newspapers owned the entirety of the older, better market but are one of many in the newer, less attractive one.

None of the other supposed benefits from the Internet to the incumbent have come to pass either. It is true that a number of newspapers, notably the *Wall Street Journal* and *New York Times,* have developed very successful online versions of their products. The notion, however, that this would halt the impact of long-term circulation declines stemming from the inability to attract younger readers is misguided. First, only the *Wall Street Journal* has been able to sustain a subscription model online, and the advertising revenues associated with even the most successful of these is a tiny fraction of what they are displacing. Newspapers' Internet revenue will remain under 10 percent of total newspaper revenue on average through the end of the decade even after a variety of Internet acquisitions they have made. Second, a dirty little secret of the newspaper business is that the demographics of the readers of their online papers are not meaningfully different from those of their off-line versions.[19] Young people are not reading the paper in print or online. They are getting their information in a variety of other ways and there is no evidence that any newspaper's Web-savvy strategies have made a dent in this trend. And since today's young people are tomorrow's old people, the implications are profoundly concerning.

The downside of high fixed cost businesses is that revenue declines fall straight to the bottom line. At the height of the Internet boom in 2000, newspapers were bitter that they were not getting "credit" in the public markets for their online revenues and a number seriously considered taking their nascent online businesses public to highlight the "value." Little did they realize that the business environment would never get any better for them than it was at that very moment—new online classified entrants still had only a few points of classified market share while the rest of their Internet brethren were using IPO proceeds to fill the print paper with unheard-of volumes of advertising. The point is that in the long run, the impact of lower barriers to entry will always overwhelm any cost benefits or growth opportunities. The precipitous decline in newspaper margins since that time tells the tale.

What does all this mean for our theory of the structure of competitive advantage generally and the future of the newspaper business specifically? The emergence of digital distribution did not eliminate significant economies of scale for the newspaper business, but it significantly lowered the barriers for non-print competitors. In a post-TV world, most local markets could support only a single newspaper. In a post-Internet world, the emergence of non-print competitors has raised the question of whether any print newspaper can be supported in certain markets given the fixed cost requirements. A number of papers both domestically and internationally have already announced the suspension of their print editions altogether.[20]

The precipitous drops in newspaper profit margins reflect both the extent of the change in the industry structure and the extent to which their managements were poorly equipped to respond. When margins are high, the hard questions are often avoided. What kinds of reporting, for instance, are true competitive advantages for a local paper? How many such newspapers really add anything distinctive to international or national news. Indeed, in a state like New York, with almost fifty daily local papers, how many separate Albany bureaus really need to exist?[21] There are three arguably national newspapers in the United States—the *New York Times*, *Wall Street Journal*, and *USA Today*—and they are among the least profitable. The other almost fifteen hundred daily papers (not to mention the more than six thousand weeklies) which represent well over 90 percent of the industry's revenues are local or at most regional.[22] From a content collection perspective, a local paper has scale advantage in dominating the intensely local scene—high-school sports, local crime, politics, and schools. This may not be what the journalists are mostly interested in covering, but if print newspapers are to survive, it will be through single-minded focus on the only area of coverage in which they have an advantage.

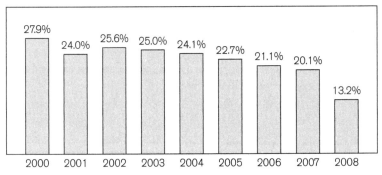

FIGURE 5.2 Newspaper Margins

Sources: Barclays Capital Newspaper Factbook (November 2008); Deutsche Bank Research Estimates, Company Filings.

Note: Includes Belo/A. H. Belo, Dow Jones, E. W. Scripps, Gannett, Knight Ridder, Lee, McClatchy, New York Times, Tribune, and Washington Post.

Becoming more responsive to the needs of the local audience is only part of the restructuring newspapers need to operate more efficiently. The biggest operating costs of a daily newspaper are on the production and distribution side. The cost structure of a newspaper is more reminiscent of a manufacturing business than a media business. It is the high fixed cost nature of this part of the business that created the barriers to entry in the first place. But just because these fixed costs represent a barrier to entry doesn't mean that the business was operated efficiently. Given that these media companies did not operate the news and content operations efficiently, it should not surprise anyone that their production and distribution operations are less than stellar. In theory, a newspaper could optimize this infrastructure by going aggressively into the third-party commercial printing and distribution businesses. Indeed, most newspapers do some of this. But there are other businesses that specialize in these areas that do this sort of thing far better. Increasingly, you are seeing major newspaper publishers—like Hearst outsourcing the printing of the venerable *San Francisco Chronicle* to Canadian printer Transcontinental—saving tens of millions by outsourcing these functions.[23]

Many who benefited from the easier life associated with the old economic order decry the "death" of newspapers. But what they are really decrying is the unpleasantness of facing real competition for the first time. The competition is not only from online classified sites but from local niche news, community sites, and even local user-generated blogs that provide alternative sources of information. The Internet has made it cost-effective for others beyond print newspapers to share their perspective on, and information about, the local scene. The local media environment in a sense will return to the era before television, when many voices are heard. Even in the national or international stage, sites like Slate, The Daily Beast, and The Huffington Post don't just provide analysis and perspective not found elsewhere, they are increasingly breaking news. Industry insiders know how many news "stories" are really slightly rewritten press releases. In the new environment, this cannot be supported any more than reportorial ego trips.

The newspaper of the future will have competitive advantages, but these will be fewer and less overwhelming and the product and operations will look radically different. Local newspapers will get their scale economies from their sales force and news coverage and will need to rely on the responsiveness of their content to their local audience's interests to secure customer allegiance. National or regional papers have always had fewer competitive advantages and may need to develop both more differentiated content and a more distinctive editorial voice to attract or even maintain a loyal readership. The fact that the highly opinionated and purely online Huffington Post recently raised equity at valuations greater than the equity of many public newspaper companies today is potentially suggestive of how the nature of newspaper content in general is likely to shift over time.[24]

In international trade, the theory of comparative advantage explains why all will be better off if countries focus on what they are best at in combination with unfettered exchange among themselves. An analogous theory is that the Internet will result in a broader and deeper reservoir of ideas for the public by virtue of the increased specialization of news providers, both online and off-line. There are some legitimate alternative theories and arguments about whether society is better or worse off without a single powerful local voice in the form of the dominant daily newspaper. There are no legitimate arguments, however, to support the notion that the Internet has helped the owners of these newspapers.

THE INTERNET AND THE ENTRANTS

For the new entrant the Internet would appear at first blush to represent a potential boon. Yet the same qualities that create opportunity for a new entrant where they previously did not exist make it difficult, if not impossible, for that new entrant to maintain barriers against the others who will surely follow. This is not to suggest that there can be no successful Internet businesses with sustainable barriers to entry. It does suggest that, if anything, establishing successful online businesses is harder, not easier, than establishing off-line businesses. And the rate of failure of these ventures is consistent with this view.[25]

Ironically, many of the qualities of Internet businesses that are viewed as particularly attractive are the qualities that make enforcing barriers to entry so challenging. Precisely because the fixed costs required to launch an online business are so low, it is difficult to achieve economies of scale. Precisely because Internet businesses are growing so fast, the benefits of any customer captivity are limited because so much of the customer base is new. The obvious convenience of Internet access and ease of navigation from site to site also undermine captivity.

Unfortunately for their investors, many executives have allowed the allure of high growth and an apparently efficient business model to cloud their strategic judgment when it comes to the Internet.

Let's take the case of comparison shopping sites. Almost all manufacturers of consumer products have their own Web sites through which they sell an increasing portion of their products directly to consumers. Retailers now also offer their full line of products to the public through their Web sites. The sites for obvious reasons do not encourage users to compare their prices with those of their competitors. It did not take long for Internet entrepreneurs to fill this gap by creating sites that would enable such a comparison across the Internet.

Given the trends of Internet usage, the Internet shopping engines experienced explosive growth even after the bursting of the Internet bubble. In addition, the capital required to launch such a business is minimal—developing a user-friendly interface on top of a search engine tailored to this purpose is not a complicated assignment. The search engine could be developed in-house or the basic technology licensed from any number of sources and then customized.

Unlike an off-line retailer, the comparison shopping engine makes money from delivering traffic to other Web sites where the transaction occurs rather than directly selling merchandise. But just as a manufacturer generally has an incentive to make its product ubiquitously available through the maximum number of potential retail outlets, e-commerce sites want traffic from as many different sources as possible. In both cases it is unusual for the source of "inventory"—whether the product itself or the online offer— to make it available exclusively through a single outlet. And not surprisingly, such exclusive arrangements, when available, come at a cost that fully compensates the manufacturer or e-commerce site. Creating sustainable, meaningful distinctions among participants, particularly in an online environment where the lowest price rather than the "shopping experience" is usually dispositive, is extremely challenging.

Shopping comparison sites have competition not only from the Web sites of the retailers and manufacturers but from various broad-based e-commerce sites like Amazon.com or even eBay. Furthermore, the giant competitors in terms of delivering traffic to other sites are the broad-based search engines like Google and Yahoo.

The sheer number of these shopping engines made it seem unlikely that any had a true sustainable competitive advantage. Although each boasts a unique "pitch" for being somehow distinctive and the "leader," at the end of the day they all do largely the same thing. It is hard to argue that there are high barriers to entry when people just keep entering. More broadly, the economics of the retail business in the off-line world are notoriously difficult, with even market leaders struggling to achieve double-digit operating margins. In the online world, with greater transparency to both the consumer and the retailer/manufacturer, one would imagine that long-term margins would be worse, not better. It is much easier and more likely to run a search on another site than to walk across the street to compare price. In summary, it is hard to imagine a business less likely to achieve a sustainable competitive advantage than comparison shopping sites.

During the first Internet boom, a number of overvalued companies overpaid for comparison shopping engines, to their ultimate embarrassment. CNET, for instance, bought a site called MySimon.com for $700 million in 2000. CNET had gone public in 1996 as an online technology information portal. At the time of the acquisition, MySimon.com was "a leading comparison shopping service on the Internet." The justification for the deal, according to the MySimon.com CEO, was that "CNET brings unparalleled experience in integrating content, community and commerce to help us create the shopping category killer."[26]

MySimon is no longer a significant player in the online shopping arena. Indeed, CNET's own business description in its last 10-K filed before its acquisition by CBS in 2008 does not even mention MySimon under either the list of "major brands" in its portfolio or even its itemization of "other brands" beyond the leading ones.[27]

Despite this track record and the structural industry characteristics, just a few years later, during the space of barely a year between 2004 and 2005, four major but completely unrelated media companies paid between $500 million and $700 million for four different comparison shopping sites with broadly similar characteristics. All the sites were experiencing revenue growth of over 20 percent and had profit of around $20 million, reflecting margins of well over 20 percent. And each of the acquirers convinced itself that these metrics justified paying over twenty times profit.

The good news about these transactions is that, unlike the previous Internet boom, valuations were based on profit rather than eyeballs or some other ethereal metric. If one believed that the current profit margin, market share, and growth trajectory were sustainable, the price paid for these properties would be quite justifiable. But if our analysis of the lack of potential competitive advantage in these businesses is correct, we would expect to see long-term margins very similar to those of off-line retailers and significant continuous movement in relative market share. Under these circumstances, these properties would be worth a small fraction of what was paid for them. The brief history of these transactions confirms our view of the fundamental nature of these businesses.

What is most striking about the miniboom of ill-advised comparison shopping deals is that they were undertaken by fundamentally different businesses, each of which was convinced of the strategic nature of the transaction. How likely is it that the same business could be "strategic" to a

2004–2005	Today
 YAHOO! / kelkoo 3/26/2004 (~$575mm) • Top-line growth north of 50% and margins of roughly 30% • Yahoo launched its own site in the U.S. (Yahoo Shopping) and acquired Kelkoo in Europe	YAHOO! / kelkoo • Sold for less than $125mm in November 2008, less than one-quarter of the original purchase price • Revenue growth estimates for Kelkoo over the next few years are less than 5% per annum, and EBITDA margins estimates range from 10% to 20%
 SCRIPPS / shopzilla 6/6/2005 (~$560mm) • Opening line of press release noted that Scripps "was moving to capitalize on the rapid growth and rising profitability of specialized Internet search businesses" • Top-line growth of 30% and roughly 25% margins	Scripps networks INTERACTIVE / shopzilla • Revenue forecast to decline in 2009 with margins less than 20% • The company in 2009 announced its intention to "competitively reposition" Shopzilla in response to poor performance
Experian A world of insight / PriceGrabber.com 12/14/2005 (~$485mm) • Acquisition rationale in press release was that PriceGrabber (1) operates in high-growth markets, (2) has strong organic growth prospects, and (3) brings potential revenue and traffic synergies	Experian A world of insight / PriceGrabber.com • Terminated unsuccessful sale process in October 2008 after announcing its sale intentions in February 2008 • Research analysts forecast revenue declines over the next couple of years
 ebaY / Shopping.com 6/1/2005 (~$480mm) • Topline growth forecast north of 20% with margins of approximately 20%	 ebaY / Shopping.com • Sharply decelerating traffic and revenue since acquisition, with revenue expected to decline in 2009

FIGURE 5.3 Case Study: 2004–2005 Online Comparison Shopping Acquisitions

diversified entertainment company, an Internet portal, an online auction site, and a credit information company? This suggests that the relentless quest for growth can blind moguls not only to the structural strength or weakness of the business they are acquiring but also to the question of whether these businesses are even relevant to their own operations. The comments of the CEO of Scripps, a small media conglomerate with cable channels, newspapers, and TV stations, at the time of the Shopzilla acquisition reflects this confusion: "In many ways, like our other media businesses, Shopzilla is a content company."[28] If content is king and growth is good, how could he go wrong?

The same fallacies that drew these companies to purchase comparison shopping sites initially attracted investors to Barry Diller's renamed Inter-ActiveCorp, once he sold most of his traditional media properties.[29] The simple notion was that the problem with media conglomerates was that they were "old" media and that the solution was to instead cobble together largely unrelated Internet businesses.[30] The real trouble, though, was that many of the individual businesses purchased, ultimately representing over sixty different brands in at least a dozen different business segments, had no real competitive advantages.[31] Some of the acquisitions were in segments, like online search, where, as we discuss shortly in the context of Google, competitive advantage was possible. But InterActive's chosen vehicle to pursue this business, Ask Jeeves, which was purchased for $1.85 billion in 2005, was hopelessly subscale. Diller has since split the company into five separate entities, which may attract acquirers for the pieces, but unfortunately will do nothing to help the underlying strength of the businesses.[32]

The Internet has not uniformly been a destroyer of media profitability. But the structural attributes of the Internet make the nature of the specific competitive advantages that support sustained superior profitability look somewhat different than they look in off-line media businesses. Where off-line media businesses are more likely to rely on fixed cost economies of scale to support barriers to entry, Internet businesses are more likely to achieve scale through the benefits of network effects. And where attractive off-line media businesses often have high switching costs or other "demand" advantages, Internet businesses are more likely to benefit from the "supply" advantage of proprietary technology that leverages the scale network effects to facilitate continuous technological improvement that other competitors—no matter what their programming skills—cannot match.

The business model of eBay is emblematic of Internet businesses with a sustainable competitive advantage. In general, it is online businesses that successfully draw their sustenance from the ability to quickly attract a critical mass of users to an "exchange" of some kind that seem to be able to create barriers on the Web. But not all exchange-type businesses draw so many users or demonstrate an ability to keep them. What the Internet giveth it also taketh away—the same qualities that facilitate the rapid establishment of critical mass enable an equally precipitous rush for the door. Unless the business establishes another leg to its competitive advantage proposition—whether through proprietary technology, some form of customer captivity, or both—the early venture backers should wait before popping the champagne. Or they should find a greater fool to sell to before it becomes apparent that the early success is not sustainable. This phenomenon is analogous to that which we see in off-line media where fixed cost scale economies are the source of advantage: Unless there is an additional element of advantage, others can eventually catch up.

Any examination of competitive advantage in Internet businesses must consider the elephant in the room: Google. Google's self-described mission of "organizing the world's information" makes clear that it is a quintessential "packaging" business, not a content company. Although Google is the poster child for an Internet business with high, and apparently increasing, barriers to entry, it is such a unique phenomenon that, unlike eBay, we cannot really say that it is emblematic of anything. Although it has not been in operation for all that many years, Google's financial and operating track record is complete enough to strongly suggest the satisfaction of our two-pronged test for the existence of competitive advantage—supernormal returns and stable or growing market share.

TABLE 5.2 Google Financials ($ in millions)

	2004	2005	2006	2007
Gross Revenue	$3,184	$6,139	$10,605	$16,594
Operating Income	$842	$2,017	$3,550	$5,084
Operating Margin	**26%**	**33%**	**33%**	**31%**
ROA			19%	20%

Source: Company 10-Ks.

Google's share of U.S. paid searches has more than doubled over a four-year period, and in 2007, it dominated with a 75 percent share.

Google has created extraordinary value in ways that are not the traditionally accepted avenues of media success, either on- or off-line. The company is considered one of very few, historically, where technology not only supports the business, but defines its strategic opportunities.[33] Although elements of the

TABLE 5.3   Google Share of U.S. Paid Searches

2004	32.8%
2005	46.9%
2006	58.7%
2007	75.6%

Source: http://www.iab.net/insights_research/iab_research/1675/113268.

Google success story are analogous to the success of a number of other media businesses, the collective strength of the franchise is difficult to analogize to much of anything. This very distinctiveness of the Google phenomenon has led many commentators—academics, journalists, bloggers, and even Google itself[34]—to try to pinpoint the origin and nature of Google's "secret sauce."

The quest to identify a single ingredient that explains Google's remarkable results and resilience is itself misguided. Google is the rare company that seems to have strong elements of all three of the most important sources of competitive advantage identified—economies of scale, customer captivity, and cost. More remarkable is that Google displays multiple manifestations of each of these categories of advantage: Google achieves scale both by the relative size of the fixed cost and network effects, it retains customer captivity of both consumers and advertisers because of habit and switching costs, and it secures a major cost advantage through proprietary technology and learning. It is worth examining each of these in some detail to better understand how Google became the shining exception to the media industry rule.

For search users, Google offers results that are superior in completeness, speed, and, most important, relevance to those of other search engines. The technologies that underlie these performance advantages have so far proved impossible for its competitors to replicate. Google's "crawler" programs, which automatically search the Web and download pages to Google data centers, are the product of continuous improvement. Google's technology in this area, which determines the completeness of search results, benefits from both its greater experience—learning-related proprietary technology—and the greater R&D resources Google is able to devote to active pursuit of innovation economies of scale. The same applies to Google's "indexer" programs, which organize the downloaded material into its databases, and the design of the hardware and software of Google's massive data centers. The efficient organization of Google's massive data centers is itself subject to a technology patent. These together account for the superior speed of Google searches. The "query processor," which organizes search results for presentation to users, benefits from similar forces that are especially difficult for competitors to replicate. Because of its greater experience with search behavior and its greater research resources, Google has a significant advantage in customizing the presentation of search results for individual users. And as Google's share of search queries expands, these advantages are enhanced.

Customer loyalty to Google's search engine is a second important factor. In the early days of Internet search, programs were relatively unsatisfactory and were unfamiliar to most Web users. Today, Google works well for most users and almost everyone has experience with search engines. As a result, the receptiveness of users to alternative search engines has been greatly reduced. At the same time, users become more effective at using particular search programs with experience. The potential sacrifice of this experience in moving to a new search engine is a further source of loyalty to Google.

The existence of this large, loyal base of customers is what enables Google profitably to devote more resources to search-related R&D than its rivals. Google's larger user base also reduces its unit fixed costs of promotion, administration, and physical infrastructure, which together with R&D represent the lion's share of its overall costs.

Finally, in search, Google benefits from certain network effects. Because Google's search engine is ubiquitous, new users are likely to be introduced to it and trained to its use, before even learning of its rivals. Portal Web sites are also more likely to use Google because of its strong position with users. These tendencies, in turn, then increase the number of Google users, which is further reinforcing.

In advertising, too, Google benefits from these same factors of proprietary technology, customer captivity, economies of scale, and network effects. The presentation of paid advertising on Google is determined by algorithms that are based on extensive response experiences and customized for advertising and individual users. The steady improvement in these proprietary algorithms over time has led to both increasing click-through rates for Google ads and steadily higher conversion rates for advertisers from clicks to sales. The latter improvements have, in turn, led to steadily higher key-word prices. In both areas, Google significantly outperforms its competitors, and the gap appears to be increasing over time. As in the case of search technology, Google advertising technology benefits from proprietary learning enhanced by economies of scale in advertising data availability and R&D investments in the active pursuit of improvements.

Although it's impossible to determine where the R&D money is spent—on improving advertising, search, or in some other highly publicized but notably unprofitable areas—the absolute numbers and increasing percentage

TABLE 5.4   Google R&D

	2004	2005	2006	2007	2008E
R&D ($ in millions)	$225	$484	$941	$1,550	$2,225
% revenue	7%	7.9%	8.9%	9.3%	9.7%

Source: Public filings; Deutsche Bank equity research, July 10, 2008.

of its skyrocketing revenues are noteworthy. The net result is that between 2004 and 2008, R&D expenditures are expected to have increased almost tenfold. Capital expenditures, estimated at almost $3.5 billion in 2008, have grown even faster during this period.

Experience with Google advertising and Google's automated programs for placing ads leads to advertiser loyalty in the same way that experience reinforces searcher loyalty. The magnitude of this loyal customer base means that Google spreads the fixed cost infrastructure associated with its ad sales and placement over far more advertisers than its rivals. Google's unit costs are correspondingly lower. Finally, in advertising, Google benefits from more than just the ubiquity-related network effects that apply to search. For example, its AdSense program, which places ads on blogs and other relatively small decentralized sites, is especially attractive to advertisers because of its wide access to such sites and ability to customize placements based on extensive experience with these sites. At the same time, Web sites are drawn disproportionately to AdSense because that is where the greatest concentration of advertisers resides. This kind of virtuous cycle, reinforced by Google's proprietary technology, customer captivity among both users and advertisers, and traditional cost-based economies of scale in R&D and other areas, suggests that its current economic performance is likely to endure. Notwithstanding the fact that Google founders Larry Page and Sergey Brin's original innovation embodied in their PageRank algorithm is fully available to their competitors.

Despite this clear story about the real sources of competitive advantage, there is an overwhelming sense in press accounts that Google must credit at least a soupçon of its success to the special mogul muscles of Page and Brin. Partly this may be because Google maintains a studied mystique around its business strategies, limiting its public utterance to enigmatic high-level platitudes like "don't be evil."[35] The company discloses only the minimum legally required, carefully guarding as trade secrets not only its software algorithms but the nature and location of its facilities and even the precise responsibilities of its leading executives.[36]

One slightly more specific core notion is a 70/20/10 rule under which 70 percent of workers' time is directed toward search, 20 percent toward adjacent areas, and 10 percent toward completely unrelated realms.[37] In theory, building adjacencies that genuinely leverage an existing competitive advantage to create a new franchise is both attractive in itself and serves to protect the core. In practice, for Google as much as others, the line between the supposedly adjacent and the clearly unrelated can be shifted to justify all manner of empire building. There is little doubt that Google's ability to manifest such a compelling and comprehensive array of competitive advantages is in part a function of the fact that it has focused—as most successful companies in and out of media do—on a highly specialized field. The fact that search broadly conceived turns out not only to be essential for most Internet users but to have remarkably broad application to a variety of tools and services required by enterprises as well explains how the business has become much larger than anyone, including the founders, imagined possible. But this should not distract from the fact that it is the specialization that facilitates the advantages.

Google's efforts to create Internet products that will be used by consumers beyond search (such as e-mail, instant messaging, maps, video, news alerts, shopping, etc.) have been active and extensive, but have not created much, if any, shareholder value. Indeed, it is rather startling just how unsuccessful a broad range of new ventures has been, despite the widespread expectation that these could leverage the Google search franchise.[38] Are Google founders Larry Page and Sergey Brin showing early signs of acting like traditional media moguls and believing that the company's economic engine is based on their personal and unique abilities? To the extent that they do stray from putting their considerable resources into digging the moat of competitive advantage ever deeper, the cost to Google shareholders from unrelated enterprises to which they deploy that genius is likely to be substantial.

The shadow of the Internet colors all conversations about the media industry. As we now turn to the specific dynamics of the individual segments that make up the sector, it should be clear that despite the handful of defensible digital business models that have emerged, this shadow is a dark one. Foundering businesses that embrace the siren song of the Internet as a lifeline do so at their peril. Moguls following this path seem unaware that the Internet can be expected to accelerate their descent into the icy depths of permanent unprofitability. Newspaper executives and analysts, for instance, maintain an obsessive focus on the point in the future when the growth from online businesses will exceed the revenue losses from their print operations. The assumption is that this moment will represent a happy turning point for newspaper publishers. In fact, if anything, it will more likely represent a dangerous point of no return as the benefits of scale and customer captivity become a distant memory.

PART II | # The Segments and the Strategies

6 | Content Is Not King: Movies, Music, and Books

Jeff Zucker: "Listen, the key to success remains the same today as it was, you know, 10, 20 years ago. You have got to have great content and you have got to have great stories. And those who can tell great stories will always succeed . . . whether it's an hour, a half hour, or three minutes. You've still got to tell a great story, and great storytelling will always win out."[1]

There are lots of kinds of media content. But it is the blockbuster, the hit, the epic that defines an era, or at least a season, that attracts the greatest fascination. The business of producing the discrete pieces of entertainment content that we watch, hear, and read is undergoing profound changes. Piracy on a scale never seen before has been made possible by the ease of digital distribution of film and music in particular. But more remarkable than these changes is the extent to which the nature and structure of these businesses have remained the same.

As much as we blame the Internet for any number of negative developments in a variety of media industries, it is important that this does not distract attention from a basic fact: Making movies, producing music, and publishing books have been terrible businesses for a very long time. To understand how the Internet may have made these enterprises even less lucrative, and to assess the prospects of various industry initiatives to "fix" their problems, it is worth considering the fundamental reasons why owners of these businesses have never generated more than anemic returns.[2]

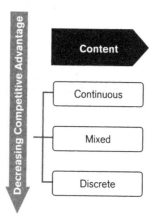

FIGURE 6.1   Content Competitive Advantage

At first glance, the making of filmed, recorded, and printed entertainment looks a lot more different than similar. The cultures and personalities that drive these organizations, for one, are quite distinct. In all, however, it is the relationships with talent that are viewed as core. Different functions develop special relationships with the artists for different businesses. In filmed entertainment, it is often the agent who is key to understanding and negotiating their manifold needs. In music, lawyers, who often perform the "business affairs" function at a label, navigate the highly arcane contract and publishing, performance and residual rights issues that arise. In publishing, it is the editor who champions an author and nurses his work through the often difficult birthing process. Although there are many exceptions, individuals who have performed these functions—none of which typically entails full P&L responsibility—have with uncanny consistency risen to the top of these respective industries. And the nature of the organizations most prevalent in these sectors very much reflects the differences in perspective occasioned by these varied backgrounds.

For all the apparent differences, there are a number of core attributes involved in putting together a slate of films, a roster of artists, or a list of titles. The largest film, music, and book companies all represent a collection of houses, labels, and imprints, respectively. This is not an accident. And it is not simply a marketing device to provide differentiated branding produced by one massive content factory. Each of the dozens of imprints at Random House has an editorial director who manages no more than five to ten editors, none of whom is likely to be able to produce more than twenty books in a year. Each of the three broad label groups at Warner Music US has its own A&R staffs that are subdivided into genre groups that on average are responsible for twenty to thirty new full-length releases annually. Each film production house, whether fully part of or with just a distribution deal at a major studio, has its own development organization whose size determines how many projects can be managed—generally no more than fifteen to twenty in a season.[3] Furthermore, it is a widely accepted axiom of movie production that at the end of the day only around 10 percent of those ideas formally put "in development" will ultimately become actual film releases and any aggressive attempt to meaningfully increase the yield on development projects will further depress financial results.

The basic management function in these content businesses is the selection and cultivation of creative material. There are individuals who are more or less talented at this, but such tasks do not lend themselves to sustainable competitive advantage. The structure of all these businesses reflects the impossibility of achieving scale economies from adding more content: A creative manager can manage only so many projects. The consumer in turn is barely aware of the production entity responsible, making any form of customer captivity highly improbable. And achieving an enduring cost advantage either through some form of proprietary technology or otherwise seems even more unlikely.

Another commonality of these hit-driven content businesses is that each has a less volatile, more attractive piece of their operations that involves the exploitation of already proven entertainment properties: In movies, it is management of the film library; in books, it is the author backlist; and in music, it is both the artist catalog and music publishing business. Based on how a new release does in the early days, it is relatively easy to project the future revenue streams from various ancillary markets over time. All the major costs of development, production, and marketing have already been incurred, so these activities accordingly generate high profitability with high predictability. There is one problem: Without new product continuously being added, these profits will decline consistently over time as the collection grows stale. Private equity investors who have looked at buying content businesses have often valued the enterprises largely based on the assumption that new content creation is shut down altogether. The result has been either that they have been outbid by a media mogul or that once they got hold of the business, they could not resist trying to produce hits themselves—generally with disastrous results.[4]

If hard-nosed private equity investors can convince themselves that they can do a better job of producing boffo box-office results, you can imagine the inclinations of more traditional media moguls. The elusive holy grail of the entertainment industry has always been a surefire way to produce hit after hit while your competitors' output reflects the hit-and-miss nature of the overall business. Freud had a word for a belief based on wish fulfillment: an illusion.[5] Such beliefs provide ready fodder for con artists, and in this regard media moguls have always been an easy mark. There is a long and distinguished history of claims to be able to predict hits. The current crop gains its patina of apparent credibility from advanced computing and statistical techniques. Before examining some of these in more detail, let's consider the overall enterprise of predicting hits.

Imagine that a mad scientist really invented a black box that you could drop a script, score, or manuscript into and quickly obtain an accurate assessment of its ultimate commercial potential. What would happen? If the mad scientist had good representation, he would either bid it out to the studio willing to pay the most to own it or just set a high license fee for usage that retained the bulk of the value created by his invention. Only the scientist would be better off.

But what if the scientist worked for a studio that refused to make the technology available to others? Even here, the benefits over time are unclear. That studio would still be bidding on projects against other studios that didn't own the black box. Some of these would presumably be offering to overpay. Smart agents would shop the black-box studio bids to other studios. Also, since the products of the black box are available for all to see, sooner or later other companies are going to learn to copy the black-box results and will bid for projects accordingly. Having the black box would stop the studio from overpaying, but how many real bargains would it get? Even if such a supernatural power were available, the lack of any other source of structural advantage would eventually overwhelm the potential benefits.

Such observations are not nearly enough to dissuade an eager mogul from exploring the possibility of getting a leg up on the competition—or at least extending his or her tenure. Unfortunately, there is no black box, nor can there be. That being said, part of the continued efforts in this regard come from the hubris of the computing and mathematical community that believes data sets are the source of all wisdom—including artistic and creative decisions.

Statistical help isn't new in the arts. Multiple regression analysis, the statistical technique that measures the predictive relationship among many variables, has been applied to the movie industry to predict box office receipts for at least thirty years.[6] Insights from these regressions have primarily affected decisions that are made in the marketing departments of studios, to help with advertising budgets and release schedules.

For example, the early regressions indicated that initial distribution of films on more screens had a significant positive effect on ultimate grosses. At the time, a release on one thousand screens in the United States was considered exceptionally large. Today, U.S. films may be released on four to five thousand screens.

More recently, "neural networking" has seemingly become a tool for the studios. Neural networks use historical data just as regressions do, but the statistician doesn't have to choose the variables ahead of time to "count." Neural networking takes advantage of the computer's ever-increasing ability to deal with vast data sets, so that for a given problem, relatively indiscriminate masses of raw data can be fed into the network, and the computer will be neurally trained to predict an outcome. The jury is out on how useful neural networks are for practitioners in many fields, because they are so complicated, it often is impossible to figure how an individual input is affecting the predicted outcome.[7] But this hasn't stopped a company called Epagogix that uses neural networking as the heart of its black-box solution to picking and fixing scripts. The company has become the consultant for numerous studio heads, hedge funds, and other players in the industry.[8] In fact, according to founder Richard Copaken, "All I do know is that in our most recent test for a major film studio, we were 100% more accurate than the studio in determining in advance of release whether these films would earn more in US Box Office revenue than their respective all-in negative cost of production (all production costs, but excluding the cost of prints and marketing). This measure typically will determine if a film will be net profitable . . . Both we and the studio were very pleased to achieve this degree of accuracy with a methodology that can be applied at the initial script stage before the studio spends the first dollar of production."[9] Interestingly, whether his method works or not (and so far, no particular movie studio's returns have mysteriously improved), this scientific black box still depends on real people reading scripts and summarizing their content.

Like movies, the music business also has had its traditional research methods and has used focus groups and phone and online surveys for years. The most widely used method is "call-out research," where fifteen to thirty seconds of a song are played over the phone line of a prescreened (for demographics and music taste) listener who then rates the tune.

But a newer, shinier black box called "spectral deconvolution" that uses massive data sets is being touted by two companies—the original one, now called Music Intelligence Solutions, based in Madrid, and a second one, to which a number of MIS's executives migrated, called Platinum Blue, in New York. Both companies analyze the underlying mathematical patterns (beyond what can be heard) in a tune, compare these to the sixty or so patterns that constituted a hit in the past, and make recommendations about where the new tune falls short. Both companies claim that they can help the music industry focus its investments in songs with a better chance of market success, and thus become more profitable. They sell their services to songwriters, their producers, and to the labels that buy the product.[10] So where is the relative advantage of using this system? Hard to know.

But there are inherent limitations to these approaches. First, and most importantly, since they depend on historical data, they cannot work unless there is substantial stability in the tastes of the buying public. If preferences shift significantly and unpredictably over time, then decisions based on historical tastes will not perform well. Thus, in music, as buyers have migrated from big bands to classic rock to heavy metal, rap, and New Age, earlier successes are unlikely to be useful for predicting current popularity. This limits the ranges of data inputs that are useful for the black-box models.

Second, there are literally hundreds of thousands of potential variables that affect success in movies, books, and music. At the same time, there are relatively limited numbers of films, books, and songs that get mass distribution and exposure (although this could change with the advent of Internet marketing). Using films as an example: The 120 releases per year and eighty years of history (1928 to 2008) provides only about ten thousand data points. Sorting among a hundred thousand potential factors with ten thousand data points cannot be done. Any combination of ten thousand of these factors will fit the data perfectly, and even searching for limited numbers of factors—say sixty—among the hundred thousand will produce high levels of spurious correlation.

For these reasons, there appear to be natural limitations on the efficacy of black-box approaches. However, even if they do not perform infallibly, statistical black-box approaches may well do better than the alternative black-box approach of using the ineffable gut instincts of selected industry executives.

Surely, the mogul will argue, there are some advantages enjoyed by the "majors" in creative content businesses. Just look at their consistently overwhelming market shares as a group in the industries of movies, music, and books. There is some truth to this observation and we will examine the financials and shares in each of these sectors, in turn. Although there are barriers to entry among these industry giants, these are not in the content component of the business but rather in the marketing and distribution component. This is part of the "packaging" function rather than the content creation function. In addition, these advantages are shared by all of the majors and have been frittered away through the absolute lack of cooperation among them. Finally, what advantages have historically been available in the marketing and distribution operations have significantly diminished over time.

These observations are consistent with the structure and results of each of these businesses over an extended period of time. All of these businesses consistently struggle to achieve even low-double-digit operating margins and generate stubbornly weak returns on investment. These results reflect the combined results of the higher-margin businesses involving the exploitation of library, catalog, and publishing assets along with the production of a new slate of product each season. An unexpected megahit or a platform shift like the introduction of the CD or the DVD can create short-term windfalls either to a particular company or to the industry as a whole. These periods of financial nirvana are fleeting, as the talent quickly moves to devour the surplus. And for every period of windfall there are periods of actual losses due to a high-profile failure or an industry-wide challenge. It will not surprise you to know that in such circumstances, talent does not raise its hand to share in the pain. Heads they win, tails you lose. The result is remarkable stability in results over time and across these industries.

MUSIC

The recorded music industry has seen steadily declining revenue and profitability since 1999, when U.S. retail shipments came in at $14.8 billion for 1.2 billion physical units. In that glorious year, there were five majors— Sony, Bertelsmann, EMI, Universal, and Warner. In recent years, the five majors became four, with Sony and Bertelsmann combining. EMI was taken private by a hedge fund and Warner Music had a near-death experience in 2004, from which it still continues to suffer. In 2007, 1.7 billion units were legally shipped, of which 23 percent were digital. Despite the 40 percent unit growth, the retail value dipped 30 percent to $10.3 billion[11] as sales shifted from higher-priced multiple-song albums physically shipped to low-priced singles digitally downloaded at iTunes and other MP3 distribution points. Even more depressing, the International Federation of the Phonographic

Industry (IFPI) estimated that illegal downloads outnumbered the number of tracks sold by a factor of twenty to one.[12]

For the decade between 1997 and 2007, the average industry profit margins were on average well below 5 percent. The industry did not achieve even a 10 percent margin in any year during this period.

Even when the music industry has had the wind at its back, returns have been good only for short periods. The arrival of CD technology in the early 1990s provided an extraordinary boost to sales and prices as buyers replaced their cassettes and vinyl albums with higher-quality CDs. Initially, returns on sales and profits did rise. But by the mid- to late 1990s, returns had declined to their normal mediocre level. Increases in the cost of CDs, as labels bid more for artists and spent more on advertising and promotion, eliminated some of the benefits. Increased numbers of CDs and artists, which reduced the average revenues per release, eliminated the rest. Despite the fact that the majors maintained price discipline, these secondary aspects of competition did their work in holding down profitability.

At first glance the other indication of competitive advantage—share stability—seems to tell a different story. Table 6.1 shows the U.S. market shares of the majors (for comparison purposes we treat Sony and BMG, which merged in 2004, as combined for the entire period) and independents between 2000 and 2007. During these years, the majors as a group remained within a 2 percent band of overall share in the fast-declining business and, in any given year, no major gained or lost more than 2.5 percent of share. The international data tells a similar story. As Warner Music takes pains to point out in its 2008 annual report, "[w]hile market shares change moderately year-to-year, none of [the majors] have gained or lost more than 3% points of share in the last 5 years."

TABLE 6.1 Music Majors Market Share, U.S. Recorded Music (Catalog and Current Titles)[13]

	2000	2001	2002	2003	2004	2005	2006	2007
UMG	26.8%	26.4%	28.9%	28.1%	29.5%	31.7%	31.6%	31.9%
Sony/BMG	33.0	31.5	31.3	30.2	29.9	27.5	27.4	25.0
WMG	16.2	16.6	17.0	17.6	16.2	17.3	18.1	20.3
EMI	9.8	11.4	9.3	10.6	10.9	10.4	10.2	9.4
Independents	14.4	14.2	13.6	13.5	13.5	13.2	12.6	13.5
	100.0%	100.0%	100.0%	100.0%	100.0%	100.0%	100.0%	100.0%

TABLE 6.2 Music Majors: Relative Share Change 2000–2007

	2000	2007	Absolute Change
UMG	31.3%	36.9%	5.6%
Sony BMG	38.6	28.9	9.7
WMG	18.9	23.5	4.6
EMI	11.4	10.8	0.6
Average			5.1

There is, however, much less stability than meets the eye for two reasons. First, when thinking about share stability in an industry, it is important to watch share shifts among the leaders over time. A quick and easy way to do this is to calculate the leaders' share just among themselves, by normalizing the numbers, so they add up to 100 percent. Then, among any two periods you are comparing, calculate the absolute value of difference, add up these absolute values, and take the average. If this number over several years is somewhere below four, there is definitely share stability; four and above indicates share instability. For context, Coke and Pepsi typically capture 1 to 2 percent share from each other over even more extended periods, with acquisitions playing no meaningful role.

The absolute numbers in Table 6.2 above do suggest borderline share stability. Although the average share shift for the 2000–2007 period is a little over 5 percent, for shorter periods within this time frame the shift is 4 percent or less. The bigger problem is that this level of stability has been achieved only after aggressive acquisitions of independents to balance any relative share loss among the majors and between the majors and the independents more generally. It is a great industry tradition for the majors to buy up successful new entrants like Sun, Atlantic, Motown, Geffen, and more recently Interscope. Labels acquired during the 2000–2007 period just by market leader Universal include RMM, DreamWorks Records, Roc-A-Fella Records, Vale Music, Arsenal Music, Sanctuary Group, ARS Entertainment, and V2 Music Group.[14] Nominal stability then is achieved the old-fashioned way—it is purchased. The overall picture, however, reflects the relentless competition among the majors and with the independents.

In the old days before digital recording and digital distribution, the majors shared a true scale advantage in the packaging and retail portions of the business compared to the independent labels and individual musicians. They supplied individual artists professional-grade production facilities and expert producers. They could mass-produce CDs accurately and cheaply and they had a sales and marketing organization that would distribute the CDs to thousands of retail outlets. These scale advantages meant the majors might have controlled the market, but it never translated into sustainable high returns because of the nature of the discrete hit business as detailed earlier and the relentless competition among the majors for talent and market position.

As fitful as the coordination among the top players has been in the past, things will only get worse in the future as the scale advantages in marketing and distribution that could have made cooperation possible disappear. These lower barriers to entry have attracted new industry participants who have started bidding for talent. In 2007, Wal-Mart made a direct deal with the rock band the Eagles, and in 2008 with another group, Journey; in both cases they cut out the artists' music label. The concert promoter Live Nation made a deal with Madonna that leaves her longtime record company, Warner, out in the cold. Live Nation now has an all-encompassing stake in Madonna's career—including the Madonna brand, albums, touring, merchandising, fan club and Web site, DVDs, music-related television and film projects, and associated sponsorship agreements.[15]

If the big and established artists are being picked off by big new competitors, the young and start-up artists are being served by independent labels as they never could before, as the fixed cost requirements of the business diminish. Small labels don't have to incur large fixed costs for a sales force if most of their artists' sales are downloaded at iTunes, with the balance at only five hundred digital sites worldwide. They can promote the indie bands through MySpace and the bands' own sites. And they can manage the artists' royalties and bookings with relatively cheap (if not free) artist management software. Independent labels have even banded together in a cooperative called Merlin. This association calls itself a virtual label and claims to have twelve thousand members that sell as much product as EMI does.[16]

MOVIES

The studios known as the "majors" are the "filmed entertainment" divisions of large media companies. Like the profits in Music, the financial returns of these divisions are not only inconsistent, but mostly, with the exception of

Fox Entertainment Group, are historically rather low. The average operating margin on sales in each year from 2000 and 2007, including Fox, ranged from a low of 2.2 percent to 9.9 percent.

The average return on assets of these divisions during those same years (where asset segment information is available or could be reasonably estimated) ranged from 1.7 percent to 11.2 percent. Without Fox, however, the yearly ROA average went up to about only 7.7 percent. And these are pretax returns; assuming tax rates of 40 percent, after-tax returns on assets averaged 4 to 5 percent—around the same as could have been achieved from investing in U.S. Savings Bonds over the same period.

The variability of these returns is attributable to the hit-driven nature of the business. The low average level of returns is a function of competitive conditions, the generally low level of barriers to entry, and intense competition among the major studios. The low barriers are apparent in the recurrent ability of independent entrants like Miramax, DreamWorks, Lionsgate, Turner, and New Line to take share. The relative stability of the majors' overall share has been sustained only through acquisition of these entrants—Miramax by Disney in 1993, New Line by Turner in 1994, which was in turn acquired by Time Warner in 1996, and DreamWorks by Viacom in 2006. The latter factor is reflected in the amount of market share that changes hands among the majors. As in music, the tendency to buy back lost share results in industry data that understates the intensity of competition.

Table 6.3 presents relative North American market shares for the six majors in 1988, 1999, and 2006. On average, roughly 5 percent of the majors' overall market share changed hands between these years. For example, Columbia (Sony) went from 23 percent of U.S./Canada box office in 1988 to 13 percent in 1999 and back to 23 percent in 2006. The results of this competition are evident in the history of the film business that we described earlier. The great recent revenue benefits of many new channels of distribution—cable, satellite, pay-per-view, DVDs, and enhanced international opportunities—have been completely offset by higher film production and marketing costs and the costs of more films released. The key to profitability in this environment has not been creativity, but the exercise of careful cost controls in production and the energetic exploitation of existing film libraries. This accounts for the higher profitability of MGM—although as a result it fell from the ranks of the recognized majors—and Fox Studios.

TABLE 6.3 Movie Majors Market Share (U.S. and Canada)[17]

Note	Distributors	1988	1999	Change from 1988	2006	Change from 1999
1	Disney	19.4%	23.0%	1.8%	16.7%	5.9%
2	Warner Bros. (Time Warner)	11.2%	20.2%	8.3%	14.9%	5.0%
3	Paramount (Viacom)	15.2%	15.0%	1.8%	11.0%	3.7%
4	Columbia (Sony)	19.6%	13.0%	8.9%	21.1%	9.4%
5	Universal (General Electric)	9.8%	13.0%	2.4%	10.9%	1.8%
6	Fox (News Corp.)	11.6%	11.0%	1.8%	17.0%	7.0%
		86.8%	95.2%		91.6%	
	Average			4.2%		5.5%

Note: 2006 studio subsidiaries.
1. Including, but not limited to Disney, Touchstone/Hollywood, Miramax
2. Including, but not limited to Warner Bros., HBO, New Line, Castle Rock, Warner Independent, Picturehouse
3. Including, but not limited to Paramount, DreamWorks SKG, Vantage
4. Including, but not limited to MGM, UA, Screen Gems, TriStar, Destination
5. Including, but not limited to Universal, Focus Features
6. Including, but not limited to 20th Century Fox, Fox Searchlight, Fox Faith, Fox Atomic

BOOKS

The consumer publishing segment that produces the latest John Grisham bestseller is known as "trade." Trade book publishing includes paper and hardback books sold to adults and to children. Trade book publishing has an industry profile similar to music and movies. Over the last several decades the industry has had mostly anemic returns. Of the top five publishers in the United States, data was decipherable for four, which on average have operating margins under 10 percent and returns on capital not much better.[18] The brightest performer in this group appears to be HarperCollins, owned by News Corp., the corporate owner of Fox—which also consistently outperforms its movie studio peers. Even Harper, however, has been unable to achieve profit margins of greater than 12 percent.

The trade book publishers may be in a very slow-growing business, evidenced by the flat or falling sales, but they are doing the best with what they've got. They've consistently kept prices up, so that the revenue growth is double the unit growth. For example, for the same period, looking at adult hardback and trade paper sales, units have grown only 1.6 percent per year, while revenue has grown 3.3 percent.[19] But when all is said and done, the overall margins and returns from this business look remarkably like those of the movie and music sectors, despite the apparent structural differences.

As depressing as these segment profiles are, all content is not equal. Continuous content businesses, as contrasted with the predominantly one-off, disjoint content businesses just profiled, are much better businesses. To be sure, music, film, and books have continuous aspects to their businesses. Around a quarter of Harlequin romance novels are sold as continuity series that are mailed out periodically to subscribing customers. Film studios are responsible for a number of long-running movie franchises or drama series, soap operas, or game shows. Even recorded music companies are able to sell some part of their product through various ongoing services, either through the mail or online. But the continuous aspects of these businesses represent a tiny fraction of the overall revenue and profit of these segments.

There are many media businesses whose core content creation is continuous in nature. Magazines, newspapers, cable channels, databases, most professional publishing, broadcast TV and radio, to name a few, all have content creation infrastructure designed to produce regularly updated versions of the same core product. This infrastructure is typically flexible enough to incorporate and integrate additional content from third parties into the mix: Newspapers and magazines use wire stories and photos, stringers, and contract writers; professional and database publishers integrate their own material with public and other sources; cable channels and broadcasters produce their daily lineups from a mix of internally produced and purchased programming. As a result, continuous content businesses typically have a significant component of their operations in the packaging side of the business as well.

The different nature of these continuous businesses translates into quite different operating structures from that of disjoint content businesses. Film, record, and book companies essentially start over from scratch each time they begin a new project. There is some shared infrastructure that is used repeatedly, but it is so generic that it can often be easily outsourced. MGM for much of its recent history operated easily without an actual studio lot. Finding adequate music recording facilities is no more a challenge than gaining access to the basic publishing software needed to turn a hundred thousand well-conceived words into a book. Continuous content businesses, by contrast, can justify investing in the dedicated equipment and resources required to produce that very particular product on an ongoing basis. Often the nature of these investments is such that they cannot be easily modified for another purpose. A large four-color printer designed to produce a high-volume daily newspaper cannot be easily retrofitted to primarily serve other kinds of printing jobs. The advertising sales force that has been calling on the same customers regarding the same basic proposition for years cannot be easily switched out en masse to market something else.

Continuous content businesses, then, by their very nature, typically entail a higher fixed cost component. A new entrant into the market can engage in a variety of strategies to mitigate the financial risks required to put this fixed cost base in place, such as undertaking market research or preselling advertising based on a prototype of some sort. But at the end of the day, if you are going to be in the business, the investment must be made. And the greater the fixed cost requirement, the greater the economies of scale and the greater the barriers to entry. Not all continuous content businesses have huge fixed cost elements. The set of *Deal or No Deal* probably does not have many other uses, but we doubt either it or a long-term contract with host Howie Mandel is very expensive. The point is, however, that as a group, continuous content businesses are likely to have greater economies of scale.

Similarly, on the demand side of the equation, continuous content businesses are more likely to be habit-forming, almost by definition. Anyone who has spent time on the phone with a customer service representative trying to turn off the cable service knows well the potential switching costs associated with canceling most subscription-based continuous content business. Most local newspaper subscribers subscribe until they move or, more and more, they die. And in the business or professional media context where the data may have been integrated into the overall work flow of the organization, these switching costs can be more than a mild annoyance.

The incremental competitive advantages of economies of scale and customer captivity potentially enjoyed by continuous content businesses over their sexier one-off sisters may sound like much ado about nothing. And to be sure, these barriers are neither overwhelming nor impervious to changes in the market environment. But these structural differences in continuous content businesses translate into meaningful differences in performance.

Let's take the example of consumer magazines targeting women. This is a sector that one might expect to have confronted dramatic change corresponding to the dramatic changes in the political, economic, and social roles of women over past decades. Furthermore, the Internet might have been expected to easily disintermediate these tired old titles by allowing women to get the information they want when they want it without lugging around a heavy magazine. The data suggests something quite different, however.

We looked at women's magazines that have traditionally been called "women's service" or "women's lifestyle." These are generally monthly magazines that cover a broad array of women's interests, including family and relationships, home decorating, recipes, and health issues. Although each title specializes in a particular age demographic, they all have very similar content. In 1998, there were fifty-three titles (with circulations over two hundred thousand and that accepted advertising) that we identified as covering women's service and lifestyle topics. By early 2007, one-third of those identified had stopped publishing, and seven new ones had entered the

TABLE 6.4 Women's Service Magazines 1998 and 2007: Ranked by Circulation[20]

Rank 2007	Rank 1998	Title	Founded
1	1	*Better Homes & Gardens*	1922
2	4	*Good Housekeeping*	1885
3	2	*Family Circle*	1932
4	5	*Women's Day*	1937
5	3	*Ladies' Home Journal*	1883
6	7	*Cosmopolitan*	1886
7	8	*Southern Living*	1966
8	n/a	*O, Oprah Magazine*	2000
9	6	*Redbook*	1903
10	10	*Glamour*	1939
11	9	*Martha Stewart Living*	1990
12	n/a	*Real Simple*	2001
13	13	*InStyle*	1994
14	16	*Shape*	1981
15	11	*Sunset*	1898

ranks. So on the surface, there seems to be a lot of product movement in this category—but it is really only on the margins. In examining the category leaders, the top five largest-circulation titles are the same in 2007 as they were in 1998. And of the top ten, nine are the same. What is most striking in this list is not only the ten-year stability, but how really old the products in this category are. Of the magazines in the top fifteen, 25 percent were founded in the nineteenth century and another 25 percent before 1940. The share stability among the top fifteen are striking as well. Even with the additions of the new titles *Oprah* and *Real Simple*, over the ten-year period, the circulation share shifts only 1.8 percent among the leaders.

But what about profitability? Surely in the new digital world, with everyone able to Google multiple sources of information on a topic of interest and dozens of independent sites targeting women—from iVillage to Daily-Candy—women's magazine publishers must be bleeding red ink. Not at all. Meredith, a public company that publishes three of the top five women's service magazines, breaks out the profitability of its publishing division. These magazines continue to show higher and more consistent profitability than even the best-run company in movies, music, or books.

So what is going on? The publishers and editors of these women's publications have clearly understood customer captivity. Women buying these publications, every month or in yearly subscriptions, make a small decision on a continuous basis. They are hooked on the kind of information and on the delivery through glossy paper with text and lots of illustrations. The managements of these very successful magazines pay minute attention to what appeals to individual segments of their readers by carefully tracking data and reinforcing that bond with readers accordingly. The best publishers can tell you how many issues subscribers read by age range or the appeal of a particular direct-mail piece to potential readers in a single state or how many print readers use their Web sites.

TABLE 6.5 Meredith Performance 2000–2007

	2007	2006	2005	2004	2003	2002	2001	2000
Operating Margin	17.3%	17.1%	19.2%	18.1%	16.9%	16.0%	17.2%	17.1%
Return on Assets	22.4%	22.2%	40.5%	37.5%	31.8%	39.3%	42.8%	43.3%

Source: Company financials, fiscal years ending June 30.

This is not to suggest that these businesses are impervious to the threats posed by digital distribution, and there are signs of trouble in the recent margin and returns trends. But continuous content businesses have tools at their disposal to protect their franchises unavailable to discrete content businesses. The long-standing relationship with their reader base both makes that base less likely to move and arms the publisher with information that ensures that the magazines remain relevant to generations of readers and to the advertisers who want to reach them. Some of this information and learning is transferable among publications within the same company, and we see ownership of these publications concentrated among five companies (Meredith, Hearst, Time, Condé Nast, and Hachette). But in the end, a customer's loyalty is to a particular title, and it is a kind of alchemy that in some cases has taken more than a hundred years to perfect.

7 | Efficient Operations in Media: Do You Think I'm Sexy?

The media moguls of history—the Goldwyns and Warners of movies, the Luces of magazines, the Paleys of television, and the Disneys of children's entertainment—typically grew to prominence with their industries. Their successors at Viacom, News Corp., Time Warner, and Disney were less fortunate. They inherited mature companies in mature industries. Opportunities to be creative on a grand scale were far more limited. However, this did not mean that opportunity had vanished altogether. Starting in 1959, Lew Wasserman created a media juggernaut, Universal Entertainment, out of an initial $11 million investment in a second-tier studio (Universal Pictures) with a second-tier record label (Decca) and four hundred acres of Los Angeles real estate. He did so in a way that did not punish his shareholders. From the end of 1959, when MCA/Universal went public, until it was sold to Matsushita at the end of 1990, its stock price rose at an annual rate of almost 14 percent compared to a roughly 5 percent annual rise in the Dow Jones Industrial Average. Including dividends, this represented a thirty-year average annual return of over 15 percent. Wasserman achieved this by an intense focus on operating efficiently.

From the very beginning of his career as an agent with MCA, Wasserman embraced professional management. Like IBM at its peak, Wasserman imposed a conservative dress code: dark suits, white shirts, and conservative ties. He insisted on clean offices with clean desks at the end of each day. There was no fraternization between managers and secretaries. As Helen Gurley Brown, later editor of *Cosmopolitan* magazine, recalled of her experience as a secretary at MCA, "[W]e couldn't attract any attention. The agents were all business."[1]

Detailed reports to higher management of financials and operating activities were frequent and comprehensive. Managers, beginning with Wasserman himself, were expected to have a detailed command of their contents. Budgets were set at all levels of the organization and compliance was closely monitored. Managers were discouraged from seeking public exposure. Indeed, MCA and later MCA/Universal were notorious for their secretive approach to public disclosure. Publicity was reserved for the stars and creative products.

Compensation was tightly controlled and focused on long-term goals. Stock grants for top managers and stock matching programs for all employees both vested over seven years. Bonuses paid in stock depended on overall corporate performance, not individual divisional performances. Unless MCA/Universal as a whole did well, individual managers would not do well. The costs of stock grants (unlike options) were fully reported in company financials. Perks were strictly limited. MCA/Universal had no corporate aircraft prior to its sale to Matsushita and afterward had one plane reserved for trips to and from Japan. Managers were motivated by a combination of generous, but not excessive, compensation and close attention paid to individual performance and achievements.

Wasserman focused on steady everyday performance, not on the allure of spectacular hits, notwithstanding the hit-driven nature of many of his businesses. His initial foray into production was for television, not theatrical films. In television, repeat business and long-term relationships with a small number of networks provided a stable revenue stream against which profits could be made by efficient cost management. This was done, according to his chief biographer, by "running Universal like a factory—the most thoroughly computerized in show business—prizing efficiency, cost-effectiveness and fully utilized facilities."[2] Wasserman himself illustrated this when he said (in a 1965 *Time* magazine interview) "[I]f you are going to manufacture anything, you ought to have the finest plant and facilities."[3]

Cost management also extended to payments to talent. Wasserman hoped by obtaining dominant share among suppliers of television programming that talent, especially writers and directors, would be forced to come to MCA/Universal for work at advantageous rates. They would be more likely to agree, for instance, to sign long-term contracts for series. In the event of success, he would be able to lock in able but unknown actors, writers, and directors at relatively low rates. Sid Sheinberg, who became Wasserman's president in 1973, had previously run the successful television division, where he signed up an unknown Steven Spielberg for a low-cost seven-year contract on the strength of an award-winning short.[4] Where money was spent on directorial talent, like Steven Spielberg once he became successful, or special effects, lesser-paid actors would be used. By offering talent the gratification of public attention undiluted by "star" executives who sought to share the limelight, and attentive treatment, Wasserman sought to economize on cash compensation.

Revenue enhancement was another of Wasserman's marked capabilities. As in the case of television production, his initial entry into the theatrical film business was designed to employ just this ability. In February 1958, before buying Universal, Wasserman acquired Paramount's film library for a $10 million down payment and payments contingent on the revenues generated that ultimately came to $40 million. He exploited the library by systematic sales to television stations amounting ultimately to more than $1 billion. Wasserman was also relentless in selling movie-related merchandise and licensing his brandable products. Marketing campaigns for Universal films were meticulously planned and staged. Wasserman pioneered the practice of wide releases, opening films, like *Jaws*, on unprecedented numbers of screens that maximized revenues in short periods of time. He even followed Disney relatively early on into theme parks, Universal City Tours, and related hotels.

The impact of these practices was apparent not just in MCA/Universal's stock-market returns, but also in its divisional operating performances. The film division produced average operating margins (on sales) of 14.5 percent from 1971 through 1989—the years for which useful segment data are available.[5] This corresponded to a pretax return on capital of about 15 percent. Both figures were well above the industry average. The music division earned average operating margins of 12 percent over the same period. Its pretax return on capital was above 20 percent.[6] Both figures were again well above industry averages. For books, data are available only from 1985 to 1989. Average returns of 12.5 percent and at least 25 percent on capital during that time were exceptional by industry standards.

Of course, Wasserman's performance was not perfect, and toward the end of his career in particular, the curse of the mogul began to take its toll. He acquired a Colorado savings and loan and a New Jersey catalog retailer—neither of which performed well. The acquisitions accelerated in the last years of his reign.[7] In 1985, Wasserman bought a toy company, which he sold at a significant loss within a few years,[8] and followed this up with the purchase of a stake in the beleaguered Coleco Industries (makers of Cabbage Patch dolls), which promptly filed for bankruptcy.[9] His labor practices were

TABLE 7.1   Universal Divisional Performance, 1971 to 1989[10]

	1985–1989		1971–1984	
	Return on Assets	Operating Margin	Return on Assets	Operating Margin
Films	9.1%	12.1%	15.3%	14.5%
Music	11.4%	8.3%	13.2%	11.9%
Books	23.8%	12.6%	n/a	n/a

questionable and many of his associates' reputations were dubious. Despite these lapses, when the entire period of his reign at MCA is taken into account, Wasserman set a widely noticed standard of performance that other moguls should have been tempted to emulate.

Wasserman may have been an icon among industry executives, but he was not a role model, at least when it comes to his single-minded focus on efficient operations. Indeed, it would be hard to identify an industry in which the ability to operate efficiently is treated with such disdain as in media. The list of epithets reserved for those dedicated to the smooth operation of the business rather than creative output is long and often profane: suits, pencil pushers, number crunchers, apparatchiks, pinheads, overhead, weenies, bookkeepers, and green-eyeshaded wonks are only the most genteel of the sobriquets.

It is easy to speculate on the source of this scorn. The cultural divide between the creatives who actually generate entertainment product and the corporate types responsible for the bottom line could not be greater. It is perhaps to be expected that the resulting lack of understanding could breed contempt when corporate directives usually come in the form of restrictions on just how creative a creative can be.

Often, however, it is the media moguls themselves who seem to deride the importance of efficiency. When, in 1991, Disney studio chairman Jeffrey Katzenberg's twenty-eight-page memo criticizing the "tidal wave of runaway costs and mindless competition" prevalent in the movie industry was leaked to *Variety*, the outcry from talent who benefited directly from the overspending was understandable—most memorable was Alec Baldwin's charge that the diminutive Katzenberg was "the eighth dwarf—Greedy."[11] More surprising was the intensity and duration of the scorn heaped by other executives who dismissed the memo as "banal," "self-serving," or worse.[12] It is as if such matters are beneath the dignity of the mogul, who should be spending his time on "vision" and "strategy." In some extreme cases, the mogul may actually think of himself as the ultimate über-creative, channeling the macromedia environment to the operating units and down to the talent themselves. The mogul's self-conception is closer to that of a prophet than to an efficiency expert.

Whatever the precise source of this predisposition to trivialize the value of professional management in media, it is unfortunate. In the absence of any meaningful competitive advantages for discrete content businesses in particular, the only sustainable distinctions in performance are those achieved by distinctions in how efficiently their operations are run. The consequences of the aggressive neglect of efficiency are apparent in the weak shareholder returns.

The fact that the sexier discrete content segments of the media industry lack competitive advantages may discourage managers who would otherwise seek careers there. There are three reasons why these concerns are often misplaced.

First, although *efficiency* sounds less fun than *strategy*, in an industry-specific context this is not necessarily so. Figuring out how to reduce raw material wastage from widget production is usually the kind of task that comes to mind when we hear the word *efficiency*. In the media context, as Wasserman demonstrated, figuring out ways to get extraordinary creative talent to remain in the fold without paying absolute top dollar or negotiating favorable revenue sharing and marketing arrangements with online partners is just as much about "efficiency."

Second, the fact that media companies systematically fail to focus on efficiency is all upside for a potential manager looking to create shareholder value. In a well-run industry without barriers to entry, the incremental opportunity to make a positive difference is indeed limited. In the media industry, there are vast differences in profitability among businesses that are largely indistinguishable. The benefits of making your particular hit-driven media business not just best in class but the best that it can be are far greater than in most industries.

Third, just because shareholders are unlikely to do well over the long term in these businesses doesn't mean that managers won't. Managers are in many ways like creative talent in that they can do very well by convincing those above that they are indispensable to the success of the enterprise or the project. Managers frequently tout their "special" relationship with talent to justify outsized paychecks. Indeed, it is precisely because media managers are often overpaid that the shareholders are left to suffer. Clever managers take credit for the hits and insist on being compensated for them, while distancing themselves from the inevitable flops. So even if you are committed only to your own wealth creation rather than shareholders', the lack of industry competitive advantages does not suggest that you should necessarily keep away. It does suggest, however, that you should take your bonus in cash.

Although efficient operations are particularly critical in segments that lack barriers to entry, this does not mean they are irrelevant to those segments with competitive advantages. Indeed, the media landscape is littered with examples of strong franchises in which much of the potential shareholder value has been frittered away through a combination of lax revenue management, waste, and imprudent investments. What constitutes efficiency varies widely by media subsector, and the overall topic deserves its own book, given the extent to which the very concept has fallen into disrepute in the industry. For our purposes, we will confine ourselves to providing a general framework for approaching consideration of efficient operations in media. We will describe the key cost and revenue levers that can be managed effectively or ineffectively in these businesses to achieve optimal financial results and provide some examples of just how great the disparity in results can be from different approaches to these factors. Finally, we discuss briefly the critical issue of designing an organization likely to facilitate efficient operations.

COST MANAGEMENT

Efficiency is widely viewed across industries as a code word for mindless cost cutting, which may or may not be fair, based on how mindless the particular cost cutting is. The source of the derision with which the term *efficiency* is met in the media industry, however, goes deeper. The concept of efficient operations is often associated with commodity businesses where the only way to scrape by is through relentless focus on controlling production costs. There is an apparent incongruity inherent in applying practices relevant to such obviously different operating environments. Creative output is anything but a commodity. It is the ultimate differentiated product. And it is the ultimate criticism of an artist to say that his or her work is derivative. So it is perhaps not surprising that there is a deep skepticism of the claim that any corporate structure that focuses excessively on cost could also foster creativity.

It is a fundamental fallacy that differentiated products, in media or otherwise, should not have efficient operations as their primary focus. A differentiated product may or may not have barriers to entry, and it is this alone that will determine whether relative efficiency will be the sole arbiter of success. Differentiated products are fundamentally different in their cost structures from commodity products, however. In addition to sourcing inputs and managing operations, which are the primary production cost elements of commodity businesses, marketing becomes a critical component. This addition entails a radical increase in the range and complexity of dimensions along which an enterprise's absolute relative efficiency will be judged.

Developing and marketing a differentiated product begins with market research and product development, moves through a packaging, advertising, and promotion phase, and ends with a distribution strategy supported by a skilled sales force. At each point along this chain, failure to operate efficiently can lead to as much of a breakdown in overall profitability as wasting money in more obvious production cost elements.

Profitable management of these three broad cost categories—goods (inputs), marketing, and operations—often involves trade-offs within and among themselves. Although there are different cost structures in different media industry segments that would need to be analyzed separately, there are enough commonalities to make some general observations.

Goods

In creative media businesses, the cost of developing product and the cost of signing talent are both core to the cost structure but are sometimes treated as a mysterious black box about which little can be done. These critical areas are often subjected to swift and radical reversals of approach—complete laissez-faire after a string of hits alternates with arbitrary and draconian cost control and micromanagement after a string of flops. In the film business, this is the source of gallows humor, since the heads most likely to roll were often uninvolved with the relevant decisions that led to the flops. It usually takes three years to take a property from concept to the screen (a year in development, a year in production, and a year for postproduction and marketing) and turnover in these ranks is such that the original green-lighting executive is long gone by the time the opening box-office tallies come in. As William Goldman famously observed: "Studio executives are intelligent, brutally overworked men and women who share one thing in common with baseball managers: They wake up every morning of the world with the knowledge that sooner or later they're going to get fired."[13] But unlike baseball managers, they are quite likely to get fired for a season they had little to do with.

This traditional approach is both wrongheaded and self-defeating. Such an operating environment breeds a fatalistic attitude in key decision makers who ultimately question whether there is any meaningful connection between their true performance on the one hand and their likelihood of advancement (or untimely demise) on the other. It is not beyond human possibility to develop a consistent and focused strategy both for developing product and signing talent that makes sense and should be broadly applicable in good times and bad.

In the case of signing talent, we again often see alternation between two misguided extremes. Media executives often seem resigned to the fact that when it comes to talent, it is only about the money. But just as often, an executive (sometimes the same one) is seen justifying his or her position or promotion based on a "special" relationship with key talent. Both phenomena contain some truth—it certainly is very much about the money and even creative artists have been known to occasionally display some loyalty—but neither constitutes a sensible cost management strategy.

Creative artists are notoriously insecure. They have all seen peers go from hot to not in a nanosecond or may have experienced their own professional near-death experiences. Money is valuable in itself but also as a reflection of the studio's belief in an artist. But a variety of other, often less costly mechanisms can deliver as much or more of a sense of security and self-worth. Indeed, once talent become unhappy, keeping them becomes impossible except at an uneconomic financial cost. So, although it may sound inconsistent with our emphasis on "operational efficiency," providing the care and attention that talent craves can be an excellent investment of management time just as those famously expensive celebrity perks can be a fantastic long-run cost saver.

These observations do not imply, however, either that one should take at face value an executive's claims to be able to "deliver" an artist or that no request of a valuable artist is too extreme. An artist's first love is to himself, not to a particular executive, agent, manager, or family member. Although consistency in managing the relationship is important, effective management should provide a web of institutional signs of commitment to an artist that minimizes an individual executive's ability to hold up the company. "Triple-teaming" talent—that is, assigning multiple executives to maintain a relationship with a single artist—may sound inefficient, but it is a very sound policy. Similarly, the long-term cost of agreeing to gross overpayment to keep a star goes well beyond that individual transaction. Nothing is secret in Hollywood. Such decisions are likely to have a multiplier effect as other talent decides to test the financial limits of a company's love. A little tough love by setting boundaries with a clear and firmly delivered no, can, ironically, serve to cement a relationship by providing clarity.

It is also important to distinguish between granting expensive perks to creative talent or staff, which can be wise policy, and providing lavish treatment of senior executives, which undermines effective operations on several levels beyond the actual cost of providing the perks. First, there is the obvious knock-on effect, as perk envy spreads throughout the management ranks. Second, it actually undermines the value of the perks provided to creatives, as management steals some of the spotlight that should be totally reserved for these creatives. Third, and maybe most important, it fosters a culture of an imperial CEO—largely detached from day-to-day operations.

Management time and attention is any company's most precious asset. On the cost management side, managers' overarching focus should be on understanding the business's core strengths and identifying where there are new niches that existing management and creative talent can fill. The flip side of this is to be able to say no—wisely and credibly. Where a project is either uneconomic or, just as important, outside the company's area of competence. Where existing management doesn't have the expertise to successfully pursue a new opportunity and outside talent is required. Where a long-standing franchise is getting long in the tooth and requires radical reinvigoration. A leader needs to be able to be close enough to the businesses to answer these questions well. The biggest potential downside of failing to "save the red carpet for the talent" is that the leader will be far enough away from the business that he or she will be at the mercy of the producer or project manager who will have very different incentives in using the company's money.

Marketing

One critical aspect of the management challenge involved is to clearly distinguish the cost of getting the product to the customer from the cost of telling the customer it is there. The effective development and distribution of creative product entails a number of distinct processes that must be managed and coordinated to achieve the best possible outcome.

The importance of efficient management of marketing expenses in media businesses should be apparent from their sheer scale. It would not be unusual for the marketing budget of a "blockbuster" film to exceed $50 million, even if that film is *Stuart Little 2* and barely manages to gross that much in U.S. ticket sales.[14] On average, the marketing costs are greater than half of the so-called negative cost of film production, and rather than focusing on efficiencies, the studios appear to be "involved in an arms race in marketing costs."[15]

At its core, effective marketing is about being honest about the product and marketing based on what you know. This may seem obvious, but there are a number of structural obstacles to achieving this result. The star or the executive in charge of the product may have an interest in either overinvesting or misinvesting marketing dollars. Overinvestment occurs where the personal shame of an overwhelming flop measured by box-office revenues leads to expenditures that have little chance of yielding an acceptable return. Misinvestment occurs where the nature of the marketing campaign is designed to satisfy the ego of the talent rather than maximize the potential interest of consumers in the product. The torrent of "for your consideration" advertisements that appear during awards season is the most obvious example of this. If such an ad really might improve the chance of gaining a film a high-profile award, it could theoretically be justified, but did anyone really believe that Tom Cruise had a shot at Best Actor for *War of the Worlds* when they took out the full page?[16]

Sometimes misallocation of marketing dollars can happen to satisfy corporate rather than talent ego. This has even less justification than talent ego gratification as corporations in content media businesses do not need to sell themselves—no one goes to see *Spider-Man* because Sony produced it. Even after Jean-Marie Messier was pushed out of Vivendi because of his media mogul excesses, some of his legacy apparently lived on. In 2006, the company launched a major corporate advertising campaign under the not-so-catchy slogan "Entertainment. It's vital." The campaign included an online video message from the new mogul-in-chief Jean-Bernard Lévy expounding on how "the entertainment focus helps his firm bridge and transcend any perceived divide between telecom and media businesses."[17]

A critical corollary to the truism about effective marketing being about marketing the product based on what you know is that the marketing plan should be adjusted based on new information. An initial marketing plan will begin to take shape before anyone knows whether they have a hit or a flop on their hands. These plans can take on a life of their own, particularly where talent is involved. This can become extremely costly if emerging facts on the ground are inconsistent with the original plan.

When it becomes certain that you have a flop on your hands, the first objective is to sell as much product as possible before it becomes clear to everyone else. Put it on the maximum number of screens early, presell as much as humanly possible, and seek out an audience that does not know any better. The second objective is to cut your losses—any planned expenditures that are not fully committed should be eliminated.

On the other hand, in the same way that buzz can quickly kill a flop, it can reduce the need for incremental marketing expense once it is clear that you have a hit. Good word of mouth is the cheapest marketing tool and it should not be wasted.

Operations

Efficient management of operational functions is subject to a number of general overarching principles that are as applicable to media companies as to other industries. The difference in practice is the extent to which media companies reject the application of these principles. This overall resistance is defended on the basis that creative businesses need to operate independently in order to thrive. There is little evidence to support this view and the counterexamples have become the stuff of legend. The financial legacy of Sony's hands-off approach to its acquisitions of CBS Records and Columbia Pictures is probably the most extreme historic example. The discovery by the private equity firm that recently bought EMI that the "fruit and flowers" cost item on the company's financials was actually a euphemism for "drugs and whores" suggests the continuing risk of ignoring more traditional operating metrics and controls in media.[18]

Operating departments do not generate outside revenues but provide internal services across an organization. The fixed costs associated with production, warehousing, fulfillment, legal, finance, HR, and even marketing should be spread across the widest possible swath of operations. Even when the idiosyncrasies of a particular division require some customization of the service or even dedicated personnel, it rarely justifies replicating a stand-alone independent functional organization. Ultimate responsibility for these functions should always be centralized with strong oversight to ensure consistency and efficiency of practices. The success with which an organization resists the pressure by individual creative units to secure control over these functions— and once secured, grow them to enhance the scale of their overall fiefdom— will likely determine whether operational efficiency is even possible.

Closely related to the question of where these operational functions should be housed within an organization is the question of whether they should be performed by the organization at all. Media companies have come very late and reluctantly to the outsourcing party. The general proclivity for empire building in all businesses seems further exacerbated by a belief that anything that even touches the core creative output should be unsullied by outside hands. The result has been a willingness to explore outsourcing only in extremis. For instance, only when facing basic questions about the viability of the business in the Internet age have newspaper companies begun to seriously look at outsourcing printing, delivery, and even certain editorial functions.[19] One wonders what might have been achieved if newspapers had considered such steps in the era when they regularly attained profit margins above 40 percent! Only if operational functions are centralized in the first place is the organization likely to have processes in place to systematically examine where outsourcing will be effective.

Beyond obvious generalized functions like payroll, any capital-intensive activities where the company either cannot fill capacity itself or does not have the scale to operate with a competitive cost structure are prime candidates for outsourcing. Sure, the tours are cool and they make executives feel more like moguls, but does anyone really believe that Columbia, Paramount, Universal, and 20th Century Fox all require major studio lots in greater Los Angeles in order to operate effectively? Production has increasingly moved on-location[20] or to lower-cost lots located elsewhere in the United States[21] or internationally.[22] Wouldn't it make more sense to contribute some portion of the studio lots to a joint operating company whose sole purpose would be to run them at optimal capacity for the shareholders and sell the excess for redevelopment? Does anyone think this is likely to happen as long as the moguls are in charge?[23]

The central financial oversight functions of operations are obviously important to the effective operation of any business. It is a truism of business that it is always easier to make a budget than to keep it. Instilling a commitment to doing the latter as well as the former is particularly challenging in media organizations. Media metrics are often articulated purely in terms of revenues, market share, and industry accolades rather than in terms of costs or contribution to the bottom line—the weekend box-office grosses, the TV ratings sweeps, award nominations. This tendency requires serious attention in the form of monthly financial review meetings that focus on cost as well as revenue, which in turn must be reinforced through a compensation structure that is consistent with this perspective.

There is another structural reason that the budgeting process of many content-oriented media businesses requires special attention. Operational costs should be budgeted for the worst-case year. In hit-driven industries, however, there is a dangerous propensity to build up the cost infrastructure as if the latest hit reflected a sustainable ongoing state of affairs. The executive in charge of a banner season or record-breaking smash in the entertainment business is viewed as imbued with magical powers and given an unhealthy level of spending discretion going forward. Belief in magic is generally short-lived, but by the time reality sets in, the damage is often already done in the form of a newly enlarged cost structure. The point is not that it never makes sense to increase a budget. Rather it is that there should be consistent processes and standards upon which to base the decision. Investments essential to reach more paying customers can be justified, as can an expanded infrastructure where higher revenues can genuinely be expected to continue indefinitely. Jack notwithstanding, magic beans are not a good bet.

REVENUE MANAGEMENT

In a culture where there is no such thing as bad publicity, it should not be surprising that there is a corresponding sense that there is no such thing as bad revenue. As a result, the biggest challenge of revenue management in media is distinguishing between good and bad revenue. At its most basic level, this can be addressed by remembering to focus on incremental contribution rather than incremental revenue. But a regular internal financial review process that appropriately addresses both the cost and revenue side of the ledger cannot in itself protect against ill-advised investment. Without an overall framework for approaching growth, an executive committed to achieving it is likely to be successful in both understating costs and overstating net revenue potential enough to secure his ambitions.

Understating costs associated with desired projects is a fine art refined by divisional executives through generations. It will be difficult for even the most perceptive senior executive to stop every possible obfuscation by those closest to the operations on the ground. One category of hidden cost, however, is particularly insidious and pervasive: the cost of management time and focus. Particularly where a project does not leverage the existing core capabilities of the organization, the costs of diverted focus are substantial and often ignored. For example, it is understandable given the magnitude of Sony's $3.4 billion write-off that the most attention has been directed toward the value destroyed by overpaying and mismanaging the acquisitions of Columbia Pictures and CBS Records. Much less has been said about the unexpected string of failures in its core consumer electronics businesses that followed, arguably as a result of the diversion of management attention.[24]

On the revenue side, beyond simply being overly optimistic about the prospects of an initiative, the most frequent source of a shortfall is the failure to fully account for cannibalization. Cannibalization can come from substitution of a new product for an old. The executive promoting an investment will always argue that the new product provides incremental value to the customer and will result in minimal cannibalization. The danger is that even where this is true, the customers may insist on volume discounts in order to purchase both products. So, for example, when one magazine owner buys its competitor, advertisers will use the transaction as an excuse to pay less for ads they were planning to buy anyway. One way to avoid this is by maintaining two separate sales forces—but even if effective, this will undermine the cost savings that justified the deal in the first place.

The best way to minimize the risk of sandbagging on either the cost or revenue side is to go back to first principles. Without barriers to entry, incremental revenue generally will not be profitable. Where there is some competitive advantage, incremental opportunities should leverage these. Economies of scale should be exploited by building on focused applications. Customer captivity should be leveraged through new products and services that reinforce the source of captivity. If there are existing resources and infrastructure that are not fulfilling their full revenue potential, these can and should be eliminated regardless of the existence of competitive advantage: This is the essence of efficient revenue management.

In either case, the point is that expansion should focus on areas where a company is already a leader or has underexploited management or physical resources. This is in contrast to two equally misguided inclinations that we frequently see in media businesses. First, if their leadership is in a segment that does not have high organic growth, the tendency is to invest in unrelated higher-growth segments regardless of whether they share any core capabilities. The shopping engine buying spree is an example of this phenomenon. Second, it is the rare media company that will simply exit a business line that is subscale where competitors have an advantage. Unfortunately, throwing good money after bad seems a preferred course to admitting defeat and emphasizing the company's own strengths. The consistently unprofitable video-game divisions of the major conglomerates are an example of this phenomenon.

With respect to deriving the most revenue possible from the products that they do produce, media companies have done a better job. The key to getting the most out of what you have is to sell as much as possible in as many forms as conceivable. The central elements of revenue maximization are the interrelated practices of price discrimination and product repurposing.

Price discrimination is another basic concept from an introductory microeconomics class. The notion is that different people are willing to pay different prices for a particular product. If a single price is charged, however, the seller is leaving a lot of money on the table. Customers who would have been willing to pay more avoid doing so, and those who would have paid something less than the list price but more than it cost the seller to produce never get to buy at all. Understandably, sellers will always want to charge each person exactly what he or she is willing to pay for their product. This is usually impossible for a variety of practical and legal reasons. But there are a number of perfectly legal ways to benefit from some price discrimination: Depending on how it was purchased, an annual *Wall Street Journal* subscription could cost under a hundred dollars or over three hundred.

In the movie business, the practice of selling the rights to a film in different "windows"—theatrical release, video on demand followed by rentals and pay-per-view, pay cable, first-run network TV, and finally syndication— is a form of price discrimination. Similarly, in the book business, the timing of release for hardcover, paperback, book-club, and remainder markets is all a way to market separately to different points on the demand curve. Sophisticated subscription businesses set individual renewal rates in part based on the length of the customer relationship, which is highly predictive of the price increase that will be tolerated without prompting cancellation. Although media businesses collectively have been sophisticated about maintaining and enforcing these price discrimination mechanisms, every once in a while they seem to forget why they have organized their sales efforts in this way in the first place. Disney's widely publicized effort to collapse the release windows—by making product available to multiple segments simultaneously— is reflective of this curious and self-defeating form of amnesia.[25]

Repurposing involves taking a core franchise product and selling as many different versions of it as possible. No one could fault the producers of *Law & Order* for failing to adequately engage in this practice around the core brand. Nor could Disney be faulted for the efficiency of its ability to monetize product extensions in every medium from toys to theme-park rides. Although media companies have aggressively repurposed to maximize revenue, they have been less thoughtful about when to produce that product themselves rather than license it. These companies have repeatedly and foolishly been unwilling to outsource production or distribution of repurposed product even where it has been evident that their own capabilities were not up to the task. Disney's decision to manage its own vast chain of consumer retail stores to sell Disney product[26] and the decision of various studios to repeat the mistake of Time Warner in the 1980s when it used its in-house arm to produce the monumentally unsuccessful video game for *E.T.: The Extra-Terrestrial* are both examples.[27]

The line between price discrimination and repurposing is a fine one. Is the sale of dubbed or subtitled films overseas or the creation of director's-cut DVD editions repurposing or price discrimination? These and numerous other examples are obviously both, to some extent. In the end, the ultimate form of price discrimination is achieved by customizing the product individually. Although this is rarely cost-effective, it is one of the few areas where digital distribution could in theory create at least some incremental opportunities to manage revenue more efficiently. Unfortunately, the impact of lowered barriers to entry tends to swamp the benefits from such customization. One counterexample is the outdoor advertising industry, where the digital billboards allow significant customization and discrimination without increasing the opportunity for entry, which is still limited by the physical space available to mount the displays.[28]

ORGANIZATIONAL DESIGN

Cost and revenue management are somewhat abstract concepts. Their actual implementation takes place in the context of a particular organizational design. Ensuring a proper fit between the structure of the organization and the activities it is meant to carry out is essential to efficient operations. We have already implicitly touched on a number of central issues of organizational design—creating proper financial incentives, fostering a culture conducive to the company's objectives, choosing functions to be outsourced—as it is not possible to discuss any key revenue or cost management concepts without integrating some discussion of organizational design. The range of topics encompassed by organizational design has sometimes been summarized by the acronym PARC: People, Architecture, Routines, and Culture. Each of these elements has been the subject of extensive research and scholarship, increasingly empirical in nature and economically grounded.[29]

In addition to the topics already covered in the discussions of efficient cost and revenue management, one additional recurring issue relating specifically to content-oriented media companies is worth noting. Specifically, all content businesses must deal with the issue of how to most effectively manage their distribution channels. Unlike the content businesses themselves, there are typically scale benefits on the distribution side of operations. It is in the content businesses' interest to work to develop cooperative mechanisms to encourage efficient distribution and to share the joint benefits of that enhanced distribution.

TABLE 7.2 Universal Organizational Design Under Different Regimes

	MCA/Universal	Vivendi Universal
Compensation	• Stock grants for top management and stock matching plan for all employees that vest over seven years • Stock grants devised to reward lifetime achievement • A rare stock bonus for management if corporation has an unusually profitable year • Cost of stock program reported in financials	• Stock options that vest over three years based on revenue growth • Stock matching for nonexecutives based on moving stock price • Options granted on meeting annual goals or term of executive's three- to five-year contracts • Options granted solely on the basis of divisional goals • Cost of stock options not reported in financials
Operational Focus	• A roll-up-your-sleeves culture where top management understands all of their businesses • Executives required to know the precise cost structure of their operations and in turn required managers to do the same	• Top management with no experience in entertainment • Top executives who delegated and let managers delegate in turn with ultimate responsibility left ambiguous
Budgetary Discipline	• Monthly corporate financial meetings with all division heads • Division heads in turn hold monthly financial meetings that include both creative executives and department heads • Budget made from the bottom up as well as from the top down	• High budget goals set in France to calm investor fears and imposed on the U.S. operations • No regular system of corporate financial meetings with division heads
Perks	• One plane after sale to Matsushita, reserved for trips to and from Japan, major Universal stars, and highly restricted executive use	• A fleet of planes were made available for use by all executives, who were charged only first-class fare

This can be achieved in a number of ways. Until recently, many of the major studios participated in an international joint venture, UIP, responsible for distributing the collective output of the founding partners Paramount, Universal, MGM, and United Artists. Snatching defeat from the jaws of victory as only media moguls can, the remaining participating studios, Universal and Paramount, have essentially disbanded the cooperative and agreed to create independent duplicative international infrastructures.[30] In magazine distribution, Hearst and Condé Nast operate a joint venture called Comag, which, in addition to distributing their own magazines, competes with a small number of the largest magazine publishers to obtain the rights to distribute other smaller competitors' product.

There is no easy way to summarize the vast array of organizational design issues that arise in media contexts. A simple comparison between MCA/Universal practices under Lew Wasserman and those under one if its subsequent owners gives a flavor of the breadth of issues implicated and their potential impact. Wasserman controlled MCA from 1962 to early 1991. Over the subsequent fourteen years it changed hands four times—from Matsushita to Seagram to Vivendi to General Electric. Throughout this period and into the present, the precise asset portfolio and ownership structure have been in constant flux, most recently in July 2008, with GE inviting two private equity firms to help finance the $3.5 billion acquisition of the Weather Channel. The table on page 139 contrasts the Wasserman approach to a number of the organizational design matters with that of a more traditional mogul—Jean-Marie Messier—who operated it under much of the Vivendi ownership regime.[31]

No single complement of design choices is likely to be perfect, and, indeed, a quality of strong management is a willingness to shift organizational structure to address the changing environment. But it is broadly evident that the choices made by someone like Lew Wasserman are far more likely to generate satisfactory returns on the underlying assets than the common alternatives. This observation is consistent with the vast disparity of returns generated by Universal under Wasserman and those of his successors. Sexy or not, efficiency matters.

8 | Putting It All Together: Networks and Databases

The raw content that is created—whether discrete or continuous—must inevitably be aggregated, packaged, marketed, and distributed, usually to local redistributors. These packagers effectively act as wholesalers of the content whose immediate client is often whoever is responsible for the actual sale or delivery to the customer: for example, movie theaters, cable operators, device manufacturers, or general or specialty retail outlets.

Packaging is frequently undertaken by the same companies that create the content or that are responsible for the ultimate delivery, but not exclusively. Certain media businesses engage in some aspect of all three elements: A local television station operator, for example, produces its own news content and possibly other local offerings, packages these with programming from various third-party providers, including the broadcast network with which it may be affiliated, and then delivers the packaged content using airwaves (known as spectrum) obtained under a government license.

Our approach is to analyze each element of the business separately because each has very different business characteristics. Content businesses, particularly of the hit-driven variety that are the subject of a disproportionate level of interest, rarely have competitive advantages. Although far less intrinsically exciting, packaging businesses, on the other hand, are far more likely to exhibit competitive advantages. Specifically, the structure of packaging businesses lends itself to scale economies and customer captivity.

Not surprisingly, packaging businesses have been far more profitable and attractive than the pure content businesses whose anemic results were

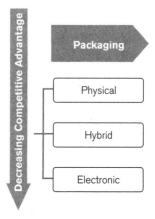

FIGURE 8.1 Packaging Competitive Advantage

highlighted in the previous chapters. Many of the largest players in movies, music, and books have built their own internal "packaging" businesses to support their own content output and also to serve independent third parties. These institutional sales, marketing, and distribution organizations are not what one typically associates with major consumer content media businesses. For book publishers they include massive book warehouse and distribution operations. Film studios require large sales organizations to negotiate release dates and terms with theater chains, cable channels, and retailers as well as the physical distribution of movie reels. Music companies still must preoccupy themselves with the delivery and placement of their CDs in stores. Not the sort of thing that draws young innocents to the glamour of media.

Glamorous or not, these businesses are consistently more financially attractive than the content businesses that spawned them. Media moguls have often sought to mask the sad performance of the content-is-king businesses by integrating their results into the far more mundane, but far more profitable, packaging businesses. It is a poorly kept secret that in particularly difficult years, content businesses become aggressive in offering attractive terms to smaller competitors to take up the underutilized capacity of their marketing and distribution organizations as a way to make their numbers.

"Packaging" encompasses a wide range of businesses and functions, but they share some common characteristics. We will focus on two categories of packaging businesses: networks and databases.

A network business is one that manages a web of customer relationships through which it distributes content. The network can involve physical infrastructure or simply an integrated sales force. In either case, there are significant fixed costs associated with maintaining the network, which are the source of the scale economies, and well-established client relationships, which are the source of the customer captivity. A new entrant, having replicated the high fixed cost of infrastructure of an incumbent, will have difficulty attracting the clients necessary to support that infrastructure in an economic way. If the incumbent has done a good job providing customer service over time, then the entrant will have to offer a lower-priced or higher-quality (more expensive) service to lure such a client away. But the incumbent, with the benefits of a lower average cost, can always match or even outdo any introductory offers of this sort. Where unattached customers are concerned, the incumbent also has a critical advantage. Because of his established infrastructure, the incumbent can serve that new customer at a much lower incremental cost than the entrant and can price his service accordingly. A company tempted to enter a market under these conditions would be well advised to think things over carefully and then look for other business opportunities.

Database businesses aggregate, integrate, and analyze large quantities of information and synthesize it in a form most useful to its customers. The data is often collected from multiple sources—sometimes many thousands—over time and must be continuously updated, cleansed, standardized, and integrated. The value of the data to customers stems from a combination of the quality, timeliness, comprehensiveness, and the ability to perform analyses on a consistent basis over time. Database businesses can have significant fixed costs in the form of the personnel required to manage relationships with data providers on the one hand and the customers on the other. The database itself may also require maintenance of a large physical infrastructure and a substantial software R&D effort to address client product needs. Database customer captivity derives from the habit that comes with regular usage but also in some cases significant switching costs that can come from changing products deeply integrated into customer work flows.

Cable channel or "category television" businesses are a quintessential network business. Although to a greater or lesser degree, cable channels produce some of their own content, each channel's identity comes from packaging that content with other thematically consistent third-party content to create a voice or brand that resonates with consumers. Channel operators generate revenue primarily from subscriber fees negotiated with cable and satellite television operators, which vary based on history, viewership, and the channel packages in which the channel is included. This is a relatively high fixed cost business because once the channel is produced, the incremental cost of adding additional homes to the network is low. Accordingly, the biggest driver of profitability is the number of homes reached, which also impacts the second major revenue stream, advertising. Scale also provides advantages in program acquisitions. Having more viewers means that established networks provide more exposure to programs than alternative outlets. Since more exposure provides program producers with greater opportunities to exploit ancillary revenues, program producers will favor large networks in offering first looks and negotiating terms. In general, the old-line TV networks still have better access to program ideas than their cable brethren, and their ratings, although falling gradually over time, still reflect the greater driving power of the programs they buy. For special purpose programming, this benefits the channel that dominates a particular niche. For example, the Sci Fi Channel is the primary destination for science-fiction program producers and its repeated programming successes in this area reflect that fact.

The attractiveness of the cable channel business, especially for specialized channels like Nickelodeon for kids or HGTV for home decor, is reflected in its financial results, which are far superior to those of pure content businesses. As anyone with a television knows, however, it is an increasingly crowded field. In addition, all channels compete with a growing number of alternative media outlets, particularly in the online and mobile contexts. The ability of this industry to maintain its performance in this changing environment is a testament to the power of its structural advantages. There are, however, significant variations in the success with which channel groups have managed the threats to their franchises. A look at the history and operations of USA Network highlights both the precise sources of competitive advantages in these businesses and the most effective strategies to protect and reinforce them.

Established in 1980 under CEO Kay Koplovitz as a joint venture of Paramount and Universal Studios, USA Network had originally been conceived of as a rival to ESPN in offering sports programming under the banner of Madison Square Garden Sports Network. However, it was almost immediately reconceived as a rival to the highly profitable TBS Superstation as well as the other general interest cable networks such as A&E, TNT, and FX. Like TBS, USA offered a mix of sports (early rounds of U.S. Open Tennis and WWF wrestling,) network reruns (*Murder She Wrote*, the network's most successful program), and both purchased and original movies. Bonnie Hammer, the current president, came to USA first as a programming executive in 1989, moved to president of Sci Fi in 2001 and then of the entire USA Network since 2004. (Both Sci Fi and USA are operated by NBC Universal—80 percent owned by GE, 20 percent by Vivendi Universal.)

TABLE 8.1 USA EBITDA vs. Cable Network EBITDA[1]

EBITDA Margin	1998	1999	2000	2001	2002	2003	2004	2005	2006	2007
Industry Average	29.3%	31.0%	33.0%	31.7%	31.3%	32.9%	34.0%	34.9%	36.4%	35.3%
USA	36.0%	41.2%	49.1%	51.6%	44.2%	38.4%	39.8%	41.1%	43.2%	45.5%
Difference	6.7%	10.2%	16.1%	19.9%	12.9%	5.5%	5.8%	6.2%	6.8%	10.2%

Increasing affiliate and advertising revenue against a largely fixed cost base produced rapidly growing profits. By the mid-1990s, USA Network was a widely admired and profitable company. USA is known for controlling its budgets, based on the theory—among other successful techniques—that TV shows make stars, not the other way around.[2]

In 2001, USA had its all-time-high EBITDA (earnings before interest, taxes, depreciation, and amortization) margin of almost 52 percent. EBITDA is the preferred metric of operating profit in the media industry because it allows executives to add back the noncash depreciation and amortization charges without offsetting adjustments for capital expenditures and other cash requirements of the business. USA still has an extremely high operating margin relative to the industry; the five-year average EBITDA from 2003 to 2007 is almost 42 percent, which is seven points above the total industry EBITDA.

Another element of USA's success as an efficient operator is that Hammer managed to develop a specialty even within the rubric of a "general interest" channel. To compete for viewers and advertisers against cable as well as the big-four broadcast networks, USA has positioned itself as "quirky" general entertainment. It developed a "Characters Welcome" brand strategy that defines the channel in many dimensions.

Creatively, USA looks for particular characteristics that have helped filter in appropriate shows. "Is there a central character?" Hammer asks. "Is this character slightly flawed but upbeat? We wanted it to have an upbeat, aspirational tone. [USA producers] weren't just accepting pitches from anyone about anything."[3]

While "Characters Welcome" describes the major characters in its most successful prime-time shows, such as *Monk,* about an obsessive-compulsive detective, or the actors who fight in the World Wrestling Entertainment, this brand positioning has also been an appeal for viewers to self-identify as "characters" themselves and as viewers interested in somewhat offbeat programming.

One of the key factors driving the extent to which packaging businesses have real barriers to entry is the extent to which the core packaging functions are performed electronically or physically. For the same reasons that we have argued that the Internet is not the friend of the business (but rather of the consumer), and contrary to popular conception, it is old-fashioned physical packaging and distribution that heighten barriers to entry. Digital technologies uniformly reduce the fixed cost element of business functions—and thus undermine scale economics—and often facilitate the ability of customers to easily switch between providers. By the time an incumbent finishes cheering the cost reductions, he will notice that the room has become crowded: with new competitors, not new customers.

With respect to cable channels, the obvious observation is that the business has always been fundamentally electronic—the signal is transmitted via satellite to the cable-head end of the local cable operator, who delivers it through the cable box to the home. But it turns out that the concept of electronic distribution is a relative one. The speed, capacity, and ease of use of the digital infrastructure are all meaningful variables in the industry structure equation. The radical increases in capacity on cable networks through a combination of the introduction of fiber to the home and the development of sophisticated software that optimizes the use of the network have changed the economics of the business. Even the once more manual process of seamlessly stitching together enough content to constitute a channel can now be performed largely in front of a computer screen.

Of course, incumbent cable programmers are best positioned to take advantage of these developments. They have the expertise, infrastructure, and relationships with the cable operators to move quickly to take up as much of the new capacity as possible with HDTV versions of existing channels and new spin-off channels targeting increasingly focused adjacent niches. The Discovery Channel, for example, started in 1985, expanded into niche categories as digital distribution came online: Discovery Kids was launched in 1996 (it became a joint venture in with Hasbro in 2009), Discovery Español in 1998, Discovery Home in 1998, Discovery Health in 1999, and Discovery Home morphed into Discovery Planet Green in 2008. In total, Discovery now operates 114 networks in 170 countries.

These are precisely the right strategies for the incumbent to undertake in order to protect its competitive advantage. Scale, however, is a relative game. And with capacity growing at the rate it is and the cost structure falling as fast as it is, it is unreasonable to expect no share loss over time from new channels produced by a combination of nimble new entrants unencumbered by any legacy cost infrastructure and rival incumbents desperately looking at ways to fully utilize their own production capacity as well as protect their home turf.

Discovery Communications, the independent operator of Discovery and its sister channels, is also perhaps the best example of the power and importance of efficient operations even while reinforcing competitive advantage. Although predominantly a cable channel operator, the company had become bloated and began to stray into money-losing auxiliary business like retail stores. Profit margins had drifted down from over 20 percent to 18 percent by 2006. A new CEO, David Zaslav, joined in early 2007 and by 2008 was able to raise margins to over 30 percent by closing the stores, consolidating production studios, and streamlining operations.[4] These results were achieved while aggressively launching new domestic channels and repurposing the library of non-star-driven nonfiction content for new international channels and other media.

The database industries have also long been essentially electronic in nature. These businesses are significantly less high profile because they typically target institutional rather than consumer markets, and almost always a highly specialized market segment. Like the cable channel business, these, too, are beginning to experience the negative impact of increasing electronic distribution. Given that these businesses grappled with changes to the electronic landscape decades before their consumer-oriented counterparts—whether a broad search company like Google or a targeted special interest site like the Internet Movie Database (imdb.com)—examining the strategies they employed to reinforce competitive advantage in the face of these trends has broader application for thinking about media and competitive advantage.

Because of the specialized nature of database industries, each with its own peculiar history and product and market dynamics, it is worth choosing one to examine in some depth. Probably the oldest database segment is the financial information industry, and Reuters is the granddaddy of these businesses. Indeed, when Paul Julius Reuter began transmitting news and stock prices in the mid-1800s between Germany and Belgium, the operation was only partially electronic: gaps in the telegraph lines from Aachen, Germany, where telegraph lines ended, were filled by an army of more than two hundred carrier pigeons.

Many think of database enterprises like financial information as "content" rather than "packaging" businesses. The core content of financial information, however, is the reporting of actual transaction prices—whether of a stock, bond, commodity, or currency—as well as information disseminated by companies and public authorities. Although today the news operations of these organizations are completely separate from their data collection, they were originally one and the same: Reporting on the prices at which a security changed hands was no different from reporting on other market developments.

The financial data content is usually created by the parties to the trade. This content is then in their hands or the hands of the trading operation or exchange through which the parties may have conducted their transaction. The fundamental business of financial information providers is the collection and integration of this content. Database businesses may enhance the aggregated database with content of their own along with software and analytic tools, but the source of their advantage stems from a packaging role.

Note that within the financial information industry there are a number of pure providers of content, whether the individual investors whose trades

TABLE 8.2 Financial Information Industry Map

Content	Packaging	Retail
Comprehensive Providers		**General High-Speed Data**
Thomson Reuters Bloomberg		Cable
Niche Providers		Telcos
Quick (Japan) Platts (Energy) Hoovers		**Specialized High-Speed Data**
IDC (Illiquid Bonds) Merger Market Deal Logic		Savvis
Financial Benchmarks		BT Radianz
Ratings Agencies Indices		**Physical Distribution**
(Moody's, S&P, Fitch) (MSCI Barra, etc.)		
Risk Metrics Markit		Mail
(Risk, Governance) (Derivatives)		UPS
Exchanges		FedEx
Equity Derivatives		
(NYSE, LSE, ECNs) (CME, ISE, ICE, etc.)		
Fixed Income		
(TradeWeb,		
MarketAxess, etc.)		
Dealers		
Money Center Banks		
Investment Banks		

Real-Time News	**News Aggregators**
Dow Jones	Factiva
AP	PR Newswire
Agence France-Press	BusinessWire
Market Participants	**Processing and Order Management Companies**
Hedge Funds	
Mutual Funds	Eze Castle Omgeo
Investors	Broadridge DTCC
Corporates	Charles River
(Company Information)	
Government	**Enterprise Software Companies**
(Economic Data)	
	TIBCO
	Sunguard
	Advent
	Specialized Software Companies
	FactSet

are the source of the pricing information or the corporations that publish information on themselves that then gets incorporated into various databases. There are also pure aggregators whose sole function is to collect data from various disparate sources and present it in an integrated form most useful to their customers. And then there are many who share aspects of both.

The broad structure of the financial information industry is common to most professional database businesses, whether in the legal, scientific, or engineering sectors—two to four broad-based content/packager leaders (in this case, Thomson Reuters and Bloomberg) that are surrounded by a significant number of successful niche content packagers. The content packagers of all sizes rely in part on pure content providers for their content and at the same time compete with some number of pure packagers.

Data collection and packaging requires a significant fixed cost infrastructure that is the source of database businesses' economies of scale. Technological developments that lower these fixed costs are frequently lauded by media moguls as an opportunity to improve profitability, but in fact these are the greatest threat to competitive advantage. When the telegraphic gap between Germany and Belgium was closed, it certainly improved Reuter's cost structure by obviating the need for managing its armada of pigeons. But the immediate loss of the seven-hour advantage it had enjoyed over a competitor who relied on local mail trains instead of birds was economically far more significant. Reuter shut down the service and soon moved to London to start the modern Reuters.

Reuters thrived in London by first using the new Dover–Calais telegraph cable to rapidly transmit quotes between the London stock exchange and Paris and then continually expanded the breadth of content and the scope of operations. Reuters aggressively built its aggregation infrastructure, extending the network of financial capitals from which it collected news and data and the corresponding sales and distribution network to the local newspapers around the world that were then the primary outlet for the information. This process of expansion and innovation had been ongoing for over a century by the time the modern financial information industry was born with the introduction in 1964 of Reuters' Stockmaster service.

Stockmaster was the first product to deliver real-time financial data internationally. Although today, installing and integrating two-way real-time data feeds from multiple global exchanges and trading floors is not a major undertaking, at the time the fixed cost infrastructure required to perform this task was substantial. Stockmaster was followed by a succession of enhanced products incorporating specialized supporting software and custom-designed terminals. The earliest and most liquid global markets were those for currencies and it was on these that Reuters had built its strongest and largest market position. In 1973, the company leveraged this position in foreign exchange by introducing the first electronic trading platform, Reuters Monitor. In 1984, Reuters went public, and just a few years later launched its flagship Reuters Monitor Dealing Service terminals, incorporating a comprehensive package of information and trading services.[5]

Up to this point in its history, the Reuters story is a consistent one of continuous reinforcement of its barriers to entry in order to remain at the leading edge of technology in organizing dissemination and manipulating large volumes of real-time data. Reuters simultaneously invested in infrastructure to support the increasingly global markets and proliferation of complex financial instruments. At the same time, they continually enhanced the power and sophistication of their products and software to counteract the increasingly ubiquitous availability of much electronic financial data from exchanges and market makers and the extraordinary decline in data storage and retrieval costs. These initiatives were almost exclusively organic and directed toward developing incremental products and services for existing customers and asset classes, on the one hand, and adding adjacent asset classes and customer segments, on the other.

The year 1981 was not only a momentous one for Reuters because of the introduction of Reuters Monitor Dealing, which by 2000 was still the company's flagship product. It was also the year that Michael Bloomberg was fired from Salomon after fifteen years at the company. Using a few million dollars in personal funds, he started a little real-time financial data business called Innovative Market Systems. The following year he sold twenty terminals to his first customer, Merrill Lynch, which also took a stake in the company for $30 million. In July 2008, Merrill sold back its 20 percent ownership in the still-private company, renamed Bloomberg L.P. in 1986, for $4.43 billion for an implied company value of $22.5 billion. Earlier that year, Reuters had been sold to the family-controlled Canadian database conglomerate Thomson for under $17 billion.

Given all we have said about competitive advantage, and Reuters' head start of over a century, how could Bloomberg have managed to build a business more valuable and profitable than Reuters with such little outside capital in such a short period of time? Reuters had always had competitors in one form or another. Niche players organized either geographically, like Quick Corporation in Japan, or around highly specialized market data, news, or software, had always managed to thrive without making much of a dent in Reuters' overall franchise. Thomson had bought an initially low-end competitor, ILX, in 1988 and spent billions more in dozens of follow-on acquisitions to augment the product offering but had never managed to develop a significant market presence outside of the United States and did not have its own news service. Others had also tried to take on Reuters more broadly, but these efforts ended up in bankruptcy or being sold for a fraction of their earlier value.[6]

To understand what made Bloomberg different, we need to look first at what Reuters was doing while Bloomberg was building its business. Once Reuters went public in 1984, it used its enhanced liquidity to grow in a new way: through acquisitions. Beginning almost immediately after the IPO with the acquisition of Visnews, later renamed Reuters Television, and Instinet, an early electronic equity trading network, Reuters' acquisition binge accelerated in the 1990s with a long list of software, data, and consulting businesses, not all of which related to the financial markets.

By the dawn of the new century, Reuters' core historic financial business, including its information and trading services, represented only one of three broad units. A second operating division was housed under the uninformative appellation Reuterspace, which was the designated home for a collection of businesses whose only common characteristic was what they were not—inclusion was exclusively reserved for those opportunities outside the institutional financial markets. A third unit was a large collection of portfolio holdings that ranged from dozens of minority positions in a "Greenhouse Fund" for start-up technology companies, to "strategic" joint ventures like Radianz with Equant, to larger controlled holdings like Instinet, which Reuters took public in early 2001. Even Instinet, of which Reuters held 83 percent and which by 2000 represented more than half of the company's book asset value and a quarter of its operating profit, was operated completely independently and had no readily discernible operating connection to Reuters' core financial business.

In facing the daunting task of taking on Reuters from a standing start, Bloomberg had three interrelated things going for him.

First, the cost of actually aggregating and managing the key data feeds had already fallen enough that the up-front cost of collecting the core content was not prohibitive. The data providers were excited about encouraging the creation of another major customer and happy to price primarily based on the number of actual users Bloomberg attracted. This lower cost of entry, however, was available to anyone—and as we have seen, many tried and failed to take advantage of it. Reuters, after all, had had over a hundred years to enhance and embed the basic data that was now so readily available. The second key to Bloomberg's success related to his previous role as a partner at Salomon Brothers, where he ultimately had responsibility for developing the firm's own computer and information systems.

Bloomberg's position at Salomon gave him a unique perspective on the needs of customers of financial data information. In his own estimation, "nobody had more knowledge of the securities and investment industries and how technology could help them."[7] Specifically he understood the frustrations of institutional customers who had few real options and felt that Reuters had grown increasingly unwieldy and unresponsive. "Our product," Bloomberg boasted after the fact, "would be the first in the investment business where normal people without specialized training could sit down, hit a key, and get an answer to financial questions, some of which they didn't even know they should ask."[8] It is not a coincidence that one of the three people Bloomberg brought with him to start the business was focused exclusively on "what our potential customers might want."[9] The selling and product development processes were then tightly linked. As Bloomberg described it, "[t]hat gives us feedback as we build—and make the customer part of the evolution process (they come to believe it is their product)."[10]

The decades of the eighties and nineties saw an explosion in the global liquidity of the financial markets and the emergence of large new classes of users of sophisticated financial information tools, most notably on the so-called buy side: hedge funds, mutual funds, and large pension and sovereign wealth funds. Although it is always great to be the leading incumbent in fast-growing markets, it poses some important risks. New customers are by definition not captive to anyone and provide an important opening for new entrants to exploit. Reuters' increasing preoccupation with entering entirely new markets and managing its portfolio of investments afforded Bloomberg precisely such an opening.

Finally, the fact that Bloomberg worked at Salomon rather than at some other financial institution is also highly relevant to his success. Reuters had built its core franchise on the back of its strength in foreign exchange and, to a lesser extent, stocks. Salomon was the leading bond house on Wall Street. The unique perspective on fixed-income markets that his perch at Salomon provided was particularly fortuitous for Bloomberg. A disproportionate amount of the growth in information needs would come from the fixed-income markets during this period. Bloomberg describes the reasons well:

> In the 1980s, bonds were coming to new prominence in the financial markets, totaling trillions of dollars. Deregulation of the housing finance and thrift industries, the repeal of withholding taxes worldwide, soaring budget deficits, and the high interest rates required to bring down inflation—all these events helped transform the government and corporate bond markets into Wall Street's hottest growth industry. Suddenly, the world's biggest fiduciaries were buying and selling junk bonds and Eurobonds. They invested in bonds created out of mortgages and car loans . . . Although not as visible to the general public, as a business, debt had become bigger than equities.[11]

More important than the growth or absolute size of the markets, the nature of fixed-income information lends itself to greater long-term competitive advantage than do the foreign exchange or equity markets. The very liquidity in the latter markets that made them so attractive for Reuters initially planted the seeds for their ultimate vulnerability.

There are lots of different currencies. But the largest five of them represent almost 90 percent of the trading volume. And if you increase the number of currencies to ten, you account for over 99 percent.[12] Any of the major international banks performs billions of dollars in currency trades in the major currencies in a day, and since it is the trades themselves that are the source of the exchange-rate data, the ability of a financial information provider to develop a proprietary information product around these securities is challenging indeed. There are obviously a lot more stocks than there are currencies, but even these number only a few thousand domestically and under fifty thousand globally.[13] More important, these are still largely traded through large exchanges that provide real-time transaction feeds on a nonexclusive basis to anyone interested in aggregating them. Again, the obstacles to developing a differentiated information product around this data are substantial.

Fixed-income markets are quite different. A single public company could have issued dozens of debt securities. Each of these securities would have multiple standard attributes with critical financial implications—not just the term of the debt, but call dates and premiums, any original issue discount, change-of-control terms, and convertibility privileges and indentures. The precise nature of these terms lends itself to certain analytic functions that allow an investor to compare the returns available from different securities from the same issuer as well as analogous securities issued by other issuers with similar credit profiles. And it is not just public but private companies that issue debt securities. And national governments. And states. And localities. And various governmental and quasi-governmental entities. Just in the United States there are almost twice as many outstanding debt securities, some of which support highly liquid markets but many of which do not, as there are equity securities globally.[14] And that doesn't count the more than one hundred thousand different global structured products that were created by slicing, dicing, and aggregating various other forms of debt obligations into now synthetic instruments that trade independently.[15] More important, debt securities do not trade predominantly on well-developed centralized exchanges but rather through trades negotiated directly by individual market participants themselves.

Bloomberg built its businesses by developing strength in segments where the incumbent did not have an overwhelming position and that lent themselves to creating sustainable barriers to entry. While targeting the growing and underserved fixed-income markets and buy-side user base, Bloomberg focused relentlessly on client needs, developing specialized software allowing customers to use, analyze, and manipulate the data seamlessly into their daily work flow. Bloomberg protested that his aim was to become "something more than a niche information provider to a group of bond-market-data junkies."[16] But this legion of users addicted to Bloomberg's elegant and useful analytic tools, linked to one another through a powerful instant messaging system, became the front line in his march toward achieving those broader market objectives.

Reuters' strategic distraction, on the other hand, became even more pronounced from the mid-1990s when the company convinced itself that the Internet was indeed its friend. Rather than direct its efforts on reinforcing its competitive advantage with its core customers, Reuters sought to establish itself as an Internet leader to a far broader range of financial customers and even to new markets outside of financial information entirely. "Whereas we have historically dealt with customers in the hundreds of thousands," exulted CEO Peter Job in one of many statements trumpeting Reuters' aggressive embrace of the Internet, "we will be able to serve tens or even hundreds of millions of people."[17]

When Reuters went public in 1984, it boasted impressive financials: solid operating margins of 21.6 percent and returns on capital of 36.1 percent. Reuters' operating margin generally remained at or above 20 percent through

TABLE 8.3 Reuters Financials 1996–2001 (pounds in millions)

	1996	1997	1998	1999	2000	2001
Revenue	£2,914	£2,882	£3,032	£3,125	£3,592	£3,885
Operating Profit	592	541	550	549	411	302
% Margin	*20.3%*	*18.8%*	*18.1%*	*17.6%*	*11.4%*	*7.8%*
Return on Capital (%)	28.2%	21.0%	34.3%	56.0%	27.0%	6.3%

Source: Company reports.
Note: Return on capital is defined as after-tax EBIT divided by the average balance of total debt plus total shareholders' equity.

1996, at which point its profitability began falling consistently. Within five years, its operating profit would be less than half of what it had been.

In 2001, Peter Job was replaced by Thomas Glocer, an American who had joined Reuters as an attorney in 1995. Glocer was confronted not only with poor performance and an unwieldy organizational structure but with the Internet bust, which cast doubt on Reuters' recent aggressive investment strategy, and which, along with the 9/11 attacks that would occur within months of his taking the helm, severely impaired the results of the financial institutions that are its core customers. Given Glocer's limited operating experience and his position as the first non-British, nonjournalist to run this culturally inflexible organization, many were skeptical of his ability to address the challenges Reuters faced.

Glocer moved quickly to radically simplify Reuters' organization, operations, and product offerings. Businesses outside of Reuters' core markets previously housed in Reuterspace, where they did not have scale, were sold. Partially owned businesses like Instinet were spun off and merged with competitors. Joint venture stakes were sold to partners. The Greenhouse Fund was shut down and liquidated. The business was reorganized around four core customer-facing markets all served by centralized shared editorial, service, and technology functions. Although some selected acquisitions were still pursued, these were of modest size, addressed a specific core product or market need, and were easily integrated into existing operations.

As Reuters had grown and added new products and purchased new companies over the years, it failed to eliminate legacy products and technology platforms. Within a few years of taking over, Glocer's team had reduced the number of product offerings from over 1,300 in 2003 to around 200 in 2005

TABLE 8.4   Reuters Financials 2001–2007 (pounds in millions)

	2001	2002	2003	2004	2005	2006	2007
Revenue	£3,885	£3,593	£3,235	£2,339	£2,409	£2,566	£2,605
Operating Profit	302	(142)	130	194	207	256	292
% Margin	*7.8%*	*(4.0)%*	*4.0%*	*8.3%*	*8.6%*	*10.0%*	*11.2%*
Return on Capital (%)	6.3%	(11.5)%	8.6%	18.4%	20.3%	28.1%	29.1%

Source: Company reports.
Note: Return on capital is defined as after-tax EBIT divided by the average balance of total debt plus total shareholders' equity.

and rationalized the dozens of different technology delivery architectures on which they ran.[18] Although the Reuters Internet initiatives had been justified in part based on their ability to improve cost efficiency, its workforce had grown from 16,546 at the end of 1999 to 19,429 at the end of 2001.[19] In 2003, Glocer announced a "fast-forward" cost rationalization initiative that would cost just over $500 million to achieve but sought to take $750 million out of the overall annual cost structure by the end of 2005. By 2004, head count would dip below 15,000 for the first time in a decade.[20]

FIGURE 8.2   Reuters Stock Price Graph 1996–2007
Source: Thomson Reuters.

The impact of Glocer's new approach on Reuters' financials was dramatic. The benefits for Reuters' shareholders were even more dramatic. After falling below one hundred pence for the first time since the mid-1980s in March 2003, Reuters' share price dramatically outperformed the market and its peers. Then, in early May 2007, Reuters announced an offer to be purchased by the diversified database company Thomson at a 43 percent premium to its share price. In a very unusual move for an acquisition of this type, Glocer was asked to become CEO of Thomson and his COO, Devin Wenig, was named the president of the combined Thomson Reuters financial division, which would now represent well over half of the combined company's revenue.

At the time of the announcement, the Thomson Reuters deal was repeatedly characterized as a "Bloomberg killer" by commentators and the press. Whether the combination would be good or bad for Bloomberg would be a function of what strategies the two clear global-market leaders now pursued in the face of this new industry structure. The term *Bloomberg killer* suggests a particular strategy, and one designed to squander the potential benefits of the transaction to both Thomson and Bloomberg. If the newly fortified Thomson Reuters focused its strategic energies at directly attacking Bloomberg where it would potentially hurt most—in its core fixed-income franchise—there would be many happy customers and many bitter shareholders.

The industry structure now faced by Bloomberg and Thomson Reuters is one in which a small number of competitors share many of the same competitive advantages and face many of the same competitive threats. Despite the inclination of testosterone-laden media moguls with a weakness for military metaphors, it is precisely the kind of industry structure in which the optimal strategy is to cooperate. How to profitably and legally manage competition in a land of a few media giants is the subject to which we now turn.

9 | Managing Competition in Media: Can't We All Just Get Along?

The most common industry structure of packaging businesses is that of a handful of competitors with shared competitive advantages. The optimal strategy for optimizing returns from such an industry structure is to develop cooperative strategies that do not land you in jail. We call this cooperation without incarceration.

The problem with the exhortation to media moguls that they should cooperate is that it is a little like telling the clinically obese that they should eat less. Although the suggested prescription is undeniably a cure for what ails, the advice is unlikely to be followed. In both cases, the chances of success increase immeasurably when you understand the underlying causes and costs of the dysfunctional behavior at issue.

The analogy between a healthy diet and healthy industry cooperation breaks down, however, on the issue of what one is trying to achieve. It is easy enough to close one's eyes and imagine a skinnier you. The exercise of reimagining an industry structure under a regime of perfect cooperation is a far more complex undertaking. If it were possible, what could be done to maximize the profits of the overall industry? There are three broad areas of cooperation to consider: revenue, cost, and risk management.

On the revenue side, the key is defining the various product niches to make sure they are fully served without redundancy and then designing a pricing strategy across all the segments. On the cost side, the range of areas of potential cooperation is vast. First, who should serve which product and geographic segments and how industry production and distribution capacity should be organized must be decided. Combining, joint outsourcing, or at least coordination of all the major operating functions from R&D and procurement to IT and overhead should be envisaged to take advantage of scale economies, enhance focus, improve efficiency, and facilitate dissemination of critical information. Standards and protocols and even advertising and promotion strategies should also be coordinated to avoid the inefficiencies associated with incompatible platforms or neutralizing messages in the market. Finally, financing and related costs can be mitigated by jointly managing the risks associated with the fluctuations in each player's performance.

Can't happen, you say, at least without going to jail for violating the antitrust laws? Not so fast. Cooperation without incarceration is not as insurmountable a challenge as some would have you believe. And the magnitude of the potential benefits associated with successful coordination of even a few of these areas compels close consideration of each individually. Even in the most potentially sensitive area of cooperation from a legal perspective—the issue of direct collusion by competitors on price—there is much that can be legitimately done by segment competitors. A strategy, for instance, that combines clearly defining a distinct market niche and publicly disseminating pricing policies will encourage others to do the same and make direct competition on price unlikely. In areas less sensitive than price, direct coordination can be consistent with the antitrust laws.

In practice, it is more often structural or cultural obstacles that impede effective cooperation than legal ones. The single-biggest overarching challenge to successful collaboration among competitors is the short-term attractiveness of reneging on the deal. This persistent dynamic among small numbers of competitors who would be best served by cooperating is best captured by a simple game known as the prisoner's dilemma.

The classic prisoner's dilemma involves two co-conspirators who are captured and can get off with light sentences if they both keep their mouths shut. Either can get off entirely by confessing and finking out the partner in crime, who will then be sent away for life. If both confess, however, the sentence will lie somewhere between the very light sentence associated with both keeping silent and the very long sentence reserved for the finked-out partner.

The dilemma lies in the fact that the "right" outcome in terms of minimizing the total jail time involves following the code of *omertà*, the Sicilian code of silence: The two light sentences together add up to the fewest number of years behind bars available in any of the options. But from the point of view of the individual prisoner, he does better if he sings like a canary. If the partner keeps his mouth shut, the prisoner will get off entirely by being a rat. If the partner confesses, the prisoner will shorten his sentence by doing the same. In no scenario will the prisoner be better off by doing the right thing and keeping mum. This perverse but unavoidable paradoxical outcome, where both players angling for their own self-interest come out worse than had they both looked out for their partner, is what economists call a "noncooperative equilibrium."

The problem faced by the prisoners is identical to that faced by two competitors who have reached an informal accord on price. If one of them cheats by lowering price and the other fails to follow suit, the price-cutter will gain a windfall in profit and market share as bargain hunters flock to take advantage. If the competitor cheats, it is better to follow suit and maintain market share albeit at a lower profit margin rather than risk becoming unprofitable by not having enough sales to cover fixed costs. Once again, everyone always has an irresistible incentive to cheat.

The prisoner's dilemma is defined by the relative payoffs associated with the various outcomes and the fact that it is a onetime game. So defined, it is a real dilemma: There is no solution to the problem and no way around arriving at the noncooperative equilibrium. In the real world, however, faced with a competitive situation that has the attributes of a classic prisoner's dilemma, there are opportunities to change the rules of the game. Those opportunities can take one of two forms.

First, businesses have the opportunity to change the payoffs associated with particular outcomes. Specifically, by making noncooperation more costly or, conversely, providing greater benefits for cooperative behavior, the perverse incentive structure underlying the dilemma can be undermined, or at least mitigated. In media, we see this kind of "outcome management" in the structure of contracts between film studios and pay-TV channels like HBO and Showtime. Under so-called output deals in which a studio makes all of its feature film output available to the channel during the window of time reserved for such exhibition, the channels pay a per-subscriber fee for each film. Although pricing is standard in the industry, a channel might be tempted to pay a higher fee to a studio with a surefire megablockbuster coming up as a way to attract more subscribers from the competitors' service. This could result in a destructive bidding war, which would undercut the profitability of the channels. To avoid this temptation, all "output deal" contracts have a "most-favored-nations" clause: Every studio is assured that they will be treated no worse than any other studio. As a result, a channel tempted to offer a bonus to get the next Harry Potter film will need to pay that same bonus for every other film from every other studio. This makes the cost of noncooperation prohibitively expensive.

Second, in the real world, competitive interactions are rarely onetime affairs. Turning the prisoner's dilemma from a static single-period game into a dynamic multiperiod game fundamentally alters the range of possible winning outcomes. To the extent that market participants incorporate the prospect of future interaction into their decision making, the prisoner's dilemma can yield a cooperative equilibrium. As Robert Axelrod, whose *Evolution of Cooperation* first brought the manifold applications of the prisoner's dilemma into the public consciousness, explains it, strategies that "enlarge the shadow of the future" are more likely to encourage cooperation.[1] By promoting the frequency and structural durability of interactions among the same relatively small group of individuals, the downside of backsliding on cooperative understandings is magnified.

Axelrod promotes the strategy of "tit for tat" as a way to foster cooperation in multiperiod games. In the context of relations among ongoing competitors, this is the equivalent of noncooperation by a market player being punished immediately—whether by matching the price cut or making a corresponding incursion into the miscreant's own most profitable market. The key to avoiding the most destructive behavior by any competitor is to signal this commitment to respond to any deviations swiftly—coupled with a willingness to quickly revert to the cooperative status quo ante. Again, there are many legal ways to undertake such signaling, whether by advertising that you "will match any competitor's price" or by announcing the establishment of an industry trade association to pursue joint standards and legislative objectives.

There is nothing structurally different about the challenges to establishing and maintaining cooperation among competitors as applied to media companies. The difference seems to lie in the extent to which media companies either fail to pursue cooperative strategies or the frequency with which cooperative regimes are foolishly undermined.

In the media industries it is not enough to engage in unbridled price competition for talent among competitors. Minimoguls in the sector have been known even to bid against themselves, as when different imprints of the same book publisher compete to pay the highest price for an upcoming novel[2] or different studio divisions or music labels battle to attract the same star for their latest pet project.[3] The insistence of studios on continuing aggressively to increase their overall film output over time in self-defeating market share wars is similarly reflective of the industry's refusal to heed the basic strategic precept to never start a war that cannot be easily won or ended. An informal accord on limiting capacity in these industries would have significant knock-on effects, as there would be less pressure for destructive competition over securing distribution shelf space in various channels.

The history of the media industry is also littered with high-profile examples of situations where both producers and consumers would have benefited from cooperative agreement on a single standard or approach. No matter how obvious the lessons of the Betamax-VHS platform war,[4] the studios were unable to halt the same saga from playing out again in the struggle between Blu-ray and HD-DVD formats resolved in 2008.[5] In both cases, an early accord would have lowered prices, increased overall profitability, and facilitated both the development of enhanced follow-on technologies and the availability of product. Although it is often assumed that if an industry operated as if it were a coordinated monopoly, the customer would lose out, this simple example demonstrates why this view is misguided.

As destructive as failing to cooperate in the first place is, the bigger tragedy is the frequency with which media companies seek to abandon successful cooperative regimes in search of elusive short-term benefit. In the perpetually challenged music industry, one of the few areas of cooperation was the standard wholesale price at which new releases were sold to retail. In 2003, Universal Music, the overall market share leader, decided to unilaterally cut this price in a misguided response to the availability of low-cost and free online substitutes.[6] Similarly, in 2005, Disney launched an effort to collapse the well-established system of release windows that has long allowed the film industry to more effectively manage revenue by price-discriminating among different potential buyer groups.[7] Finally, in 2008, NBC announced that it was considering ending its participation in the well-worn coordinated mechanism for selling advertising on all the major television networks.[8]

This litany of self-defeating strategic behaviors might lead one to believe that sustainable cooperation is just not possible in media. The case of how the major television networks cooperated successfully for decades demonstrates both some of the myriad ways in which constructive cooperation is possible even in media as well as some of the key threats to maintaining that cooperation.

The economics of the broadcast networks are complex in that they are inextricably intertwined with those of local television stations that reserve a portion of their programming for product delivered by the networks. Government rules limit the number of stations maintained by a single owner so that today the network-owned station groups are limited to serving 39 percent of the population. In markets where the network doesn't own a station, it affiliates with another station that receives a network's programming in exchange for the right to sell a portion of the available advertising time.[9] The overall network economics that must be looked at in terms of

TABLE 9.1 Television Broadcast Industry Map

Content	Packaging	Retail
Film and Television Studios	**Networks**	**Owned and Operated**
Warner Bros. (Time Warner)	ABC (Walt Disney)	NBC TV stations (WNBC/KNBC)
Columbia (Sony)	CBS (CBS Corp.)	CBS TV stations (WCBS/KCBS/KCAL)
CBS Paramount (CBS Corp.)	NBC (GE)	Fox TV stations (WNYW/KTTV)
NBC Universal (GE)	Fox (News Corp.)	ABC TV stations (WABC/KABC)
Fox (News Corp.)	CW (CBS/Time Warner)	And Others
ABC Television (Disney)	MyNetworkTV (News Corp.)	
Paramount (Viacom)	**Independent, Non-Network Syndicators**	**Affiliate Station Owners**
MGM	Sony Pictures Television	E. W. Scripps
Lionsgate	Warner Bros. Television Distribution	LIN Television
Dreamworks	Debmar-Mercury	Local TV
And Others	Entertainment Studios	Hearst-Argyle
Independents	Trifecta Entertainment & Media	Belo Corp.
Endemol	And Others	McGraw-Hill
Brillstein		Sinclair Broadcast
Harpo Productions		Gannett
Carsey-Werner		Gray Television
Classic Media		And Others
And Others		**Independent Stations**
		KTVK-TV (Belo)
		KNWS (Johnson)
		WAXN (Cox)
		WCIU (Weigel)
		KTXA (CBS)
		And Others

the combined impact of this broadcasting ecosystem involve the network itself, the owned and operated stations (O&Os in industry parlance), and the affiliates. The industry map above summarizes the traditional broadcasting television industry structure.

The network business has a number of characteristics that would suggest the existence of competitive advantages, most notably in the areas of economies of scale, customer captivity, and governmental protection.

There are significant fixed cost components to operating a network, relating to the programming, distribution, and marketing infrastructure. Programming costs, whether on a national level, in purchasing film rights and developing new television shows, or on a local level, in producing local news and community interest programs, do not generally vary with the size of the audience.[10] The network infrastructure at both the national and local levels is likewise fixed by whatever it costs to lease distribution capacity to deliver the network's programming to the local station or for its local stations, in turn, to transmit their local signals. Finally, the cost both of advertising the network's shows and of the ad sales force required to maximize the yield on the available inventory does not really change much with the size or success of the network or stations.

Network customer captivity is not overwhelming—few watch a show because it is on a particular network, and even before the advent of the automatic "clicker," getting up to change the channel was not an insurmountable burden—but successful series are by their nature more than a little addictive. And networks have successfully used their established addictive shows as a means to launch the next generation of most promising entries.

The government licenses but does not own or control the airwaves. It has strictly limited the number of licenses and terms under which these are made available, in theory to protect the public interest. Although there is a legitimate debate over whether the massive bureaucracy dedicated to awarding and reviewing these licenses has benefited the public, there is no debating the extent to which these capacity constraints have imposed significant barriers to entry.

The existence of these formidable barriers shared by the major networks did not ensure their financial success. The broadcasters could easily have wasted the opportunity to achieve superior returns by directly and unrestrainedly competing for advertisers, programming, viewers, and affiliates. The result would have been a profit profile similar to that experienced by businesses without any competitive advantages at all. The networks instead experienced an extended run of remarkable returns through a comprehensive system of perfectly legal cooperation along all major dimensions of potential competition that lasted until relatively recently.

ADVERTISERS

The "up-front" season during which the networks market the virtues of their upcoming season to major advertisers has itself become quite a media extravaganza. What occurs during these few weeks is that advertisers commit to purchasing a set amount of advertising during the season before they know how the shows will do. Behind the glitz is a highly successful, closely coordinated system to ensure the highest prices possible for advertising with the least incentive among networks to undercut one another. Because the up-front purchasing opportunity occurs at virtually the same time for all networks and during a limited time period, the ability to bargain by ad buyers is severely limited. If the advertisers do not make a deal during the up-front season and time is instead purchased closer to the actual broadcast date, then all networks price ad slots at a "spot" rate—which is typically higher than contract rates.

The up-front season occurs in the context of a general industry agreement on capacity developed under the guise of a public interest code of conduct to "protect" viewers from too many advertisements—no more than fourteen minutes in a typical broadcast hour. With the limited number of minutes available for sale preagreed, the tight time frames of the season make it relatively difficult for advertisers to successfully pit the networks against one another on price. Furthermore, the capacity not presold is available later only through the ongoing spot market, which, in the case of hit shows, can be bid up to astronomical levels, particularly if significant up-front sales have severely limited the advertising time still available for sale. The networks further limit capacity by using unused advertising space as the official currency to true up any shortfalls in promised viewership in connection with earlier advertising sales.

PROGRAMMING

The same tight time frames of the advertiser up-front season have been used to constrain the ability of producers to induce networks to bid against one another either for pilot ideas or for promising new series once the pilots are completed. The incentive to take a bird in the hand given the financial downside of failing to obtain any deal is fairly compelling. Furthermore, until relatively recently, networks never bid against one another for existing successful series when the time to renew with producers arrived—the only instances of a show moving from one station to another were when the previous network actually canceled the show.

VIEWERS

If there were a single owner of all the networks, how would it program the week? It would obviously not put all its biggest blockbuster series on at the same time, but would instead space them to ensure maximum total viewership.

The separately owned networks have tried to achieve the same result through carefully timed public announcements of their scheduling intentions. The networks long divided the sports programming available across the week and across the year, reflecting this approach to maximizing overall viewership while avoiding destructive price competition for sports programming.

AFFILIATES

Consistent with their approach to all other aspects of their competitive interactions, the networks did not allow local stations to force them into unproductive bidding wars. The prevailing culture of cooperation notwithstanding, stealing an affiliate was also a fairly complex affair because of a variety of cumbersome governmental requirements involved in shifting or adding affiliates. So once again, rules instituted to protect the public really served primarily to protect the interests of the incumbent networks.

All of these various mechanisms of cooperation that characterized the first half century of the broadcasting industry have come under increasing pressure in the last decade as changes in technology, regulation, and industry structure lowered the barriers to entry. Falling barriers to entry fundamentally change industry economics for the worse.

But continued cooperation is often the best financial defense against such changes. Unfortunately, the most frequent reaction is a rush to abandon the previous cooperation in the misguided hope that thereby some kind of sustainable competitive edge can be retained. The predictable result is the acceleration of an industry decline that could have been profitably slowed down.

The signal event in the recent history of the broadcasting industry was Rupert Murdoch's daring entry into the market with a fourth network, Fox, in 1986. Despite Murdoch's reputation for ruthlessness, the early years of Fox respected the cooperative regime long established by the three incumbent networks. Murdoch's network relied on the purchase of a group of independent stations and affiliations with other, generally weaker, UHF stations. Just as he did not compete for affiliates, Murdoch did not compete for programming but instead relied on talent discarded by the majors and genres viewed as beneath their dignity. The first established star Fox hired was Joan Rivers, to host a late-night talk show. Rivers had already been passed over by NBC in favor of Jay Leno to follow Johnny Carson on *The Tonight Show*. The other programs in its first years were also ones that the established networks had either rejected outright or were not likely to run. *Studs, Married with Children,* and *The Simpsons* were either too vulgar (though this may be hard to believe from the vantage point of the twenty-first century) for the other networks, or in a cartoon format that they reserved for Saturday-morning children's shows or Disney specials. By going down-market, Fox reduced direct competition with the other networks. Although Murdoch did offer a discount to the established advertising rates of 20 percent, by tying the modest price cut to the rate card set by the incumbents, he signaled a strong willingness to play by their rules.

If the nature of News Corp.'s entry into the broadcasting market in the mid-1980s reflected the constructive cooperative regime prevalent at the time, Murdoch's decision to outbid CBS for the rights to NFL football in the mid-1990s signaled and promoted the decline in the network business's attractiveness. Under the earlier regime, when NBC sought to acquire football programming, it did not bid directly against the incumbent CBS. Instead it helped incubate the new AFL, which then merged with the NFL. NBC thus acquired football programming without a bidding war. When ABC wanted in, it offered football on Monday night, both expanding the football audience and avoiding direct competition with NBC and CBS. Murdoch in contrast started a bidding war.

Rather than representing the logical culmination of a sensible Trojan-horse strategy, the move revealed mounting tensions within the industry caused by the relaxation of regulation and the explosion of cable channel competition. Technology had also not only begun to reduce many of the fixed cost elements that gave the businesses economies of scale but introduced devices like the time-shifting DVR that threatened the entire advertising model upon which the broadcast business was founded. In subsequent years, bidding wars over affiliates, talent, and programming became commonplace. And the once sacrosanct up-front sales season convention now has become a subject of controversy within the industry.

The financial data on the broadcasting network industry is consistent with this picture. A highly successful individual station once could achieve profit margins of 50 percent. Given the modest capital requirements of operating these businesses, this could translate into returns on capital of well over 100 percent. Today, station profit margins are less than half the levels once achieved. Market share positions among the networks were consistent from the 1950s until the mid-seventies, with CBS on top, followed by NBC and then ABC. The total number of viewers during that period continued to grow as TV households increased rapidly. In the subsequent fifteen years

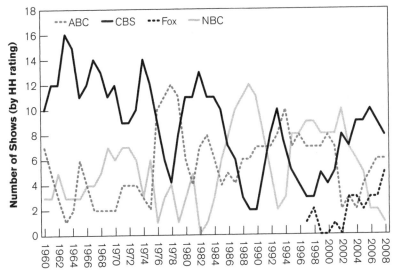

FIGURE 9.1   Prime-Time Top Twenty Shows by Season[11]

through 1990, each of the three networks had a lead position for about five years. Since the 1990s, there has been no dominant network among these three, nor have challengers such as Fox or the subsequent less successful entrants, the WB and UPN, achieved either dominance or a stable share.

Looking at the number of top-twenty prime-time shows produced by each broadcast network makes the same case with even more volatility among the networks.

The broadcasting industry history demonstrates that cooperation in media is possible, but that continued cooperation in the face of declining competitive advantages is particularly challenging. These challenges come from two sources.

First, the key to sustainable cooperation is a regime under which the benefits of that cooperation are perceived to be shared fairly. Changes in the environment are likely to impact market participants differently and potentially require realignment to reestablish a cooperative equilibrium. Even the introduction of a new cooperating industry participant, as was the case at least initially with Fox, requires some redistribution of the benefits of the prevailing regime. It may not be a coincidence that Murdoch, without the decades of shared history of cooperation in TV broadcasting—preceded by decades of prior history of cooperation in radio broadcasting—was the first to break the tacit understanding that members of the club did not steal programming from one another. Or maybe Murdoch felt that at that point he had earned the right to be a full member of the club but was not getting his fair share of the benefits.

Second, it is true that when barriers to entry are gone, there is little point to cooperation. No amount of cooperation among any realistic number of the dozens of TV content production companies with pilot-pitch ideas will improve the terms they obtain from the networks. Without competitive advantage, the exclusive operating focus should be on efficiency, and wasting time pursuing pointless cooperation is inconsistent with that imperative. But companies with long-standing high barriers to entry can easily confuse lower barriers with none. Network broadcasters continue to have competitive advantages, even if they are not what they once were. The slow decline in these advantages certainly makes for a number of critical challenges in establishing or reestablishing a cooperative regime. But the potential benefits relative to the alternative may be that much greater. And the abandonment of the cooperative imperative will certainly accelerate the decline in returns available to shareholders.

The implications for Thomson Reuters and Bloomberg's approach to their new competitive landscape seem clear. Like broadcasters, financial information providers face declining barriers to entry in certain key parts of their business. It does not make sense to engage in fierce bidding wars for every new proprietary data set or interesting piece of software that comes on the market any more than it makes sense for the networks to bid up the price of talk shows or network news anchors. Nor does it make sense for Thomson Reuters to take on Bloomberg's core fixed-income franchise or for Bloomberg to try to re-create Reuters foreign exchange franchise any more than it makes sense for the networks to outbid one another for football rights or to all decide that they want to be number one on Thursday nights.

Rather, shareholders—and even customers—will be better off if each company focuses investment on a combination of reinvestment in the areas of its own greatest strength and defensible adjacent niches. All the while both should signal through the nature of pricing and product introduction and positioning which markets, product sets, and capabilities will be their areas of focus and which they will they implicitly defer to the others' leadership.

A clue to the likely nature of the competitive interaction between Thomson Reuters and Bloomberg is found in Bloomberg's autobiography, in which he lays out his overall strategic approach. "Doing things differently has been basic Bloomberg from day one. If the world's going left we often go right," the sometimes bellicose and boastful executive began.

In football, going around the line when you are a light running back makes more sense than going up the middle through the heart of the other team's defense. For us too. If our competitors' strength is their balance sheet, we try non-capital intensive strategies. If they concentrate on one part of the world, we focus on another. Letting them define the rules is a sure way to come in second. And in life, unlike in children's games, second place is first loser![12]

Beneath the sports analogies and excess testosterone that characterizes much of Bloomberg's competitive banter, a broader substantive theme emerges. It is an approach that reflects the wisdom of a remarkably successful entrepreneur, politician, and executive: the avoidance of destructive conflict through carefully managed cooperation.

10 | All (Profitable) Media Is Local: Newspapers, Theaters, and Communications

In Chapter 4 we described why media moguls' unfortunate habit of extolling the imagined virtues of globalization is fundamentally misguided. Global barriers to entry, we showed, are structurally more difficult to establish and defend. In this chapter we focus on the logical corollary to these observations—namely, why intensely local media businesses are inherently more likely to develop and sustain competitive advantage.

Logic aside, many instinctively resist the idea that local media is better media for several reasons. First, they point to the recent challenges faced by many forms of local media like newspapers and local television broadcasting. Second, they suggest that the focus on all things local is inconsistent with our view that economies of scale are generally the most important source of competitive advantage. Third, they note the apparent contraindication in the fact that the most successful mass media products and brands by their nature resonate beyond local boundaries. Finally, it is argued that even if local may once have been superior, the emergence of the Internet—the ubiquitous media without borders—has nullified the application of this insight to media contexts. Less substantive is the gut instinct that local is, well, less cool, less fun, and generally less alluring. We address each of the more substantive arguments below.

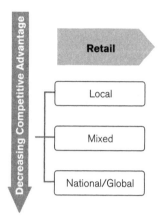

FIGURE 10.1   Retail Competitive Advantage

LOCAL IS DYING

We have already discussed the factors that led to the decline in profitability of newspapers and broadcasting in some detail.[1] What is most remarkable in some ways about both of these stories is not how far these businesses have fallen, but how resilient they have been in the face of the numerous competitive threats they experienced. Let's take an even closer look at newspaper performance to highlight this point.

Various experts had been writing the newspaper sector's obituary regularly since readership began falling in the 1960s and with even more frequency once circulation began consistently declining in the 1980s. Based on these unambiguous trends, one might imagine that the decade of the 1990s would have been a financially bleak one for the industry. In fact, newspaper stocks not only outperformed their sexier media conglomerate peers during this period, they outperformed the market as a whole.

The public markets' willingness to so reward the press was driven not by any romantic attraction to a business widely viewed as facing at best a slow death but rather by the stubborn facts on the ground. Those facts did not include superior revenue growth. Indeed, newspapers as a group managed to grow their top line to barely half of what the media conglomerates achieved during the same period. But, because of the largely fixed cost structure described and resulting economies of scale, a disproportionate amount of these modest revenue increases fell straight to the bottom line. As a result, newspapers improved their margins by more than 50 percent during the decade of the 1990s. The industry gave back more than half of these margin

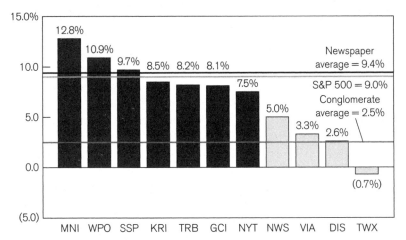

FIGURE 10.2 Total Shareholder Returns: Newspaper vs. Conglomerates vs. S&P (1995–2005)

Note: Total shareholder returns include capital gains and dividends. Represents time period of 12/31/95–12/31/05.

gains between 2000 and 2005 as the impact of the Internet on the business began to be felt. But despite the fact that newspaper margins in 2005 were back to the levels of 1995, the faster-growing media conglomerates could not deliver comparable returns over the period.

The broadcasting business, which, during this period, faced collapsing viewership that was more dramatic than the corresponding newspaper circulation declines, managed to generate even higher financial returns because

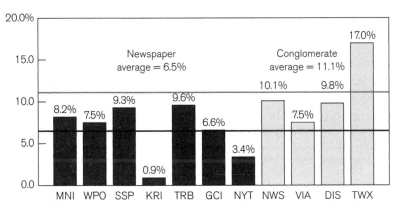

FIGURE 10.3 Revenue Growth: Newspaper vs. Conglomerates (1995–2005)

Note: Revenue growth represents period between calendar years 1995 and 2005.

the business had fewer hard capital needs in the absence of printing presses and the like. Even by 2005, with the newspaper and broadcasting industries facing actual revenue declines, both sectors still managed to generate returns far superior to those experienced by the media conglomerates. On average for that year, Tribune and Gannett (the two largest newspaper/broadcasting conglomerates) achieved almost double the return on capital and return on sales of News, Disney, Time Warner, and Viacom. These results reflect the power and resilience of the structural advantages afforded by competitive advantage.

As notable as these general sector observations is the fact that within these industries the level of resilience in the face of current trends is directly tied to the level of localism of the product. Even in 2008, newspaper companies that focused on dominating smaller local markets—Gannett, Lee and McClatchy, for example—maintained 20 percent margins, while sexier national and big-city newspapers struggled with profitability in some cases.

SCALE DEMANDS GLOBALIZATION

Scale, we have noted, is a relative concept. As such, absolute bigness does not necessarily connote scale. Indeed, one could be plenty huge and fail to establish similar relative scale nationally or globally to, say, what a home-town newspaper manages to achieve locally. This basic confusion between size and scale seems endemic to the media sector. And something about the media sector manages to make moguls out of the hardest-headed financial executive one could imagine. The case of the movie-theater industry demonstrates both phenomena.

In the mid-1990s, the largest private equity firms took note of the attractive cash-flow characteristics of the movie-theater business. They were particularly impressed by the fact that despite all of the other changes in the media environment, 8 to 10 percent of the public continued to go to the movies each week, as they had for decades. Each tried to outdo the other by competing aggressively on price for every chain that became available in the apparent belief that the biggest would be the best. In so doing, these financial whiz kids misunderstood the source of the attractiveness of the sector. The end would come predictably and painfully.

The movie-theater business had become widely fragmented after the Supreme Court ordered the five major film studios to spin off their theater operations in the late 1940s. By the mid-1990s, no cinema circuit represented even 10 percent of the screens in the country. The five largest chains constituted only about a third of the market.

TABLE 10.1 Largest Theater Chains—1995[2]

Circuit	Number of Screens	% of Individual Total	Number of Locations	Average Screens per Location
1 United Artists	2,295	8.9%	423	5.4
2 Carmike	2,037	7.9%	467	4.4
3 American Multi-Cinema	1,632	6.3%	233	7.0
4 Cineplex Odeon	1,631	6.3%	357	4.6
5 Cinemark USA	1,224	4.7%	164	7.5
All U.S. Theaters	**27,805**	**100.0%**	**7,744**	**3.5**

Looking at the actual financial performance of the industry giants of the time, a single notable economic fact stands out. Largely rural and regionally focused theater groups like Carmike and Cinemark generated almost double the profitability of the sexier nationally oriented big-city circuits like United Artists, AMC, and Cineplex Odeon.

The company financials also immediately reveal the source of the dramatic margin differential between the two groups of companies. Local scale allows circuits to drive better deals with the movie companies, the local concession distributors, and the commercial Realtors with whom long-term leases are typically negotiated. Furthermore, fixed marketing costs, all of which are dispersed on a local or regional basis, are spread more effectively across more theaters, as are the fixed overhead costs required to manage the regional operations.

No matter, as far the budding minimedia moguls in private equity were concerned. They seemed to take as their role model AMC—despite its weak financial performance. AMC had pioneered "multiplexing" and was busy building larger and larger theater complexes so that its average number of screens per theater location was among the highest in the industry. Given the fixed costs of operating a single location, multiplexing offers significant efficiencies, but these are available to anyone who wants to build an enormous theater. Furthermore, the relative impact of theater size compared to regional concentration is demonstrated by the fact that Carmike still managed to have double the profit margins while averaging only about 63 percent of the screens per theater as AMC. Two-thirds of AMC screens

TABLE 10.2 Select Cinema Profitability ($ in millions): Fiscal Year 1994[3]

	Regional Focus				National Focus					
	Carmike		Cinemark		United Artists		AMC		Cineplex Odeon	
Revenue	**$327.6**		**$283.1**		**$622.7**		**$564.7**		**$539.4**	
Costs										
Film Rental	114.7	35.0%	84.0	29.7%	239.6	38.5%	182.7	32.4%	204.8	38.0%
Concessions	12.2	3.7%	17.6	6.2%	27.2	4.4%	26.5	4.7%	21.7	4.0%
Theater Ops	127.8	39.0%	87.6	30.9%	226.9	36.4%	226.8	40.2%	231.7	43.0%
Leases	—	—	29.6	10.5%	17.0	2.7%	11.4	2.0%	—	—
Subtotal	**$254.8**	**77.8%**	**$218.7**	**77.3%**	**$510.7**	**82.0%**	**$447.3**	**79.2%**	**$458.2**	**84.9%**
Depreciation + Amortization	22.5	6.9%	15.1	5.3%	63.0	10.1%	37.9	6.7%	40.7	7.5%
G&A	5.1	1.6%	17.1	6.0%	32.5	5.2%	39.8	7.0%	15.9	2.9%
Other	—	—	1.3	0.5%	12.2	2.0%	0.2	0.0%	2.9	0.5%
Total Costs	**$282.4**	**86.2%**	**$252.4**	**89.2%**	**$618.4**	**99.3%**	**$525.2**	**93.0%**	**$517.7**	**96.0%**
EBIT	**45.2**	**13.8%**	**30.9**	**10.9%**	**4.3**	**0.7%**	**39.5**	**7.0%**	**21.7**	**4.0%**

were distributed across the twenty largest American cities. And AMC did not stop at its national borders, developing a multiplex in Japan and further aggressive international plans elsewhere.

Kansas City–based AMC's strategic approach is reflected by its fateful decision to build at untold cost an enormous state-of-the-art twenty-five-theater complex on Forty-second Street in the heart of New York, a market with no paucity of existing screens. The massive construction project involved literally moving the facade of an existing building down the block to accommodate local concerns. AMC had no presence in the New York market. Loews, which was the leading theater operator in New York at the time, built a competing multiplex across the street to send AMC a message. Even before Loews's competitive response, the AMC project could not have realistically provided a sensible return on investment.

The late 1990s saw deal after deal in the sector as a who's who of private equity moguls bid against one another for theater chains, then bid for more and sometimes merged with one another. At the same time, AMC had set off a "megaplex building frenzy,"[4] increasing the number of screens from 27,843 to 37,131 nationally between 1995 and 1999, far outstripping the modest growth in attendance.[5] The result was over a dozen bankruptcies and restructurings.[6]

A new wave of financial players have now moved in, engineering further consolidation, so that the top-five circuits now represent about half of the nation's theaters. The relevant market shares, however, are in the regions. There is some evidence suggesting these new owners have assimilated the historic lessons of focusing on local dominance, avoiding destructive competition, and managing overall capacity. For example, AMC—now owned by a combination of buyout firms J.P. Morgan Partners, Apollo, Bain, Carlyle, and Spectrum, having merged with Loews, which itself had merged with Cineplex Odeon—has abandoned its strategy of global domination and closed or divested all of its subscale holdings in Japan, Hong Kong, and Spain and just retained its business in Mexico. AMC's international segment went from an average negative operating profit of –3 percent from 2000 to 2003 to a positive operating profit in 2007 of 29 percent.[7] Both Regal and AMC, now the two largest circuits, shut a large number of theaters outside of their core regions a few years ago, significantly improving profitability and reducing the absolute number of industry screens for the first time in a decade.

But the call of the mogul is never far. Starting in 2002, the number of screens started to creep up again. Not at the rate it did previously, but steadily. While most analysts had anticipated that the industry restructuring would result in a reduction of five thousand to ten thousand screens nationwide, after dropping two thousand screens the industry has added almost twice that

TABLE 10.3 Regal EBIT Margins 2002 to 2007[8]

	2007	2006	2005	2004	2003	2002
REGAL	12.22%	12.74%	11.41%	13.17%	15.50%	14.43%

and is at an all-time high.[9] This trend has continued even as movie attendance has been slowly declining since its peak in 2002. Furthermore, some companies like Regal that had benefited for many years from focused regional operations prior to 1995—and had consequently been one of the nation's most profitable chains—seemed to forget these lessons under the spell of a mogul's desire to grow. After emerging from bankruptcy in January 2002, Regal achieved average margins of 15 percent during 2002 and 2003. At the time it still enjoyed the benefits of heavy geographic concentration. Nearly 40 percent of its screens were in the southeast United States (an area with just 22 percent of the U.S. population) and a further 9 percent were in the states of Washington and Oregon (home to 3.3 percent of the U.S. population). From the end of 2002, Regal aggressively pursued a national expansion strategy, growing rapidly throughout New England, California, and states like Hawaii where it had previously had no or marginal presence. By 2005, the profit margin had declined substantially and it has never fully recovered.

MASS MEDIA REQUIRES MASSIVE MARKETS

Movie theaters exhibit the ultimate mass media. But as we have just demonstrated, the most successful of these are the most intensely local. The very unattractiveness of truly mass media stems from the fact that, after being held up by the talent, these businesses must rely on a network of powerful local distribution franchises in order to secure the attention of consumers. Mass media may need to reach massive markets to succeed, but to do so it will perpetually remain at the mercy of the individual artists who will drive demand for the product and those who control the local infrastructure that allows it to get into the individual customers' hands.

The counterargument here is that movie theaters are an increasingly irrelevant "old media" distribution mechanism. We are now in an era of instantaneous global communications, this line of reasoning goes, making these kinds of gatekeeper institutions anachronistic. Although not without rhetorical merit, this analysis is simply inconsistent with the facts.

If movie theaters as an institution are admittedly a bit "old school," it would be hard to argue that the location in which most media is consumed is as easily disposable: the home. Even with the explosion of mobile communications, the continuing investment of consumers in progressively more complex devices to enjoy media in the home reflects the vitality of this entertainment venue. And for the foreseeable future, the only way to deliver the kind of increasingly rich content demanded is a wire into that home. Let's turn and look at the businesses that provide this all-important link from the home to the world of mass media.

Modern electronic links to the home come in two basic flavors—hardwired, which includes cable and landline telephone, and wireless, which includes satellite, local broadcast TV, and cellular. In fact, all connections to the consumer, whether through the home, office, or directly, fall into one of these two categories. In practice, the networks in which these links are embedded are a mixture of both. Landline telephones are connected to switches that are generally connected to other switches by high-capacity fiber optics, but in some cases interswitch transmission is by high-capacity (wireless) microwave connections. Sometimes the final connection to a handset or other device is wireless, as in the case of wireless home telephones or Wi-Fi computer links. Cellular telephone networks consist of wireless connections from individual devices to base stations, but base stations are generally hardwired with high-capacity fiber to switches, which, in turn, are part of high-capacity fiber-optic networks. Even satellite networks receive programming at ground stations via hardwired connections. Cable programming, especially local-TV programming, arrives at cable systems via wireless transmissions. From an economic perspective, however, the form of transmission makes surprisingly little difference.

The critical aspect of electronic links to homes, offices, and individuals is the fundamental economies of scale that characterize local connections. Once a connection has been made from any network to an office or house, a second connection of the same kind is wasteful. And once any particular home is connected to a network, it is most efficient to connect adjacent homes to that same network since these homes can share a common infrastructure. The cost of any incremental capacity involved is cheap relative to the cost of the basic infrastructure. This basic economic observation applies equally to hardwired connections, such as telephone or cable, in which the local infrastructure consists of an area-wide access line with many individual offshoots as well as wireless connections where end users can share a common local transmission facility.

If competing local infrastructures are available, then the one with greater local penetration will be the more profitable. Since the cost of the local infrastructure is largely fixed, the competitor with greater local market share will enjoy greater revenue against the same fixed cost. This fundamental advantage will be reinforced by the economics of servicing the local infrastructure. Technicians dispatched to repair local links will be greater in number for the dominant local competitor than others. They will spend less time in transit and can be deployed, given their greater numbers, more heavily and rapidly in emergencies. The result will be better local service quality and more rapid repair at lower cost.

An entrant seeking to attack a dominant local competitor will, therefore, be at a significant local disadvantage whatever his global level of resources. He will have to build an expensive local infrastructure and carry the resulting fixed costs until he can attract a local customer base equivalent to that of the local incumbent. These businesses are typically characterized by significant customer captivity that reinforces the advantages of local scale. If customers are reluctant to incur the costs of switching to the new entrant, then a local incumbent who offers equal prices and service quality will keep the vast majority of his customers. The entrant will attract too few customers to support his infrastructure and will be faced with an endless period of future losses.

In landline telephony and local cable, this is exactly what has occurred. Local telephone companies have enjoyed upward of 90 percent market shares in their service areas since the 1920s. Cable companies have also maintained 90 percent market shares in their franchise areas. Most facilities-based competition, like Winstar during the telecom boom of the late 1990s or RCN, the cable "overbuilder," have either gone bankrupt or limped along with negative returns on capital invested. International telecommunications giants, like Deutsche Telekom, NTT, or BT, have never seriously attempted to compete outside their traditional service areas. As a result of these monopoly positions, landline telephone companies earned returns on capital of roughly 22 percent during the late 1990s and early 2000s, corresponding to average sales margins of 26 percent. More recently they have faced intensified competition from the cable companies as well as customer migration to cellular. Yet from 2005 to 2007, returns on capital averaged roughly 16 percent with sales margins at 18 percent.[10]

Cable company returns are difficult to calculate given the intricacies and distortions of official cable system accounting; however, returns on capital from 2005 to 2007 appear to have averaged at least 20 percent and operating margins on sales have exceeded 20 percent.[11] Notably, cable companies with tightly clustered regional focus, like Cablevision and Insight,

TABLE 10.4 Japanese and Korean Cellular Companies, 2007[12]

Japanese Company	Share	Return on Sales	Return on Capital
DoCoMo	48%	20%	17%
KDDI	33%	14%	n/a
SoftBank	19%	11%	6%

Korean Company	Share	Return on Sales	Return on Capital
SK Telecom	51%	23%	15%
LG Telecom	15%	9%	6%

achieve margins compatable to or better than industry "leaders" many times their size, like Comcast and Time Warner Cable.

Cellular telephone markets have been more competitive with multiple viable providers in each local service area. However, dominant local providers earned outsized returns on capital as a consequence of their local economies of scale. This is most readily apparent in the national data.

In Japan, DoCoMo, with a market share of roughly 50 percent, had an operating margin in 2007 of 20 percent and a return on capital of 17 percent. SoftBank with 19 percent market share had a 2007 operating margin of just 11 percent and a return on capital of 6 percent. In Korea, SK Telecom, the dominant competitor with 51 percent market share, earned a return on capital of 15 percent compared to the 6 percent return of LG Telecom, the second local competitor.

Looking at the same phenomenon within one company but across countries, at Vodaphone in 2007, the company enjoyed local profits that were closely related to local market share. In Italy, a market share of 61 percent was associated with an operating margin of 38 percent. In Germany and Spain, with average market shares of about 48 percent, the company has operating margins of 28 percent. And in the U.K., a local market share of 38 percent led to an operating margin of 15 percent. Below 15 percent market share, profits were zero.[13] In the United States, the locally dominant cellular companies associated with the regional Bell companies, Verizon and Cingular, have always been far more profitable than the less dense national competitors like AT&T and Sprint. And it is they who dominate the U.S. cellular market today.

In contrast, "national" telecommunications providers, like the long-distance companies, have been barely profitable or unprofitable. As a result, AT&T has been absorbed by BellSouth/Southwestern Bell and MCI has been taken over by Verizon. Sprint limps along on the edge of bankruptcy.

Software-based global Internet providers like Skype and Vonage have never made money. In television, local stations have always been more profitable than the national networks of which they are a part. Only satellite TV, which has a significant local sales and service presence, has earned high returns on capital among the national media. And, not surprisingly, the need for a significant local presence has meant that the satellite broadcasters are either monopoly (BSkyB in the U.K.) or duopoly (DISH Network and DirecTV in the United States) providers in each national market.

It is hard to imagine a more massive market than the global communications network that connects us all both to media and to one another. The increasing facility of this infrastructure to provide more and better products and services to satisfy once unimaginable customer desires has changed our collective sense of the possible in media. It has also led many to assume that the most successful companies will be those that provide the most media to as many people as possible internationally. The data demonstrates, however, the continuing truth that in communications as elsewhere, high profitability is associated with local, not global, presence. Attractive businesses are consistently characterized by density of coverage within tight borders rather than breadth of international footprint.

THE INTERNET KNOWS NO BOUNDARIES

The foregoing examples will surely be inadequate to sate the global ambitions of the most committed media moguls. Even if they grudgingly concede we may have a point in these particular cases, they may still argue that these illustrations are largely of historical relevance. The emergence of the Internet, the moguls will insist, has made all reference to borders—whether local or even national—largely irrelevant.

The concept of "local," however, applies not only to geographic but psychographic and demographic "spaces" as well. Let's return to one of the earliest Internet spaces to gain traction and scale: job boards.

In our earlier discussion of the newspaper sector we described the development of the online classified business and the emergence of Monster .com as the early leader in the job boards industry. Job boards are a classic network effects business: The more job seekers come, the more employers are interested in posting jobs; the more posted opportunities, the more likely applicants will look. This virtuous liquidity circle typifies network effects businesses. Although Internet businesses do not generally have significant fixed costs, Monster did also benefit from the ability to spread its substantial sales and marketing budget across a larger customer and user base, giving it some traditional scale economies as well.

Behind these apparent advantages lurked some threats to Monster's initial dominance. The key to sustainable barriers to entry is to secure multiple sources of competitive advantage. The unemployed tend not to be too picky about how many job sites they choose to post their résumé on or how many they search. And employers are rather unsentimental about where to buy space to post the next set of jobs based on a combination of price and effectiveness. Similarly, job sites are not too complicated and do not lend themselves to any truly proprietary technology. Without either significant demand or cost advantages, Monster needed to rely largely on the benefits of scale through reinforcing the fixed cost and network effects elements of the business.

Dice operates a business model almost identical to that of Monster, with a single important difference: It focuses on the niche of technology jobs. Those looking to fill technology jobs have a number of qualities in common. They are interested in a lot of practical job-related issues like industry and salary trends. But they are also nerds, and have a wide range of other common interests that they might like to share with like-minded community members (when is that next *Star Trek* movie coming out anyway?). The sense of kinship heightens the level of customer captivity achievable in niche media. A clever niche business works hard to keep community members coming back for regular updates (reinforcing habit), integrates its tools and information into users' daily work flow (increasing switching costs), and amasses a compelling collection of information and services (amplifying the cost of searching for a satisfactory alternative). And Dice is a very clever niche business.

The value of these business characteristics to employers who might want to consider Dice as a resource to fill technology jobs is substantial. The unemployed, we have noted, are not terribly selective in making their résumés available. The holy grail for a corporate human resource professional, particularly one seeking to fill highly skilled positions for which there is a scarcity of qualified applicants, is the passive job seeker. Passive job seekers are reasonably happy in their current position and sensitive to their current employer thinking that they might be looking around, but willing to consider new challenges opportunistically. Dice does everything it can to encourage the tech geeks who frequent the site to make their résumés available. Employers in turn are willing to pay more for access to a database that includes résumés not obtainable elsewhere, and that posts jobs likely to elicit interest from candidates not likely to be cruising general interest job boards.

But wait, the clever reader might say, surely the economies of scale asso-ciated with a niche job board cannot possibly approach those available to a general interest site. The fixed costs associated with a single Super Bowl ad for Monster must overwhelm the entire marketing budget for Dice. The key here is to remember again that scale is a relative concept. Dice does not advertise on the Super Bowl not because it lacks scale, but because that is the wrong venue for it to reach its target audience efficiently. Dice adver-tises in venues that predominately attract techies—on sites like TechTarget, for example—not on TV, radio, and newspapers. The company is focused exclusively on how to market effectively to its core audience. Monster's scale relative to its largest direct competitor, CareerBuilder, is actually minuscule compared to Dice's scale relative to the next-largest pure-technology-oriented employment site. And Dice has buttressed the moat around its core franchise by leveraging its strength in adjacent niches like engineering and jobs requir-ing security clearances.

Dice went public in July 2007, a few years after Monster had spun off its distracting employment agency businesses and begun divesting its other noncore businesses. As a result, we are able to compare the performance of the two businesses fairly easily for the recent 2005–2007 period. Not surprisingly,

TABLE 10.5 Dice vs. Monster Performance (2005–2007) ($ in millions)

	2005	2006	2007
Revenue			
Dice Holdings	$62	$104	$144
Monster Worldwide	818	1,117	1,324
EBITDA[1]			
Dice Holdings	$22	$38	$63
Monster Worldwide	189	299	336
EBITDA Margin[1]			
Dice Holdings	35.4%	36.2%	43.5%
Monster Worldwide	23.1%	26.8%	25.4%

Source: Company filings, JPMorgan Research.

Note: Dice financials are pro forma for eFinancialCareers as if it were owned on 1/1/05, discontinuation of CyberMedia India as of 1/1/06, and includes the add-back of deferred revenue.

(1) EBITDA excludes stock-based compensation and is adjusted for restructuring and other nonrecurring expenses.

given the inherently stronger barriers available to a leading niche media business than to a leading general interest media business, Dice is consistently, considerably, and increasingly more profitable.

So, rather than supporting the supposition that the Internet would rewrite the rules of competitive advantage, the Monster/Dice case study instead strongly reaffirms their validity. Even in the purely geographic rather than psychographic or demographic context, the notion that the Internet eliminates borders is fundamentally misguided. In the job board category, homegrown sites are consistently leaders within their national geographies. Even a company like craigslist, which gets significantly more attention than its modest overall market share justifies, still has been unable to replicate its strong initial impact outside its base in San Francisco. Among employment sites in the largest English-speaking markets—the United States, U.K., and Australia—there is little overlap among the leading players. The top players in the U.K., totaljobs .com, and Australia, Seek, do not even operate in the other markets.[14]

None of the substantive arguments proffered against the proposition that local media is better media has, well, much substance. It may be that these oft-heard propositions justifying a misguided march toward national or global domination are mere pretexts for the real driver of mogul behavior. Global businesses may not generate superior returns but do generate higher salaries, higher profiles, better seating, and better parties. Who wouldn't rather be an international man of mystery than, say, the king of southeastern movie theaters?

Local just ain't sexy. Sure, you can find a local executive with more money than sense who thinks it would be cool to buy the local newspaper. But it took almost two years for Gannett, the largest newspaper company in the world, to realize that it would be unable to attract any serious media mogul to take the CEO slot, and it settled for an internal candidate. This occurred despite the fact that Gannett outperformed the conglomerates over the previous decade and even in 2009 boasts higher margins than hit-driven content businesses like movies, music, and books.

Craig Dubow has now been Gannett's CEO since 2005 but he remains almost as anonymous as he was before. Similarly, Glenn Britt is the CEO of Time Warner Cable, the leading public pure cable company with well over $30 billion in value. He may be an excellent operator, but because he has publicly eschewed any mogul ambitions in purchasing media content assets, there are barely a handful of people outside of the cable industry who have ever heard of him. Although CEOs with a greater taste for the limelight shy away from local media, investors with an interest in the sector do so at their own peril.

11 | Reinforcing Competitive Advantage in Media

We have repeatedly made the point that the appropriate strategies for reinforcing competitive advantage vary depending on the source of that advantage. In case study after case study we have emphasized the importance of relentless vigilance among those media companies fortunate enough to benefit from barriers to entry.

In the analytical framework of this book, the two extremes are represented by those without barriers to entry who should focus not on strategy but on efficiency and those with unique barriers who should focus relentlessly on reinforcing them. Although there are plenty of companies without any competitive advantages, there are precious few whose advantages are completely unique to themselves. After Microsoft in operating systems and Intel in chips, it is hard to come up with industries in which a single competitor absolutely dominates with stable market shares, say, north of 70 percent.

In media, the best businesses we have profiled—with the possible exception of Google—share at least some aspects of their competitive advantages with others. And even where the particular advantage is singular, the company operates within a broader media ecosystem in which there is a tug-of-war among various links in the value chain, each of which wants to capture its fair share.

In the last chapter we suggested that it is intensely local businesses that have the greatest opportunity to achieve sustainable leadership. And while the source of these businesses' advantages is clear enough and the optimal strategies for reinforcing them obvious enough, continuing success is often a function of successfully managing that broader ecosystem. In online job boards, this has taken the form of an informal armistice between leading niche businesses and leading general interest ones in which both avoid direct conflict. In cable, it has taken the form of avoiding destructive competition on price with the only other wire into the home provided by the local phone company. In newspapers, it has taken the form of increasing outsourcing of and cooperation with businesses that were once viewed as direct competitors. In movie theaters, it has taken the form of a variety of partnerships and alliances to create the most compelling local entertainment venue possible.

In the history of media, there have been products and sectors in which a single player has enjoyed overwhelming market share. These periods of euphoric hegemony, however, have uniformly been short-lived. The failure to sustain these powerful advantages has generally not come from a misunderstanding of the nature of the barriers faced by competitors or obvious negligence in reinforcing them. Rather, more often it has stemmed from a mogul-like insistence on ignoring the pressures of the broader competitive ecosystem by refusing to share the spoils equitably. Nothing is forever, but the end is usually accelerated by giving an incentive to all those upon whom you ultimately rely to conspire for your downfall. Nowhere is it more true than in media that hogs get fat, but pigs get slaughtered.

For those with short memories, which is to say everyone, the case of Nintendo's global dominance of the home video-game segment in the late 1980s and early 1990s is instructive. On the back of a dwarf plumber named Super Mario and a hundred-dollar console system that alone could play it, Nintendo achieved market shares in excess of 90 percent in both the United States and Japan.

Nintendo's innovation was to incorporate improved-chip computing power into the game cartridges, which had the joint benefit of ensuring that unapproved games could not run on their system and lowering the hardware costs. The popularity of Super Mario and availability of low-priced consoles quickly gave Nintendo a dominant share of the market. In 1989, 9 million systems and 50 million game cartridges were sold. In the United States alone, 70 percent of American households with boys between eight and fourteen years old owned a video-game system of some kind, and 90 percent of these were made by Nintendo.

It is not difficult to identify the sources of competitive advantage enjoyed by Nintendo. Its large scale did provide efficiencies in spreading the cost of marketing and developing new games and even new console systems. But more powerful than the fixed cost economies, which in the context of the overall industry cost structure were relatively modest, were the network effects afforded by the huge installed user base. The best game writers wanted to produce games for the most ubiquitous system, which in turn made more videophiles want to use it. This is precisely the kind of virtuous circle that characterizes network effects businesses.

These scale economies were reinforced by customer captivity—once you owned a console you were reluctant to switch. But this benefit was not as strong as it first seemed. By the time that Nintendo achieved its dominance, the industry had already experienced two of the boom-and-bust cycles that would continue to characterize the sector. When a new technology emerged that was available to all console producers, the incumbent advantage would be limited as customers chose among various new-generation machines. Indeed, given the relatively narrow age group composing the core user base, many selecting a new-generation machine would likely be first-time buyers with no prior allegiance at all. This fact highlights that Nintendo had no technological advantage—the chip technology it cleverly harnessed to quickly build its market position was widely available.

The relevant competitive ecosystem Nintendo had to manage was not simply the much smaller console producers like Atari, Sega, and Activision. Even more important were the game writers who created the content and the retailers who distributed both the consoles and the games. The most complex strategic decisions Nintendo faced were not about how to reinforce its competitive advantages, but about how to manage its relations with these constituencies. Nintendo decided to treat them badly.

Although Super Mario had been produced by Nintendo itself, the company knew its continued success was tied to the ability to reliably produce new hit games that adequately fed the needs of its voracious and dominant installed base. To ensure that it was never short of compelling games for its system, Nintendo knew it could not count exclusively on its own ability to produce hit after hit and needed to license independent game writers. Game writers in turn were desperate for access to Nintendo's installed base. Although Nintendo charged a seemingly reasonable license fee of 20 percent on the wholesale cartridge price of thirty dollars (for a six-dollar fee), licensees were required to use Nintendo to manufacture the cartridge (with a minimum ten-thousand-unit run paid up front) at a cost of fourteen dollars per unit. Nintendo in turn contracted manufacturing out at four dollars so that it made sixteen dollars on units sold and still made ten dollars on unsold inventory while taking absolutely no risk. The game producers, who were limited to making five titles a year, in turn could easily lose money if the game was not a hit.

Such was the power of Nintendo at the time that it was able to abuse retail giants like Wal-Mart and Toys "R" Us with the same impunity that it did small game-development shops. They were forced to pay when the consoles arrived at the store—virtually unheard-of in the industry—install expensive prominent displays, and adhere to Nintendo's "suggested" retail price. Deviations could be punished by skimping on the offending chain's allocation of hot game cartridges. Nintendo's ability to use artificial cartridge shortages against retailers had the corollary effect of further infuriating the game writers, who relied on unit sales to cover their development and production costs.

Not surprisingly, game writers and retailers did everything possible to encourage and promote the success of the next generation of console games produced by competitors. When Sega packaged its new-generation player with Sonic the Hedgehog for $150, the broader ecosystem worked hard to ensure that the era of Nintendo's global supremacy would come to an end, which it promptly did. If Nintendo had aligned its interests with the rest of the value chain, everyone would have been better off. Nintendo would not have ensured a position of permanent leadership, but it very well could have sustained it through one or two more product cycles. Note that it would not have been just game writers and retailers who would have been better off—even consumers could have benefited from a broader array of product availability without needing to purchase multiple competing platforms, each with its own proprietary games.

Nintendo's approach in the eighties and nineties has reverberated through the industry for years—a culture of cutthroat competition and aggressive winner-take-all bargaining across the value chain does not dissipate easily. The game console sector accordingly has been characterized by significant shifts in market share, particularly between platform cycles, and generally low profitability. But every console cycle offers an opportunity for reform and redemption and Nintendo's approach to the latest one suggests that they may have learned some lessons from their previous decade's performance. As Sony and Microsoft fought it out on the usual battlefield of harnessing the latest ultra-high-performance graphics chips to create a gaming experience of ever-increasing sophistication, Ninetendo did something highly uncharacteristic: It got out of their way rather than piling on. Nintendo decided instead to target a market that had the virtue of being both ignored and much larger—the rest of us who are not hard-core gamers. The accelerating complexity of the game consoles had unattractive side effects on both the demand and supply sides of the business equation. First, consumers of previous platforms had started careers and families and cut back on game time, so found it difficult to keep up. Second, as consoles became more powerful, making games for them got steadily more expensive.[1] In introducing the Wii, Nintendo was able to make a cheaper, less powerful console to create a new, relatively low-priced, motion-sensitive game experience that powerfully appealed to an expanding audience for gaming.[2] The result was that by the end of 2008, Nintendo's share of the annual console-unit sales approached fully half of this broadened marketplace, almost doubling the share it had enjoyed just five years earlier in 2003.

The magnitude of Nintendo's success in the console market allowed it to challenge the long-established dominance of the leader in a related ancillary market—publishing video games. Electronic Arts (EA) had for years enjoyed overwhelming advantages in market share and financial performance in comparison to its smaller peers. During the five years between 2001 and 2005, EA generally maintained more than double the market share of any of its competitors. The company's operating margins (as high as 27 percent in 2003) were not only far in excess of those of its competitors, some of whom were not always profitable, but dwarfed even the most efficient operators in the other arguably analogous content businesses we have looked at: movies, music, and books.

The first question is how anyone could have established such a leadership position in the video-game industry in the first place. Might it be that content really is king when it comes to game software? The business, after all, looks like a mirror image of those discrete content businesses that we have relentlessly derided as being without advantage. Game software, from Super Mario in the eighties to the contemporary Grand Theft Auto franchise, is no less a hit-driven business than movies, music, or books.

The numbers, however, suggest that there is more to the story. The stark contrast of these results with those of other hit-driven businesses suggests that there must be something different either about the structure of this industry or about this content particularly. In fact, there is something quite different about both.

On the content creation side, much of the structure of the video-game business does not look that different from movies, music, or books. There are plenty of independent game developers and independent game publishers. Over time, the most successful ones have been bought up by larger businesses, while the less successful ones have closed down. This process has not decreased the number of independent players over time because new ones have emerged to take the place of those that folded up or folded in. The fixed cost infrastructure required to manage, manufacture, and distribute video games worldwide, however, is on a completely different scale from other content businesses. Physical games must simultaneously reach a wide range of mass-market retailers (who are responsible for up to 20 percent of game sales) like Wal-Mart, toy stores, consumer electronics retailers, drugstores, and specialty game outlets as well as all the other traditional retail outlets for buying or renting music, books, or videos. This complex rollout must be coordinated with a multifaceted marketing and promotional strategy customized to the various markets being served and serviced.

Starting in the early 1980s, EA invested aggressively in dozens of countries to create the first global sales force dedicated to placing its product prominently in hundreds of thousands of retail locations. The company's resulting ability to simultaneously ship and promote singularly massive volumes of a particular game made EA the partner of choice for any software developer or independent publisher whose livelihood hinged on per unit royalties from sales. Furthermore, EA established overwhelming positions in key gaming genres like sports by buying up the bulk of important licenses. The distribution infrastructure generally allowed the costs of these licenses to be spread more widely, but dominating niches further enhanced the efficiency of marketing and promotion efforts around brands like EA Sports.[3]

TABLE 11.1 2005–2007: Percentage of Sequels Twenty Top Sellers: Video Games vs. Movies[4]

	Video Games	Movies
2007	95%	50%
2006	80%	30%
2005	85%	15%

By contrast, in the movie business, for example, no major studio has or can have these kinds of scale advantages relative to its peers. Each has comparable distribution reach and none has the practical ability to "corner" a genre. This distinction is a function of the lower relative fixed costs associated with physical distribution, the open-ended nature of the potential content that can appeal to a particular genre, and the general lack of any consumer association between the film or genre and the identity of the studio. Note that even the exception to this last rule—Disney and children's programming—has not proved a barrier to competitor studios establishing their own successful children's franchises.

Despite the similarities in the content creation aspects of the business, the nature of the content itself also has some important differences from movies, music, and books. The predominance of series within overall industry sales makes the entertainment software business look a lot more like a continuous than a discrete content business.

The impact of the effectively continuous nature of game software content has a direct impact on the barriers to entry in the sector. Sequels or series engender significant customer captivity. If you loved *Rocky*, you are more likely to see *Rocky II, III,* and *IV,* and eagerly anticipate *Rocky: Resurrection.* Game franchises share this quality. In addition, there is a stronger "word-of-mouth" marketing effect in games than in films, as once a gamer becomes somewhat skilled at a particular title, he or she is highly likely to want to encourage friends to do the same. This in turn enhances the collective desire to get the next version when it becomes available to maintain and improve his or her skills. In addition, although "star" software development teams are reputed to have similar personal characteristics to entertainment figures, their leverage in negotiations regarding the next edition of Super Mario compared to Sylvester Stallone's regarding his participation in the next *Rocky* is limited. This phenomenon ensures that shareholders rather than celebrities can keep more of the value created.[5]

Despite these observations about the video-game industry, there are still plenty of smaller independent game producers. Occasionally these players produce something that becomes a franchise property. Our point here is not to argue that small independents can't sometimes come up with hits, only that as an ongoing enterprise, these businesses are significantly less profitable than the market leader. Whenever one of these smaller players generates a franchise property, it will be less effective at profitably exploiting it. This is why small

TABLE 11.2 Game Publisher Operating Profit Margins: 2005–2008

	EA	TAKE-TWO	ACTIVISION	THQ
2008	–18%	7%	–8%	–42%
2007	–17%	–14%	15%	–3%
2006	5%	–16%	5%	5%
2005	11%	–4%	2%	7%

players who produce franchise properties typically get bought up by larger ones and why smaller players who do not get bought up eventually die off.

The 2008 stalemate in negotiations between Take-Two, a subscale player with a single great franchise in the form of Grand Theft Auto, and Electronic Arts reflects exactly this dynamic. Take-Two wants its shareholders to be paid for all the incremental value EA can generate from the GTA franchise. EA believes that since no one else should be able to achieve these benefits, it should retain them for its own shareholders. Both companies are in a sense correct. If history is any guide, Take-Two's threat that it will succeed in getting some other media mogul to overpay despite not having any ability to do more with the franchise than the current operator is highly credible.

The superior performance of EA between 2001 and 2005 stemmed from the collective impact of scale economies and customer captivity. Its absolute and relative performance since 2005, however, highlights the potential fragility of even the most apparently impermeable barriers to entry. The sources of these challenges stem from the structure of the video-game business, changes in the overall technological environment, the response of competitors to EA's dominance, and EA's management of its leadership position.

First, the overall dynamics of the video-game industry are driven by platform cycles. Scale and customer captivity to some extent are up for grabs each time a major platform shift takes place. It was Nintendo's failure to recognize its own vulnerability to this shift that allowed others to exploit its arrogance to their own advantage in the early 1990s. And it was EA's correct assessment of the success of the Sony PlayStation 2 (PS2) in the early 2000s that allowed it to produce an overwhelming market share—greater even than that of Sony itself—of the games used. Failing to pursue a similar strategy in anticipation of the launch of Wii allowed Nintendo to achieve an overall market share of video-game publishing approaching that of EA. EA did not have one top-ten game for the first Wii platform in contrast to its ownership of five of the early top-ten PS2 titles.[6] During the 2008 Christmas sales season, EA had only one hit on the industry top-ten list, while five of the bestselling titles were from Nintendo.[7]

Second, a still-small but increasing portion of the video-game business is being captured by online gaming generally, in particular a segment known as Massively Multiplayer Online Games (MMOG). As computers get more powerful and networking interactive technology improves for the average home user, downloadable games and games played in a virtual reality allow game designers to bypass retailers entirely, and are marketed directly to consumers over the Internet by the publisher. Revenues are generated through either subscription or advertising revenue. In 2008, 22 percent of the most frequent game players said they pay to play online games. This is an increase from 19 percent in 2007 and 8 percent back in 2004.[8]

As we have seen elsewhere, electronic distribution undermines barriers to entry and here the significant distribution advantage that EA enjoyed and defended for many years is threatened by the growth of these games. Furthermore, MMOG involve continuously developing original story lines in persistent fantasy worlds without specific endings and integrating input from hundreds of thousands of hosted players. As a result, different programming skills are required. Notably, many of the most successful MMOGs to date have not been produced by the largest publishers. The dominant market share leader in MMOG is World of Warcraft, whose parent, Vivendi Universal Games, was not among the top-five game publishers.[9]

Third, EA's competitors were well aware of their scale disadvantages and actively looked for ways to overcome them, some more rational than others, but all of which caused harm to EA. A number of competitors built up their own dedicated global direct-sales infrastructure, while others aggressively bid up the cost of key game licenses. Most notably, two of the other top independent game publishers—Vivendi and Activision—combined to create Activision Blizzard.[10] As a result, in a few short years, when one takes into account the explosion of game share of Nintendo itself, EA went from having an overwhelming market leadership to being one of three players of comparable size.

Finally, although most of the phenomena described here were out of EA's control, neither the outcome nor EA's response to these market dynamics was a foregone conclusion. EA responded to potential threats to its singular dominance by trying to take on all comers and cede no ground. The company sought to maintain its commanding lead across all platforms and across all genres. As EA's mogul-in-chief John Riccitiello articulated his none-too-modest ambitions: "We want to be the number one entertainment company in the world."[11]

Rather than choosing its battles carefully and offering targeted incentives that advanced cooperation with competitors and other players in its ecosystem, EA invested aggressively on all fronts in the hopes of achieving an unachievable outcome—perpetual all-encompassing dominance. So, for example, EA reported over half a billion dollars in losses in a predictably failed effort to dominate the online gaming space, despite having no significant competitive advantages in this domain. The reporting of the losses stopped after 2003, but the incurring of the losses undoubtedly has endured—the company has simply opted to bury them in its overall results.[12]

Furthermore, if EA had offered more generous distribution terms to its competitors, they might have been more willing to avoid building up their own competing direct-sales infrastructures. And there is a variety of informal signals that EA could have employed to encourage competitors to focus on genres and platforms that were less central to its own franchise.

None of these types of strategies would have eliminated the inexorable industry trends, but they could have substantially slowed them. EA's diffuse response to these challenges may well have also resulted in a general loss of focus on operating efficiency and even contributed to its inability to adequately anticipate the startling success of Wii, in contrast to the way it had effectively managed the introduction of the PS2 in 2000.

The broad moral of both the EA story and the earlier Nintendo one is that by cooperating with members of the competitive ecosystem, one can still meaningfully defer, if not alter, the inevitable fate of those with singular overwhelming competitive advantages. In the Nintendo case, which involved entertainment hardware rather than software, another overarching truism should have colored the company's thinking: With respect to any device, no matter how brilliant, innovative, or successful, eventually everything is a toaster—just another generic appliance. These lessons are often sadly lost on media moguls, as the manner in which the contemporary version of the Nintendo case is playing out with the iPod at Apple demonstrates.

The launch of the Apple iPod in 2001, followed in 2003 with the iTunes system that allowed users to legally download music for ninety-nine cents a song, is widely credited with the resurgence of Apple. This view overstates the long-term impact of the iPod given the questionable strategic approach to the music industry the company took and understates the much more significant impact of Apple's recent decisions to reverse similarly misguided approaches to its PC business by adding Intel chips and supporting Microsoft Windows. Although the iPod has been a wildly successful product launch, Apple's refusal to share the potential benefits with the music companies suggests that it will be short-lived.

Music companies were desperate for a solution to protect them from the accelerating rate of theft of their intellectual property online. They saw a potential solution in the elegant iTunes digital rights management (DRM) system developed by Apple called FairPlay, which undermines piracy by limiting to five the number of computers that can play downloaded songs. As the only credible game in town at the time, Apple refused the music companies' request to share in the equity of iTunes and establish it as the sole ubiquitous standard through which music would be made available online. Indeed, Apple's sole interest was in selling iPods, and it not only refused to share equity, but insisted that music be made available at a single low price and that iTunes be incompatible with any other music players.

Left with no other options, the music companies reluctantly agreed to participate with iTunes on a nonexclusive basis but quickly set about aggressively looking for ways to undermine Apple's dominance of the MP3 music player market. They encouraged the development of alternative digital music outlets, including partnerships with MySpace, Amazon, Wal-Mart, and others, most of whom agreed to the variable pricing that the music companies sought. In addition, the companies have agreed to allow these competing services to sell songs without DRM limitation in order to help them catch up to Apple—while mostly refusing to allow Apple access on the same unrestricted basis.[13]

An objective Apple shareholder might fairly react to this analysis: If the iPod represents a strategic failure, then I hope Steve Jobs has plenty more just like it! The music business was bigger than the PC business in 2007 and the market share of the iPod has held fairly steady at around 70 percent. Many observers view the iPod boom as having spawned a renewed interest in the Mac.[14] Apple stock was under ten dollars a share when the iTunes store opened in April 2003 and was over one hundred dollars by the end of 2008. What's not to like? To answer this question fully requires that we look a little more closely at the history of Apple and what else has happened at the company since 2003.

Apple is a company that has repeatedly pulled defeat from the jaws of victory by refusing to play nicely with others.[15] The company saw its market share collapse in the early eighties with the introduction of the IBM PC that ran on the Microsoft operating system and Intel chips. Convinced that its superior product attributes and marketing would more than counterbalance the economies of scale available to its much larger rivals in the operating system and semiconductor markets, Apple resisted working with these rivals for almost twenty years as it watched its global PC market share dwindle to around 2 to 3 percent.

The two fateful decisions relating to these markets were connected— without a more powerful chip, the Mac products could not effectively support running both operating systems. In 2005, Apple finally abandoned their use of their PowerPC chips in favor of Intel.[16] Although the company had been working with Microsoft since 1997 when it accepted a $150 million investment and Microsoft committed to developing versions of its core software products for the Mac,[17] Apple did not actually start supporting Windows until 2006.[18]

Apple's 2008 results are highly instructive in identifying the primary source of increased value. Although it is true that Macs are now a minority of the company's revenues, they continue to represent the vast majority of the company's profits. iPod margins are far below that of the Mac and the iTunes business barely breaks even. Between 2006 and 2008, Apple's operating income rose from $2.453 billion to $6.275 billion as operating margins rose from 12.7 percent to 19.3 percent. During this time iPod dollar sales rose by only 19 percent and iPod prices fell by 14 percent. In contrast, Mac dollar sales rose 94 percent and Mac prices rose by 6 percent.[19] Furthermore, any suggestion of a "halo effect" from the iPod seems inconsistent with the fact that Mac sales were accelerating dramatically while iPod sales were relatively flat even in the face of significant price cuts.[20] In 2009, iPod sales are projected to decline even in the face of further price cuts—Mac sales are expected to continue their robust growth—suggesting that the maintenance of share has come at a cost.

The iPod has been a success and no one can deny the marketing genius of Steve Jobs. But in a world where everything eventually becomes a toaster, the "bring 'em on" ethos that many media moguls share with former president George W. Bush is as self-destructive in business as it is in government. The objective should be to delay the inevitable, not to accelerate it.

Local media franchises usually do not face the same inevitability of becoming the equivalent of a toaster. But they, too, must remain vigilant. And vigilance is as much a function of continuously reinforcing the key sources of advantage as it is a function of reaffirming one's commitment to cooperating with those who operate in the same broad competitive ecosystem. Falling prey to the mogul urge to dominate the broader universe rather than clearly delineating your region of advantage and signaling a willingness to remain happily and profitably within its boundaries is the surest way to accelerate the destruction of a perfectly good media franchise.

PART III

Good Mogul/Bad Mogul: The Sources of Success and Failure

12 | Bad Mogul: Media Mergers and Acquisitions

The single most consistent reason for underperformance in media companies is bad acquisitions. Having spent as much time as we have emphasizing the impact of misguided strategies pursued by media moguls, this may seem an odd statement. "Great, I can forget about all this fancy talk about competitive advantage, cooperation, and efficiency," a mogul might understandably react. "Just don't do stupid deals." In fact, the analytic framework outlined in the first two sections of the book is inextricably intertwined with the central question of why moguls relentlessly undertake inherently foolish deals or overpay for ones that might have made sense at a different price.

In a world where economists can be found on as many sides of an issue as politicians, it is a relief to find a topic on which there is effective unanimity. Mergers and acquisitions (M&A) do not create value.[1] Although some intra-academic squabbling persists over the question of whether the value lost by the purchaser in these deals is fully counterbalanced by the windfall obtained by the seller,[2] no one seriously argues with the proposition that buyers end up worse off with remarkable consistency.

The stupidity of much M&A has been a frequent subject of not only academic research but general interest business books and the press. The focus of this work has often been on particularly egregious deals, but has sometimes entailed more systemic approaches, alternatively using the tools of economics, psychology, and sociology to draw conclusions. What then justifies rehashing this vast literature to make essentially the same point with respect to the media industry?

The extent to which media moguls have abused M&A to the detriment of their shareholders sets the industry apart from all others. The distinction stems in part from the depth of the media industry's obsession with growth at all costs and its reliance on M&A to achieve it. This difference is unintentionally highlighted by data included in a recent book by the leading global consulting firm.

The Granularity of Growth is a gift to investment bankers from McKinsey & Co.[3] The book provides the strongest possible case for making acquisitions, almost without regard to quality, relevance, or price. Broadly, the authors argue that "sustained positive revenue growth," regardless of its nature or source, has been the key to achieving superior performance.[4] *Granularity* distinguishes among three "cylinders" of potential revenue growth: growth from acquisitions, organic growth in line with the sector (what they term "portfolio momentum"), and organic growth achieved through market share gains.[5] It concludes that it basically does not matter which of these spurs the top-line increases as long as they are spurred.

The views expressed in *Granularity* are based on a proprietary database of hundreds of the largest companies, developed by a dedicated cadre of analysts in India who scrubbed financials to ascertain the precise source of each dollar of revenue growth. They draw a number of interesting lessons about where growth has come from historically (mostly portfolio momentum and very little share gain), how the most successful companies achieve it (firing in the top quartile on any two cylinders or in the top decile on one), and what practical strategies improve the chance of growing (basically anything that moves a company from low-momentum portfolio segments to high-momentum ones).

Investment bankers love *Granularity* because it provides an intellectual foundation to justify the relentless pursuit of that activity on which they thrive: doing deals, any deals. With revenue growth as the prime directive and organic share gain identified as the least significant factor, companies are inevitably led to aggressively make acquisitions at all cost, preferably in sectors experiencing high organic growth, while selling off any businesses in slower-growth sectors.

This recommended approach of relentless portfolio realignment is consistent with the ideal *Granularity* holds up to companies as a model to emulate: private equity firms.[6] It is not a coincidence that private equity firms are investment banks' biggest clients. They are literally in the business of doing deals—buying and selling and buying again, the faster the better to be able to raise the next bigger fund to do even more. *Granularity* glosses over a stubborn fact about private equity firms, however, that makes them a rather odd role model. Although the authors mention in passing that private equity firms "still produce a decent return,"[7] as a group they actually underperform the market significantly. The average absolute return of these funds may seem high, but it is not nearly enough to justify the incremental risk associated with the leverage employed. Borrowing similar amounts to invest broadly in the stock market would yield far superior performance.[8]

Although most of the data upon which *Granularity* is based is presented on an aggregated basis, it does include one highly relevant chart that distinguishes the sources of growth by industry sector.

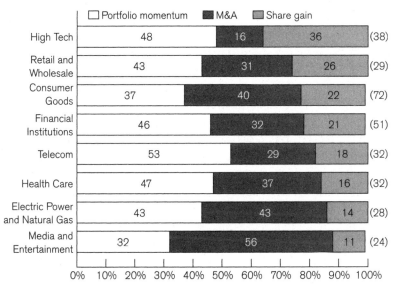

FIGURE 12.1 Differentiation by Growth Cylinder and for Selected Sectors Percent (Number of Companies)

Source: *The Granularity of Growth.*

Sample: Granular growth decomposition database.

Note: Numbers do not always add up to 100 percent because of rounding.

What is striking here is that media alone among sectors has relied on acquisitions to generate more than half of the growth achieved during the period. No other industry comes close. Despite the apparently nonironic use of the word *granularity* in the title, the authors make no note of this stark fact or otherwise comment on whether the overall observation that is the basis of the book—that there is a strong positive correlation between revenue growth and total shareholder returns—holds true for each of the sectors reviewed. Based on our earlier review of this question, there appears to be a correlation between these factors among the largest media companies, but it is decidedly negative.

Even if we had access to the proprietary McKinsey growth database, this would not be the place to take up all of the issues raised by the analyses presented in *Granularity*. It does, however, provide us with an excuse to get granular with respect to how and why media moguls manage to destroy value through acquisitions with such shocking consistency. The urgency of this examination is highlighted by a largely ignored report in 2004 by a young media research analyst, Douglas Shapiro, at Bank of America Securities. In the report, Shapiro asked a question that strangely no one else had asked before in an industry that relied so heavily on acquisitions to generate growth: How would the stocks of the largest media companies have performed if all these deals had been left undone? [9]

In the report, Shapiro meticulously unwound the contribution to the bottom line from the series of major acquisitions made over the previous decade by Time Warner, Viacom, Disney, and Comcast. The dramatic results are reproduced on the following page, showing not only that the shareholders would have been better off on average if the deals had been avoided, but that in the case of Viacom and Time Warner, the stock prices would have been well more than double their levels at the time of the report.

The extent of value destruction from these deals in the worst cases is the most striking aspect of this analysis. Equally noteworthy, however, are the reasons that M&A did not appear to destroy value in the best case. According to Shapiro's analysis, if Disney had not bothered to do the $19 billion acquisition of Capital Cities/ABC in 1995 (the largest deal in history at the time) or the $5.2 billion acquisition of the Fox Family cable channel in 2001, shareholders would have been roughly in the same place. This result, by media industry standards, is a home run. What is most remarkable, however, is that Disney managed to stand in place only because

TABLE 12.1 Summary of Results: The Impact of "Unwinding" Big Media Mergers

	Viacom		Disney		Time Warner		Comcast	
	Actual	Hypothetical	Actual	Hypothetical	Actual	Hypothetical	Actual	Hypothetical
Market Cap	$61,712	$28,767	$55,897	$54,741	$80,939	$54,411	$61,286	$36,964
EV	$68,110	$20,461	$65,874	$46,199	$94,439	$68,438	$65,875	$28,945
EBITDA	$6,705	$2,014	$5,171	$3,627	$9,800	$7,102	$7,247	$3,184
EV/EBITDA	10.2	10.2	12.7	12.7	9.6	9.6	9.1	9.1
Shares Outstanding	1,762.7	371.3	2,217.3	2,264.8	4,697.5	1,263.4	2,248.2	1,069.6
Current Price	$35		$25		$17		$27	
Implied Price		$77		$24		$43		$35
PPS % Variance		121%		-4%		150%		27%

Source: Company reports, Bank of America Securities LLC estimates as of July 7, 2004.

the unexpected explosive growth in the value of Cap Cities' 80 percent stake in ESPN managed to cancel out the dramatic underperformance relative to the prices paid for both the ABC network and the Fox Family Channel.

What is striking about the Disney case is that all the assets that were supposed to create "synergies" apparently destroyed value for shareholders. Putting a studio together with a broadcasting network, it was thought, would make both stronger. In fact, Disney studios' margins declined after the deal and ABC quickly went from being the number one network to the number three network. Fox Family, it was thought, would become far more valuable under the ownership of the leading family entertainment franchise in the world, yet its ratings actually deteriorated after the acquisition.[10] To top it off, the offsetting source of value creation at ESPN was unrelated to the fact that Disney owned it. Even if one believed that Disney's ownership of the Anaheim Ducks could theoretically help the leading sports cable franchise, because of Hearst's 20 percent ownership stake, ESPN had to be operated completely independently with any affiliate transactions with its majority owner closely scrutinized.

The Disney case underscores an important aspect of the dangers of media moguls' excessive reliance on M&A. There is often a basic confusion regarding what the true source of value creation from a transaction might be. It is the combination of a fanatical desire for growth with a misdirected understanding of the potential benefits from strategic combinations that has made acquisitions a particularly deadly tool in the hands of an unrestrained media mogul.

What makes a particular acquisition "bad"? Consistent with our overall approach, it will not surprise anyone that we like deals in which the return on investment exceeds the company's cost of capital. Shapiro pointed out in his 2004 report that the media companies he looked at consistently maintained returns far below their cost and more recent research that has focused on the same central issue demonstrates that this has not changed since then.[11]

This sounds sensible enough, but it begs the fundamental question of why media deals fail so consistently and so spectacularly. To answer this question in more concrete terms, let's get even more granular and examine the largest media deals in history. A half-dozen transactions greater than $50 billion in today's dollars have occurred in the history of the media industry. All have ended in tears, at least for the acquiring shareholders.

TABLE 12.2 The Disney Magic: The Operational Impact of Disney Acquisition and Ownership

Disney Studios—Before and After Cap Cities/ABC Acquisition[12]					
	1993	1994	1995	1996	1997	1998
Revenue	3,673	4,793	6,001	6,471	6,981	6,586
EBIT	622	856	1,074	895	1,079	749
Margin	16.9%	17.9%	17.9%	13.8%	15.5%	11.4%

ABC Network Relative Performance—Before and After Acquisition by Disney[13]					
	1993–94	1994–95	1995–96	1996–97	1997–98	1998–99
ABC						
Ranking	#2	#1	#2	#3	#3	#3
Rating	12.5	11.9	10.6	9.2	8.4	8.1
CBS						
Ranking	#1	#3	#3	#2	#2	#1
Rating	14.1	10.9	9.6	9.6	9.6	9.0
NBC						
Ranking	#3	#2	#1	#1	#1	#2
Rating	11.1	11.6	11.7	10.5	10.2	8.9

Part-Year Disney Ownership   Under Disney Ownership

TABLE 12.3 The Dirty Half Dozen ($ in billions)[14]

Rank	Date Announced	Target Name	Acquirer Name	Nominal Value	Real (Inflation Adjusted) Value
1	01/10/2000	Time Warner	America Online Inc.	$175.87	$229.17
2	07/08/2001	AT&T Broadband	Comcast Corp.	76.06	94.26
3	04/22/1999	MediaOne Group Inc.	AT&T Corp.	60.55	80.14
4	06/24/1998	Tele-Communications, Inc.	AT&T Corp.	45.02	60.76
5	06/20/2000	Seagram Co Ltd.	Vivendi SA	43.17	55.08
6	09/07/1999	CBS Corp.	Viacom Inc.	39.37	51.58

COMCAST-AT&T BROADBAND: THE WINNER'S CURSE

Although not the biggest single transaction, we start with AT&T-Comcast for two reasons.

First, embedded within this deal are three of the six largest media deals in that the company that Comcast devoured had already been responsible for two of the other largest media deals. The price Comcast paid was less than that paid in total for the two earlier megadeals. To the extent that we conclude that Comcast still paid too much, it will be very safe to assume that the other transactions were even more misguided.

Second, in many ways, Comcast-AT&T seems like a textbook case of the right kind of M&A to pursue. Strategically sensible and flawlessly executed as it was, if this deal destroyed value, it highlights just how high the bar is set for any deal to be in the interests of the acquiring company's shareholders.

In the late 1990s, Comcast was one of a half-dozen midsize cable companies with between 3 and 6 million subscribers.[15] The largest of these had around half the subscribers of the two industry giants, Time Warner Cable and AT&T, which had entered the industry through its daring acquisition of Tele-Communications, Inc. from John Malone. Although Comcast was publicly traded and widely held by investors, the founding Roberts family absolutely controlled the business through a dual-class stock structure similar to that found in many media companies. Investors, however, did not mind that the Roberts family managed to control around 90 percent of the vote while owning less than 5 percent of the equity for the simple reason that the family ran the company extremely well. Comcast had among the highest margins in the industry and the stock had delivered compound annual returns in excess of 20 percent since the company's IPO in 1972.

Being the best-run midsize cable operator may have satisfied the other shareholders of Comcast, but it was not enough for the Robertses. They felt, with some justification, that they deserved to be among the industry leaders in size as well as in performance. To remedy this injustice, in March 1999, Comcast announced a stunning takeover of MediaOne for $53 billion in stock for a total value of $60 billion including MediaOne's debt. The transaction represented an almost 50 percent premium to MediaOne's share price just a month earlier. Furthermore, the Roberts family proposed to give MediaOne shareholders 67 percent of the economics of the combined company without any of the vote. The Roberts family, by contrast, would have been diluted to a mere 2 percent economic interest while retaining 82 percent of the vote.

There was one problem. Michael Armstrong, the then CEO of AT&T, didn't want the Robertses to join the club and didn't much like being a couple million subscribers smaller than Time Warner Cable either. So he decided to offer to pay more for MediaOne. Around $10 billion more, in fact. And AT&T was offering to pay about $20 billion of the purchase price in cash, rather than the 100 percent nonvoting stock deal Comcast had proposed. Using nonvoting stock to buy a company larger than itself was one thing. It would be another matter entirely for Comcast, which then had a total market capitalization of not much more than $20 billion itself, to come up with a proposal that would be genuinely competitive with AT&T's enhanced stock and cash offer.

For its troubles, Comcast received $1.5 billion from MediaOne, the largest breakup fee ever recorded at the time, and an agreement to sell them some cable systems that AT&T did not want. For some, that might have been enough. But hell hath no fury like a media mogul scorned. Comcast was seething. Armstrong had justified his company's diversification from telephony into cable at previously unheard-of prices by spinning visions of an integrated bundle of high-tech voice, video, and data services. Unfortunately, it soon became apparent to investors that Armstrong didn't have the first idea of how to operate a cable company, much less offer these services. AT&T cable profit margins were not much more than half of those achieved by Comcast.

With AT&T's shareholders revolting and its stock price languishing, the Roberts family approached Armstrong about taking the entire cable business off his hands. Armstrong feigned interest and then turned to the media mogul's preferred solution to a fundamental strategic or operating problem: financial engineering. In October 2000, he announced his intention to issue special "tracking" stocks to reflect the underlying value of the four distinct parts of AT&T's business—consumer, business, wireless, and cable. Ultimately, once investors "understood" the true value of the overall enterprise through the prices of these tracking shares, the businesses would actually be separated. Financial engineering is a corporate form of blaming the victim: The problem isn't bad management, it's stupid investors. Once you explain it to them slowly, the theory goes—whether through tracking stocks or selling stakes in underappreciated businesses to venture capitalists or whatever— the problem will be "solved."

Once this announcement was made, the Roberts family again tried to engage Armstrong about a combination, without success. Once AT&T filed its preliminary proxy in May 2001 in connection with its plans, the Roberts family approached the company once more about putting the businesses together. AT&T imposed preconditions on any conversations, and the Roberts family would not agree. As the September 2001 AT&T shareholder vote approached, the Robertses seethed still more.

The Roberts family faced a dilemma. They really wanted to own these assets. But how can you make a company sell a division that it doesn't want to sell? Comcast could wait for the ultimate spin-off of the soon-to-be-renamed AT&T Broadband, but that newly independent entity might remain equally unreceptive to their approaches. In addition, if a transaction were completed too soon after the separation, there was a risk that the tax-free nature of the spin-off would be invalidated—with Comcast on the hook for the bill. So Comcast decided to do something to get the company's attention. In early July, it publicly announced an offer to buy AT&T Broadband for almost $60 billion, representing thirty times EBITDA or significantly more than double the multiple that cable stocks traded for in the public markets at the time.

Now Armstrong was seething. Although the company couldn't be forced to sell a division, if the shareholders rejected the proposed company restructuring, he and his board would be humiliated. So Armstrong delayed the shareholder vote and directed his advisers to solicit alternative proposals. For almost six months, AT&T tormented Comcast: first, with extended negotiations over the terms under which it could get access to the same confidential company information it was now providing others and then with a series of "final" bid dates after which all of the parties were told to try again. By the time Comcast "won" its prize on December 19, it had increased its already breathtaking offer by more than $10 billion, substantially increasing the amount of stock it would issue to AT&T's shareholders and almost doubling the amount of debt and liabilities it would take over to $25 billion.

As a final treat for their trouble, in addition to paying what would now amount to a truly heart-stopping price, AT&T forced Comcast to accept their beloved friend Michael Armstrong as chairman of the combined company and agree to limit the Roberts family voting power to a mere 33.3 percent to go along with their now under 1 percent economic interest.

The Roberts family had attained their longed-for prize. They now controlled and ran the biggest cable company in the world. But for all of the talk about the genius of engineering the only successful hostile acquisition of a division of another company in history, at the end of the day Comcast ensnared its corporate prey the old-fashioned way: It overpaid.

Comcast justified the price it paid by identifying well over $1 billion in cost savings. AT&T was notoriously poorly run. Simply applying Comcast's profit margin to AT&T's revenue yielded a potential benefit of $1.6 billion.[16] In addition to the benefits of increased operating efficiency, Comcast pointed to a number of "synergies." Much more will be said shortly about what kinds of synergies should be believed and what kind should not. The good news about Comcast's acquisition is that most of the synergies were in highly credible cost categories: integrating the national sales and advertising platform, using the combined buying power to negotiate better programming deals, and rationalizing the operating structure of adjacent cable systems. The bad news is that the vast majority of the cost structure of the cable business resides at the local level within each self-contained operating system. Having lots of self-contained systems does not have much impact on this core cost structure except in the case where systems are next to one another and their overall operating configuration can be combined.

For argument's sake, let's say that Comcast was able to add $2 billion in EBITDA to AT&T under its ownership by achieving efficiencies and synergies—more than even they claimed could be achieved at the time.[17] Since AT&T had announced its intention to list its cable business separately, there was a wide range of analysts who published estimates of what it would be worth in the public markets, all of which hovered around $50 billion. Comcast paid $72 billion and it would require an investment of at least $2 billion to $4 billion to achieve the hoped-for cost benefits. Although it would have taken several years to attain the full benefits of the combination, if we simply assume that these were immediate, Comcast would have obtained $2 billion in EBITDA each year for the extra $25 billion it paid. That is an 8 percent annual return in terms of EBITDA (2/25 = 8 percent), but EBITDA is an industry convention that does not take into account capital expenditures, working capital needs, and other cash items. Actual cash, of the kind that Comcast would have gotten if it had invested in a government bond instead, is typically less than half of EBITDA in the cable sector, so the real return on the investment is likely less than 5 percent.

Ouch. But how can a strategically brilliant, flawlessly executed transaction end up being such a dud? Most companies are acquired through an auction of the kind ultimately undertaken by AT&T or simply by paying a significant premium to the stock price in the case of a stand-alone public company. Being able to operate a business better or achieve synergies is a great thing that does create value. The question is, who gets to capture that

value? If there are multiple interested owners who can produce comparable efficiencies and synergies, they will bid up the price to reflect the value they can create. When the smoke clears, the selling shareholder has all of the benefit regardless of which potential buyer ended up paying the last dollar. Why don't they just split the value? The answer is that if Cox, Time Warner Cable, and Comcast all think they can create $2 billion of incremental EBITDA by owning AT&T Broadband, there is no reason for AT&T to stop until it finds out who is willing to pay them for all of it. Where one potential buyer is more efficient or has more synergies, in theory it can pay a dollar more than the next-best buyer can afford and keep the rest for its own shareholders. The problem here is that it is hard to know enough about the next-best buyer's cost structure or how he or she looks at it. So most times, once all the strategizing and machinations are over, the buyer just hands over his wallet and asks the seller to give it back when he is finished.

There are exceptions to these rules, and we will discuss them shortly. So-called mergers of equals, where no premium is paid and the respective shareholders benefit pro rata from the combination, are the most obvious example. The point, however, is that they are very much exceptions.

The moral of this story is that you can want a thing too much, and media moguls frequently do. This tendency within the media segment is heightened by the peculiar ownership structures that prevail, under which absolute decision-making control is often maintained through supervoting shares. Although the moguls share the potential negative economic consequences of foolish deals through their ownership, the psychic benefits of amassing an ever-larger kingdom over which to rule are not shared proportionately with the other shareholders. This disparity encourages even more systematic overestimation of the economic benefits of combinations.

There are other structural deal-related issues that stem from supervoting stock in mogul hands. For example, while the Robertses own a tiny portion of the overall economics of Comcast, this stake still represents a disproportionate amount of the family's personal wealth. Although other shareholders can easily diversify their holdings by simply selling a portion of their stakes and buying other securities, this is more difficult for the Robertses. Given the public focus on the significant disparity between their economic ownership and their nondilutable blocking stake in the company, as well as the potential negative signaling effects, they are understandably reticent to sell shares. This could encourage them to pursue diversifying acquisitions through the company rather than on their own, even if these are not necessarily in the other shareholders' interest. Comcast's failed attempt to acquire Disney was viewed by many shareholders in precisely this way. Although Comcast abandoned the transaction in the face of fierce shareholder opposition, the company has never disavowed the "strategic" justification for having pursed the deal in the first place.

AOL-TIME WARNER: THE MYTH AND REALITY OF SYNERGIES

The combination of AOL and Time Warner has already been the subject of a half-dozen books, and with good reason.[18] The epic drama that ultimately resulted in a historically unprecedented destruction of value is chock-full of vivid characters and life lessons related to every aspect of corporate governance and decision making. The central figure in this saga was Jerry Levin, a media mogul who proved to be the perfect mark for the con of the century. Brilliant, isolated, arrogant, and emotionally fragile after the death of his son, Levin had grown increasingly frustrated with his inability to bring Time Warner into the digital age. AOL chief Steve Case drew him in by first feigning a lack of interest in running the combined company and then convincing him (yes, prodigious amounts of alcohol were involved) that by "using the new technology to give people access to news and information, and to one another, Time Warner could reduce ignorance, intolerance and injustice."[19]

Levin's justification for the transaction is unusual only in its mad, messianic formulation. The basic description of the hoped-for synergies, however, was quite consistent with those promised in most mega-media combinations. It is the synergistic aspects of the AOL–Time Warner deal rationale that are the focus here. When Levin's vision was translated in calmer moments into specific itemized lists of supposed deal benefits by investor relations professionals, the presaged synergies almost precisely mirrored those touted in the other large media deals that came before and that have unfolded since.

Of all the iconic moments that defined the AOL–Time Warner combination, one perfectly captures the parties' approach to synergies. The scene took place in an elevator of the Equitable Building in New York as the principals and their investor relations teams ascended to the formal public unveiling of the "strategic merger of equals to create the world's first fully integrated media and communications company for the Internet Century." On the way up, the AOL team mentioned, in passing, that the announcement would include a commitment to achieve $1 billion in synergies. Given that AOL was nominally paying a premium of $60 billion, AOL thought it important to quantify the benefits above and beyond the current public valuation of Time Warner. This was the first Time Warner's respected head of investor relations had heard mention of estimated synergies. She was, to put it mildly, apoplectic. No operating executives at Time Warner, the company that was contributing over 80 percent of the revenue to the deal and that would be overwhelmingly responsible for delivering these results, had been consulted. The numbers had been developed entirely by the investor relations professionals at AOL. How, she wanted to know, could this estimate seriously be presented to public investors? An argument ensued. Levin was silent. The elevator arrived at its destination and Time Warner's CFO, the only inside executive whom Levin had included in any of the negotiations, raised his hand to silence the group and bring the matter to a close. "We'll handle it," he said dismissively, and the group exited to face the waiting crowd.

Synergy is a term misused almost as much as *strategy* in mogul circles. A synergy is a financial benefit, to either the top or bottom line, attainable only through a particular corporate combination. In M&A, synergies are what make the value of the whole greater than the sum of the parts. Performance improvements that could be undertaken by a company on its own may attract a hungry suitor and help justify a particular transaction, but it is not a synergy as such. A true synergy must entail achieving either cost savings or new revenues that are possible only because of the combination.

In many media megamergers, as in the AOL–Time Warner transaction, the synergies are often an afterthought. Even in cases where there is more advance thought given to quantifying the precise magnitude of specific synergies than in AOL–Time Warner, that exercise is often treated as completely distinct from laying out the mogul's all-important strategic vision. Once big-picture strategy is laid out, synergies are discussed in the context of hopefully satisfying investors that the numbers can bear the burden of achieving the moguls' worldview. This tendency to treat strategy and synergy as largely unrelated in itself suggests a fundamental misunderstanding of the nature of both concepts.

Strategy and synergy have an important, tight structural connection. Earlier we showed why strategy is irrelevant in the absence of competitive advantage. Similarly, synergies of any magnitude are simply not possible in the absence of competitive advantage. As a result, a transaction cannot be strategic without synergies and the extent of the synergies defines just how strategic the proposed deal is or is not. Furthermore, it is almost impossible to create competitive advantage through a corporate combination where none existed before. To see how and why this is so, we need to look at how each of the sources of competitive advantage operate in the M&A context.

The competitive advantage that is the greatest source of cost synergy is economies of scale. Economies of scale exist when a company benefits from being able to leverage a relatively large fixed cost infrastructure across a bigger customer base. An acquisition by a company with economies of scale provides an opportunity to spread those costs over an even bigger customer base by eliminating much of the duplicative infrastructure of the target. Time Warner and AOL were largely in completely different businesses, so scale could not justify a combination. When analysts, with the quiet guidance of company executives, estimated the specific sources of the promised synergies, they did not hold up to close scrutiny.

Putting together businesses that already have scale in distinct segments does not increase their combined scale in either one. The impetus for Levin to pursue the transaction was the repeated failure of the company to derive any benefit from existing businesses—magazine publishing, movies, music, and cable—in trying to establish a successful online service. Although there could be some savings from folding Time Warner's modest online operations into AOL, this would be far less than the hundreds of millions in benefits promised from reducing expenditures while suddenly generating hundreds of millions in new advertising revenue from these hitherto unprofitable sites. Even the "no-brainer" corporate overhead expense reductions were wildly overstated, as very different kinds of lawyers and HR professionals are needed, for instance, to manage issues that typically arise in the music and movie businesses as opposed to a consumer online service.

The aspect of scale, or at least size, that the companies emphasized was in the areas of sales and marketing. Again, however, where the products and distribution channels are dissimilar, it is unclear what significant cost or revenue benefits accrue from the combination. If it were cost-effective to market AOL software by including samples with Time Inc. magazines, presumably the independent companies would have negotiated a mutually agreeable commercial arrangement to do so. If New Line Cinema or Warner Music thought it should allocate more of its marketing budgets to AOL, it could always have done so. This kind of cross-promotion is not free—it uses up limited advertising inventory that could be sold to someone else. If the combination forces divisions to suboptimize their respective sales and marketing strategies, it represents a dis-synergy, not a synergy.

TABLE 12.4 $1 Billion in Proposed AOL–Time Warner Synergies

Area	Revenues/Costs	EBITDA	Rationale
Ad Sales Upside	$200.0	$160.0	$200 of $600mm in est. revenue upside at TW Online properties (CNN, CNNfn, CNNSI, *Time, People, InStyle, Entertainment Weekly*)
	120.0	120.0	More deals on AOL, ICQ through TW relationships
Higher Broadband Penetration	120.0	72.0	1mm more broadband subs for TW relationships from AOL upgrades $500K average for year paying $20 more per month
Incremental Subs	25.0	12.5	New subs to AOL and magazines (through cross-promotion)
New AOL Premium Services	60.0	30.0	2mm AOL subs sign up for $5 incr. fee by year-end 2001 (for AOL TV, real-time stock quotes, etc.)
Music	25.0	6.3	Downloads on early generation music devices
	10.0	2.5	Increased Warner Music sales using AOL platform
	$590.0	**$403.3**	**Total Revenue Upside**
Reduced Operating Expenses	$200.0	$200.0	Sales & Marketing, AOL (distribution of AOL software)
	100.0	100.0	Sales & Marketing, Time Warner (movies and music)
	125.0	125.0	Reduced spending on TW online initiatives (Entertaindom)
	50.0	50.0	Overhead (Finance, Legal, HR)
	50.0	50.0	Reduced customer support cost (in COGS)
	25.0	25.0	Reduced cost of content purchased by AOL ($600mm over 4 years)
	25.0	25.0	Reduced cost of member subscription and renewal
	25.0	25.0	Reduced telecom/technology costs across AOL Time Warner
	$600.0	**$600.0**	**Total Cost Savings**
	$1190.0	$1003.3	TOTAL SYNERGIES

Source: Adapted in Harvard Business School Case 9-701-036 from Merrill Lynch Research.

The other sources of competitive advantage can rarely justify an acquisition by themselves, although they can reinforce the benefits that accrue from scale. Customer captivity is an important source of competitive advantage, but it is one that does not travel well. Customers are captive to a particular product or service. But how does subscriber loyalty to *Sports Illustrated* increase captivity of customers to any other Time Warner products or to any other business the company may buy? Subscription businesses often have strong customer captivity and AOL–Time Warner made much of the supposed benefits of amassing subscription relationships with over 100 million consumers. But given that Time Warner never got much out of having both magazine and cable subscribers, it was a little unclear how adding ISP (Internet Services Provider) subscribers to the mix would change the dynamic.

Although proprietary technology can be obtained through an acquisition, it can often be more efficiently obtained through a license. There was no proprietary technology to speak of at Time Warner or AOL, although clearly Levin wanted the Internet know-how that had eluded his own management ranks. Overpaying superstars is a far cheaper way to secure management capabilities, whether in technological or other domains, than pursuing a misguided corporate combination. To the extent that either company benefited from regulatory protection, the deal reduced this, as the companies needed to make a variety of governmental accommodations in order to ultimately secure approval.

If a transaction is uniquely strategic, this should manifest itself in a unique ability to reduce the combined cost structure through the benefits of scale. If someone else can take out more costs and you still pay more than they were willing to pay, it is a sure bet that your shareholders will be worse off for it. Although revenue synergies are theoretically achievable, banking on them is a risky proposition. Whereas a combined cost structure can be mapped out with reasonable precision in advance, revenue synergy estimates must rely on market research and mogul instinct, both of which systematically overestimate the benefits and underestimate the risk of revenue dis-synergy. If the merging businesses previously competed and there are customer overlaps, there is always a risk that these joint customers will seek bulk discounts. If the merging businesses have no customer overlap and revenue synergies are to come from cross-promotion, one should ask why these were not sought from a commercial agreement between the parties before the transaction.

In AOL–Time Warner, one of the very few areas of genuine potential synergy was in broadband, where Time Warner already had a thriving service called Road Runner, and AOL was just trying to define its own strategy. Rather than combine their efforts after the merger, each division continued to work completely independently. Given Yahoo's subsequent success as a broadband marketing partner to AT&T, it is not clear that a transaction would have been necessary to achieve the potential benefits. But the fact that the two sides refused to cooperate when combined in a single company highlights a key cultural obstacle to achieving potential synergies even when they do exist. Because true synergies are overwhelmingly of the cost variety, the difficulties of agreeing on whose ox will be gored—which generally translates into whose head count will be reduced—diminishes the likelihood that genuinely strategic deals will get done in the first place. Instead, diversifying, visionary transactions are favored in which everybody is a winner—except the shareholders.

At the time of the AOL–Time Warner deal, Co-Chief Operating Officer Bob Pittman was quoted as telling skeptical investors that "if he couldn't generate $1 billion in synergies out of a company with $40 billion in revenue and $30 billion in cost he should be taken out and shot."[20] In the end, like most great con jobs, AOL's fleecing of Time Warner's shareholders involved a piece of clever misdirection. By focusing attention on these hastily invented synergies and a futuristic vision of the combined companies, AOL's leaders, Case and Pittman, ensured that no one would direct their attention to the critical issue that sealed the fate of Time Warner's shareholders: the value of AOL.

Although AOL appeared to be buying Time Warner at a 71 percent premium, actually Time Warner shareholders were also effectively buying AOL at a 42 percent discount. As it turned out, this was not nearly enough of a haircut to AOL's trading price. Through a combination of virtuoso salesmanship and fraudulent accounting, AOL had convinced the market that its pre-announcement value of almost $200 billion was justifiable. In 2009, even after adding over a billion dollars in incremental Internet acquisitions to the division, what is left of AOL is likely worth substantially less than $15 billion.[21]

VIACOM-CBS: THE SMARTEST GUY IN THE ROOM

Sumner Redstone is a very smart man. He built a small regional theater chain into one of the world's largest media conglomerates through a series of highly complex, tax-efficient transactions. Redstone's autobiography catalogs all of the lesser moguls—each, he insists, a "close personal friend"—whom he bested in some negotiation or other. Whatever one might think of the book, Redstone's cool description of the succession of "friends" he dispatched on the way to building his vast empire leaves little doubt that the title—*A Passion to Win*—is at least justified.

At the time of Redstone's announcement of the acquisition of CBS in 1999, he exerted absolute control over Viacom through the only class of securities that had any vote at all. The seventy-six-year-old mogul's stake was worth $9 billion. The initial conversations between the companies began when CBS CEO Mel Karmazin approached Redstone about a relatively small part of Viacom: its television stations. These nineteen stations represented less than 4 percent of Viacom's revenue, which otherwise encompassed Paramount studios, Blockbuster video stores, the bouquet of MTV cable channels, Simon & Schuster book publishing, and related Internet sites.

Recent regulatory rule changes had allowed owners to operate more than one station in a market, creating significant cost savings from eliminating the duplicative infrastructure. Combining Viacom's small station group with CBS's would have clear synergistic benefits of the most unambiguous kind. During the course of discussions over the best way to realize these benefits, Karmazin raised the possibility of combining the two companies.

The possibility of putting Viacom together with CBS intrigued Redstone. Karmazin was a Wall Street darling, and bringing him into the company would quiet concerns about succession, given Redstone's age. The recently announced AOL–Time Warner merger, coming a few years after Disney's purchase of CapCities/ABC, now left Viacom as one of the smaller media conglomerates. Redstone was sure that he would be able to leverage the company's new heft in other ways as well.

But above all, Redstone liked to win. As much as he liked to crow, with no small justification, about outsmarting others, Redstone seemed to equally enjoy deriding the foolish deals of others. Having repeatedly and publicly bragged about not having taken Steve Case's bait, thus managing to avoid the sad fate of Time Warner's shareholders, Redstone was not about to announce a deal that anyone could second-guess.

So Redstone made two demands as a precondition to any combination with CBS. First, CBS shareholders could receive only no-vote shares in the deal. Second, Redstone would not pay any premium whatsoever to CBS shareholders. To an outsider, these requirements seemed completely unreasonable and certainly unprecedented in the media industry. Redstone was in effect insisting that he be able to take over control of one of the most storied entertainment franchises in history without paying anything extra for the privilege. Karmazin agreed and the sides negotiated a series of complex temporary governance protections for the CBS shareholders—and management independence for Karmazin—before the final agreement was announced. Redstone had won again. Or had he? By the time Redstone announced that he would not be renewing Karmazin's contract as CEO of the company in 2004, the value of his stake in the company had declined by almost $2 billion. The next year, Redstone would announce his intention to split Viacom and CBS up again, with CBS looking more or less like it would have looked had Sumner simply sold the stations Karmazin approached him about originally. What went wrong?

Redstone did not pay a premium to the market for CBS, but the market was valuing CBS at a premium to Viacom. The deal was announced at the peak of an unprecedented advertising boom corresponding to the Internet bubble. CBS, almost all of whose revenue came from advertising, was trading in the public market as if that boom would continue indefinitely. As a result, although CBS shareholders as a group would own 54 percent of the equity (but none of the vote), CBS had contributed only 45 percent of the profit to the overall enterprise in the year of the acquisition. This disparity would grow over time as broadcasting revenue (CBS's primary contribution to the combination) grew less than 5 percent annually between 2001 and 2004 while cable channel revenues (the main contribution from the Viacom side) grew more than 15 percent annually.

Before the deal, Viacom had the least advertising exposure of any media conglomerate. After the deal, Viacom was the most advertising-exposed. Once the advertising boom ended, Redstone experienced a multiplier effect of value destruction. First, when the smoke cleared after the collapse of the advertising market, it became clear that he had given away more than half of his company for assets that were generating barely a third of the profit by the time Karmazin was dispatched. Without realizing it, Redstone had paid a massive premium for the CBS assets. Second, as market sentiment moved away from advertising-supported media, these businesses began to trade at a discount rather than at a premium to other kinds of media assets. The issue was not simply the market's perception of the current stage of the advertising cycle but a realization that secular trends were moving advertising dollars away from traditional media assets like many of those favored by CBS.

At the time of the CBS-Viacom announcement, the focus of the multimedia investor presentation was the synergistic value of the absolute scale afforded by the combined operations. Cross-promotional opportunities not unlike those touted in the AOL–Time Warner deal were center stage. The same supposed benefits of a studio owning a broadcast network that had done nothing for Disney after it bought ABC were again highlighted. Content is king. Lots of brands. But the real hard synergies were largely limited to those that resulted from combining the TV-station operations that were a modest part of the overall transaction. And the resulting sprawling operations would be significantly more difficult to manage. On paper, the deal was indeed a textbook case of shrewd media deal making. But the combination of few genuine synergies with the increased organizational complexity gave Redstone almost no margin for error. The subsequent history has shown that the passion to win can sometimes be deadly.

VIVENDI–UNIVERSAL: THE MASTER OF ILLUSIONS

We introduced Jean-Marie Messier in Chapter 1 in connection with his head-scratching $2 billion acquisition of an educational publisher, Houghton Mifflin. Messier's largest head-scratching acquisition was the massive three-way merger he engineered between Vivendi, Seagram (which had purchased Universal Studios from Matsushita five years earlier), and Canal+ (the largest French pay-TV operator, in which Vivendi already had a stake). The Vivendi portion of the transaction was valued at $44 billion, including $8 billion in Seagram debt, while the Canal+ portion represented an additional $15 billion.

Messier's acquisition of Seagram contains echoes of all the other value-destroying deals we have highlighted.

First, he overestimated the potential for synergies. There was little connection between the collection of largely European media and communication assets owned by Vivendi and the Universal portfolio. Messier insisted that the European distribution would somehow add synergistic value to Universal, which was primarily involved in U.S. film, music, and theme parks. These hoped-for synergies were almost entirely to be achieved by generating new revenues rather than eliminating costs from duplicative infrastructure. Notably, the most hyped synergy was the supposed value to an Internet platform created in conjunction with Vodaphone called Vizzavi, with 1.6 billion euros in committed funding from the partners. Vizzavi had been launched only in 2000 and was soon recognized as a failure, having never even entered the ranks of the top-ten French portals.[22] After investing 600 million euros, Vivendi was able to get its partner to take its stake for 142.7 million euros in 2002.[23]

Second, he wanted it too badly and he paid too much. The premium represented close to 50 percent above what the company had been trading at before deal speculation began. Long-suffering Seagram shareholders were thrilled initially and research analysts pointed out that the price was well above any reasonable basis for valuing the company.[24] Conversely, the English-language press expressed shock at the price and profound skepticism that the transaction would end well for Vivendi's shareholders. The *Financial Times's* Lex Column opined: "[T]he details [of the supposed synergies] are extremely sketchy. Consider . . . that Seagram has signally failed to find another buyer, Mr. Messier is giving too much value away."[25] An anonymous analyst was more direct: "This deal makes me weep. There are any number of obstacles why it could blow up: management is one, valuation is another and the man on the street is just not ready for the kind of services it will offer."[26]

Third, when being paid in shares rather than cash, deals that seem too good to be true probably are. As Sumner Redstone and Gerald Levin learned, when stock is involved, everyone is both a buyer and a seller and the outcome is a function of the assets sold, the assets received, and how they are run afterward. Shareholders of both AOL and CBS clearly did better in those deals than they would have done on their own, at the expense of shareholders of Time Warner and Viacom. In this case, everyone came out a loser because Seagram shareholders ended up with a stake in a company that Messier proceeded to drive to the brink of bankruptcy over the subsequent two years. At the time of the deal in 2000, Seagram had consistently and dramatically underperformed the market since CEO Edgar Bronfman had taken the reins from his father in 1994.[27] The premium being offered would go part of the way to making that back—except that Bronfman had placed the combined company in the hands an über–media mogul upon whose ambitions French corporate governance placed few meaningful constraints. By the time Messier was finally forced out of the company in 2002, the value of Seagram stock was far below what it had been before it obtained its "premium" in the original deal.

All of these value-destroying attributes of the largest media transactions are interrelated. Synergies can justify a financial premium, so overestimating synergies leads to overpaying. Belief in these synergies also provides a psychic cushion that leads moguls to minimize the real risks that flow from both the market's possibly incorrect assessment of relative asset value and the potential future mismanagement of the combination. With respect to the latter risk, the challenge of effectively managing such a wide-ranging collection of assets is often underestimated. The lack of real cost synergies in itself is strong evidence of the absence of operational connections between the units. Part of the objective of spinning fanciful synergy potential on the announcement of media deals may be not only to justify an otherwise unjustifiable price, but to justify the practicality of actually managing the assets together.

Shareholders have come to expect a certain amount of salesmanship in their CEOs. And since this is Hollywood, maybe they are even willing to allow some extra leeway for media moguls. Sarbanes-Oxley has added urgency to the question of when aggressive marketing, even by media moguls, becomes unacceptable deception. For regulators in the United States and France, Messier, who cannot serve as an officer or director of a U.S. company until 2013 and has paid millions in fines for his failure to provide transparency to shareholders, was viewed to have definitively crossed that line.[28]

Messier was known as the Master of Illusion in France,[29] but a variation of the core illusion inherent in Vivendi's acquisition of Seagram is shared by many other moguls and those who invest in them. The core content asset that Messier was hoping to leverage across his planned global distribution network was the fabled Universal Studios. That business was under largely the same ownership and management for almost thirty years. Starting with Matsushita's 1991 purchase of MCA, a dizzying succession of moguls have convinced themselves that they had the secret to unlocking hidden value from the studio.

The Japanese believed in the benefits of combining hardware and software; Seagram sold its book division but doubled down on music through the acquisition of PolyGram; Vivendi had a base of European distribution and content assets and added more afterward along with stakes in various U.S. content and distribution businesses; GE left the music and games behind but brought to bear an existing television network and cable channels and then added Internet assets, a Hispanic broadcast network, and some new cable channels; and now Comcast wants to connect the largest network of cable systems to the content factory.

The diversity of mogul approaches to the optimal configuration of media assets is reflected in the succession of strategic decisions relating to USA Networks made by this succession of owners of Universal Studios. Under MCA,

USA Networks was a 50/50 venture with Paramount when Matsushita bought Universal. Seagram bought out its partner to become the full owner in 1997 only to sell 55 percent of it the following year. Much of this divested USA stake was then bought back by Vivendi in 2001 (for over twice what Seagram had sold it for). General Electric, the current owner of Universal, bought in most of the outstanding USA stake in 2005.

As hard as it is to believe, this summary significantly simplifies the level of activity around the Universal asset over this period. Standing back and looking at the actual performance of the film studio in this time frame, however, one is struck by the apparent lack of any correlation between the results and either the ownership structure or the asset mix during this period. For all of the change going on around the business, two things remained remarkably consistent: The senior corporate decision makers remained thousands of miles away from the Los Angeles–based operations and for most of this period the same individual ran the business day-to-day.[30] The factors that actually drove performance in a given year were how many films were hits and how well the operations were run both in terms of cost efficiency (notably managing risk of flops by cutting losses quickly, avoiding expensive talent bidding wars, and using marketing dollars effectively) and revenue efficiency (by wringing every last possible dollar out of a hit across windows and platforms and using those successes to effectively develop new products to capitalize on audience goodwill). The ability to perform along these dimensions does not appear to be impacted significantly by the particular conglomerate ownership and asset mix.

Just as the line between selling and deception can be a fine one, the line between illusion and delusion can be as well. It is not always clear whether the moguls who pay huge premiums for these sexy media assets based on imagined synergies are kidding themselves, their shareholders, or both. In the case of Messier, the decision to use billions of dollars of the company's money as well as millions of his own to buy back stock as the shares sank further and further suggests a genuine belief that with just a little more time the hoped-for synergies would manifest themselves.[31] The incremental 6.4 billion euros in debt that resulted from these buybacks played a significant role in undermining the company's solvency.

The largest media conglomerates have made similar investment choices in recent years as the market has become more skeptical about the prospects for growth and synergies and more concerned about the looming threats to their established franchises. In total, the largest media companies

TABLE 12.5 Universal Studios Ownership Time Line[32]

	Existing Portfolio	Selected Acquisitions	Selected Divestitures
MCA (1962)	Universal Studios Putnam Berkley (Books) Universal Music Group 50% of Cineplex Odeon 50% of USA Networks		
Matsushita (1991)	Entertainment Hardware	1992 – Sci Fi Channel for USA Network (Undisclosed) 1994 – Minority Stake in Interplay (Undisclosed) 1994 – KB Theatres (Undisclosed)	1992 – Select Cineplex Odeon Theatres
Seagram (1995)	14.2% of Time Warner	1996 – Rising Tide Records (Undisclosed) 1996 – 50% of Interspeed ($0.2BN) 1996 – 50% of Brillstein-Grey (Undisclosed) 1996 – Interbrew Productions (Undisclosed) 1997 – 50% of USA Network ($1.7BN) 1998 – PolyGram NV ($10.2BN) 1998 – Wet 'n Wild (Undisclosed) 1999 – 50% of B&M (Undisclosed)	1996 – Putnam Berkley ($0.3BN) 1998 – 55% of USA Network 1998 – Cineplex Odeon ($0.4BN) 1998 – 14.2% of Time Warner 1999 – Select PolyGram Library Assets ($0.3BN) 1999 – Wet 'n Wild

Vivendi (2000)	Echostar	2000 – 51% of Canal+ ($11.5BN)	2001 – Havas Advertising ($0.4BN)
	Telepiu	2001 – Houghton Mifflin ($2.3BN)	2002 – Publishing Div. ($1.7BN)
	Telecom Hungary	2001 – MP3.COM ($0.4BN)	2002 – Echostar ($1.1BN)
	Havas	2001 – Elektrim ($0.5BN)	2002 – Houghton Mifflin ($1.7BN)
	MediMedia	2001 – USA Entertainment ($10.7BN)	2003 – Telepiu ($0.8BN)
	49% of Canal+	2002 – 41% of Groupe Cegetel ($4.3BN)	2003 – Telecom Hungary ($0.7BN)
	Vivendi Telecommunications	2003 – SportFive ($0.3BN)	2004 – Keolis ($0.5BN)
		2003 – Maroc Telecom ($1.4BN)	
GE (2004)	NBC with 29 owned and operated stations	2005 – 5.4% of VUE ($3.2BN)	2005 – 51% effective interest in Universal Studios Japan ($0.2BN)
	4 cable channels: CNBC, MSNBC, Bravo, and Telemundo	2006 – iVillage ($0.6BN)	2005 – Vogue Pay TV
		2007 – Oxygen Media ($0.9BN)	2005 – GameWorks (Undisclosed)
		2008 – Weather Channel JV w/ Blackstone & Bain Capital ($3.5BN)	2005–2008 – GigaTV (Undisclosed)
			2006 – Select Local TV Broadcast Stations ($0.6BN)
			2007 – MovieLink

bought back billions of dollars in shares even as their stocks have declined. There is nothing wrong with share buybacks in themselves—indeed, this form of return of capital would have been a far preferable use of resources than the misguided acquisitions detailed in this chapter. The shareholders hurt by buybacks of an overvalued stock are those who do not take the opportunity to sell. The fact that the moguls responsible for the latest wave of buybacks have uniformly not sold themselves—some have actually bought more shares—suggests a fragile grasp on reality similar to that of Monsieur Messier.

In the era of Sarbanes-Oxley, with prosecutors of the ferocity of Patrick Fitzgerald on the lookout for white-collar criminals, the difference between illusion and delusion for a CEO can represent the difference between incarceration and freedom. For shareholders, however, as a practical matter there is little difference at all.

13 | Media M&A That Works: One That Happened and One That Didn't

The legacy of the largest media deals in history is not a proud one. It would be a mistake to conclude, however, that media M&A can never create value. The case studies of the last chapter are cautionary tales but also provide clues as to when an acquisition should be pursued. Acquisitions are generally successful for one of three reasons.

First, strategy matters. If an acquirer is uniquely positioned to benefit from a combination—typically by being able to eliminate more duplicative infrastructure in a sector with economies of scale—both buyer and seller can benefit from a deal. Where the next-best buyer's price is topped modestly, and the bulk of the value of those synergies that are exclusively available only to the most strategic buyer are preserved for its own shareholders, an acquisition can make sense. Unfortunately, often several interested parties bring broadly comparable synergies to the same transaction, which inevitably results in a bidding war among them that shifts all the potential value to the seller.

But even being clearly the most strategic buyer is not enough to ensure that shareholders benefit. If the next-best buyer bids irrationally, or the seller has unrealistic expectations, the most strategic buyer must still be prepared to walk away. And as the Comcast–AT&T Broadband deal showed, even great operators with compelling strategic logic can want an asset too much.

Second, opportunistic situations arise. The challenge to making M&A work for the buyer is that the potential benefits from strategically sensible deals typically go disproportionately to the seller because of competition. A variety of circumstances can arise that limits that competition and increases the opportunity for a buyer to secure more synergy value for itself. A seller may have legitimate noneconomic objectives—a continuing role for certain key shareholders, a desire to retain certain cultural or operational features of the business for a time—that may provide an advantage to a particular buyer. In sales of broadly owned companies, these kinds of advantage are not unheard-of, although they are very rare. Even if the company is private but owned by a number of family members with different objectives, it is very difficult both practically and legally for the seller to aggressively pursue anything but the highest price in a sale.

Sometimes otherwise interested parties may be preoccupied or financially constrained. A difficult economic environment can provide a unique opportunity for well-capitalized companies to pursue targets if their likely strategic competitors for the prize are simply not in a position to participate. Although sellers usually try to time a transaction to maximize participation by interested parties, this is sometimes out of their control.

Third, there is nothing wrong with being smart or lucky. Every once in a while an asset that derives no strategic benefit from being part of a particular acquirer ends up being intrinsically much more valuable than expected. This is often explained in hindsight as the result of extraordinary vision but is more likely the result of luck. The ultimate value of ESPN was not really anticipated by Disney and Disney's ownership has had no apparent impact on its operations. Even Hearst's incredibly successful acquisition of a 20 percent stake of ESPN in 1990 for well under $200 million occurred only because a favorable tax ruling allowed the company to efficiently redeploy proceeds from an earlier cable system sale. The transaction occurred after CapCities/ABC declined to meet the modest asking price for the stake and it failed to attract interest from other parties for a year.[1] Indeed, early and substantial losses at ESPN were a major factor in driving ABC's 1985 sale to CapCities in the first place.[2] In any case, the dramatic appreciation of Disney's 80 percent stake in the channel was enough to counterbalance the significant underperformance of those core businesses imagined to be strategic in the overall CapCities/ABC acquisition.

Identifying undervalued assets is an important and valuable skill but not one that investors particularly look for in operating executives rather than investing professionals. It may make sense to invest in Berkshire Hathaway based on this quality in its CEO, Warren Buffett, but no media executive has shown an ability to systematically identify such opportunities. Where private equity investors have outbid strategic media companies for assets, it has in part been a function of their lower cost of capital through the aggressive use of leverage. Just as significant a factor has been situations in which these investors have taken a more aggressive investment thesis on a sector than the strategic operator. The track record of such calls has been decidedly mixed, but the broader point is that media management teams, in contrast to private equity firms, are generally backed for their operating skills rather than for their skills in outthinking the market.

One might conclude from this constrained list of circumstances in which acquisitions might make sense that we have eliminated all the fun stuff. And to be sure, part of the point of this book is to warn against the kind of fun had by media moguls at the expense of shareholders. But it would be wrong to assume that the only deals that would pass muster for a mature media company are inexpensive consolidating transactions where there is an idiosyncratic opportunity to avoid competition.

ONE THAT HAPPENED: DOW JONES–CBS MARKETWATCH

In 2004, Dow Jones shocked the media world when it announced that it was buying CBS MarketWatch for just over half a billion dollars. Since the Internet bubble had popped a few years earlier, no traditional media company had dared take on a major new media asset, particularly at a premium value. Dow Jones was about the last company anyone expected to blow open the wave of Internet 2.0 merger mania that followed. The conservative, family-controlled company, which owned the *Wall Street Journal*, some community newspapers, and a newswire business, had been more or less out of the acquisition business for over a decade—and for good reason. Its last major acquisition had been a Reuters competitor called Telerate that it was forced to sell at a loss of over $1 billion, costing the company president at the time his job.[3]

CBS MarketWatch was a leading personal finance site with its own reporters who tried to break market-moving news. The company was "1999's first hot initial public offering,"[4] skyrocketing from its offering price of $17 a share to $130 in its first couple of hours of trading. The stock settled at a valuation of over a billion dollars.[5] After the bust just a couple of years later, the company struggled like all its peers, cutting staff and falling as low as a few dollars a share.[6] MarketWatch nonetheless continued to grow and in 2004 was expected to have just over $80 million in revenue and $12 million in EBITDA.

Paying $519 million, or eighteen dollars a share, for the stock of a company that had $12 million of EBITDA seemed like a lot of money. Dow Jones itself traded in the public markets at the time at around thirteen times EBITDA rather than the forty-three times EBITDA it looked like they were paying. To this day, the conventional wisdom in some circles is that Dow Jones overpaid for MarketWatch in the same way it had for Telerate. A closer look suggests otherwise.

The cash on MarketWatch's balance sheet and the value of its tax shield made the effective price closer to $400 million. A number of parties participated in the auction for MarketWatch. These included some of the founding partners who still had minority stakes like Viacom (which owned CBS by this time) and Pearson (owner of the *Financial Times* newspaper). In addition, a number of other national news organizations like the *New York Times* and Gannett, owner of *USA Today* and a number of CBS station affiliates, also participated. All of these companies were "strategic" to one degree or another, having some existing infrastructure supporting personal finance content on- and off-line. There were around $10 million in costs that any of these buyers could have taken out of the company. These costs would come from eliminating duplicative public company costs, some overhead, and shared infrastructure. Most would also eliminate a $4 million annual royalty fee for the use of the CBS name.

Dow Jones may have benefited from these categories of synergies a little more than its competitors. Its existing personal finance Web assets might have been a little bit greater and the degree of overlap in overhead could have been a tad more pronounced. And replacing CBS with Dow Jones in the name of a U.S.-focused personal finance Web site was probably more valuable than replacing it with the *Financial Times* or even the *New York Times* or *USA Today*. But any of these companies could have taken out around $10 million in these cost categories, give or take a few million. As a result, in an auction, the benefit of these synergies would likely go entirely to the seller.

Dow Jones, unlike any of these companies, however, operated a real-time newswire service. This involved an entirely distinct pool of hundreds of dedicated reporters located across the river from those writing for the *Wall Street*

Journal. In addition to the reporters themselves, the operational and physical infrastructure required to run a real-time wire service was substantial. The only other companies to have a real-time wire service of scale were Reuters and Bloomberg, both of which had much smaller consumer-oriented operations and neither of whom was participating in the auction.

Dow Jones could take out an additional $10 million in costs that no one else participating in the auction could. The entire news operations of CBS MarketWatch could be performed without meaningfully increasing the size of Dow Jones's existing infrastructure. This significant advantage allowed Dow Jones to pay what was effectively a lower multiple than its own stock was trading at for a much faster-growing, highly strategic asset. Dow Jones paid pennies more than the next highest bidder, also suggesting that it was able to retain most of the value of the last $10 million of synergies that were unique to it for the benefit of its own shareholders.

In addition to these cost benefits, Dow Jones management hoped for a variety of potential revenue synergies. Might they be able to sell more *Wall Street Journal* subscriptions through the MarketWatch site? Would they be able to get higher advertising rates on MarketWatch because of what they are able to charge on WSJ.com? Wisely, Dow Jones left this speculative "upside" outside of the valuation it used to justify its purchase price. As Gordon Crovitz, who ran the Dow Jones electronic businesses at the time of the acquisition, told us, "In the end, we underestimated what we could achieve on the cost side and overestimated what we could do with revenue. The fact is that the consumer personal finance market is very different from that targeted by the online or print *Wall Street Journal.* Although we ultimately did improve MarketWatch's yields by including it in our advertising network, doing contortions to try to convince advertisers or readers that these markets are really the same ends up being not a good use of energy. I am just glad we sold this deal based on what we could deliver on costs and were able to bank the modest revenue benefits for our own account." [7]

ONE THAT SHOULD HAVE: MICROSOFT-YAHOO

One of the implications of our perspective on what makes a deal "strategic" is that eliminating overlapping infrastructure will be core to achieving the potential combination benefits. Most of that infrastructure is typically people. And more often than not, it is the buyer who gets to decide what part of the overlap is superfluous. It does not require unreasonable cynicism to consider the possibility that one reason that smart deals don't happen is that those likely to be eliminated fight to make sure they don't. Entrenched management can hide behind the shield of maximizing shareholder value to justify saying no to a strategic takeover, but a board would be wise to take an active role in ensuring this is not a pretext.

Let's look at Microsoft's attempted acquisition of Yahoo. In January 2008, Microsoft CEO Steve Ballmer announced an offer to acquire Yahoo for thirty-one dollars per share or $44.6 billion. This represented a premium of 62 percent above Yahoo's closing price of $19.18 per share. Yahoo was the leading Internet portal, offering users an entry point to the Web, a variety of search capabilities, messaging and chat-room services, free e-mail, and a wide range of shopping, information, and entertainment services. Microsoft hoped to combine Yahoo with its own MSN portal to achieve the scale necessary to compete effectively with Google in offering search-and-display advertising. Microsoft's announcement stated: "We believe . . . that the combination of Yahoo! and Microsoft creates a more credible alternative to an increasingly dominant player [Google] in the advertising industry . . . and are excited about what our two companies can do together to collectively forge growth opportunities in online services, search and advertising."[8]

Microsoft expected to create "synergies" with an annual value of $1 billion by achieving economies of scale in bringing customers to advertisers and "from eliminating redundant operating expenses, redundant capital expenses, and ensuring appropriate headcount allocation by function."[9]

If this were indeed the limit of Microsoft's synergy ambitions, then the deal was a typical example of mogul empire building at the expense of shareholders. MSN had been a continuous money loser for Microsoft since inception. In 2006, an attempt to improve the situation by generating its own search and ad-placement technologies (and withdrawing from an agreement to use Yahoo in these areas) had clearly failed. The offer to Yahoo was an attempt to redress the situation. But the premium of $17 billion above Yahoo's market value would hardly improve things if $1 billion were the true extent of synergies. This represented a pretax return of just 6 percent ($1/17 = .059) or an after-tax return of 4 percent on the $17 billion premium paid.

In fact, the potential benefits of combination were far greater than $1 billion. In 2007, Yahoo spent $1.6 billion on sales and marketing, $1.1 billion on product development, and $.6 billion on general administration.

Almost all of these $3.3 billion in expenditures were duplicated at MSN. Either they could be eliminated entirely, or offset by reductions at MSN, or, if retained, could generate greater efficiency and/or revenue enhancement by being applied across the increased joint number of users and advertisers. At a minimum, therefore, Microsoft should have expected to gain $3.3 billion in synergies by eliminating redundant expenses and, in its own words, "ensuring appropriate headcount allocations by function."[10]

The return on Microsoft's premium investment of $17 billion would have been really 20 percent pretax ($3.3 billion divided by $17 billion) or about 13.5 percent after-tax. This would have increased over time as the cost of the eliminated staff and outside services grew with wages and benefits. In addition, there were genuine (albeit smaller) revenue synergies. The effectiveness of Internet advertising has grown steadily over time as data from user behavior has been analyzed to improve ad placements and appearances. The amount of user experience has been an important part of this process, as shown by the greater rate of improvement of Google compared to smaller rivals. The combined Yahoo and MSN operations would have benefited from significant economies of scale in this area. Thus the acquisition premium offered by Microsoft (even when it later revised its offer to thirty-three dollars per share) was well justified economically.

The overall deal was almost equally well justified. A total of $9.2 billion of the $44.6 billion purchase price was covered by net cash holdings of $1.25 billion (cash of $2 billion less debt of $.75 billion) and securities (chiefly $7 billion of Yahoo Japan stock and $.75 billion of Google stock). The Yahoo Japan stock was especially valuable, since it operated the dominant auction site—the U.S. eBay position—in Japan. The net cost of the Yahoo acquisition was, therefore, just $35.4 billion. Postmerger operating income, including only the cost synergies of $3.3 billion, would have been almost $4.3 billion per year. That represents a pretax return of 12 percent or roughly 8.5 percent after-tax. Both numbers are well within reason for a company like Yahoo, with high returns on invested capital and high single-digit to low double-digit growth.

Of course, the ugly reality that underlay these numbers was that most of the fourteen-thousand-plus Yahoo employees (or an equivalent number of MSN employees) would lose their jobs. Microsoft attempted to sugarcoat this reality by pointing out that it was a growing company with expanding job opportunities that might absorb many of the displaced employees. Indeed, the point of providing the low synergy estimate may not have been just to manage analyst expectations so that it could easily outperform in the future, but to soften the blow of what was certainly coming Yahoo's way in the form of massive cuts. Even internally, Microsoft avoided providing any specificity around where the "synergies" would come from.[11] The following year Microsoft announced a ten-year exclusive agreement in search, which reproduced some of the benefits of an actual combination of the two companies. In addition to not capturing all of the potential benefits, however, the terms of the operating agreement were much less attractive to Yahoo's shareholders. Yahoo's share price has stubbornly remained well below twenty dollars a share.

But those at Yahoo seem not to have been persuaded, and with good reason. The exchange of catty letters between angry (and poorer) shareholder Carl Icahn and the board strongly suggests that these issues remained at the forefront of Yahoo's mind. *Portfolio* magazine published an amusing "translation" of one of the letters to Icahn from Yahoo chairman Roy Bostock. These letters are carefully crafted by lawyers and PR experts, so it often takes some work to divine the subtext. To rebut Icahn's charge that the board had not aggressively pursued the Microsoft deal, Bostock noted that they had in fact met with Microsoft and shared their "perspectives on transaction synergies, and other non-price deal terms." *Portfolio*'s interpretation of what Bostock really meant: "We explained . . . what protection conditions were non-negotiable, and which synergies were off-limits for at least three years."[12]

Yahoo rejected the Microsoft offer and moved decisively to thwart its implementation by intensifying its involvement with Google. The deal failed, and Yahoo's postdeal value fell well below. While one mogul—Ballmer—may have been operating sensibly, another—Jerry Yang of Yahoo—was not. In mogul dealmaking, it takes two to tango and asking for two good dancers is usually asking too much for the structural reasons outlined here. Yang may have in some sense been trying to do the right thing for the legacy of the company he created. But although Yang may not fit the standard profile of a media mogul, as the *Financial Times* pointed out with respect to his decision making, at least as far as shareholders are concerned, "entrenchment and attachment amount to the same thing."[13]

14 | Good Mogul: The Outperformers

The metaphorical media mogul who is the archetype of this book is surely to be feared—maybe by competitors, business partners, wives, subordinates, and assorted "close personal friends," but most strongly by shareholders. What these moguls have in common is the aggressive pursuit of strategies that have no logical connection to value creation and an apparent lack of interest in those that do. In place of effective strategies to bolster barriers to entry where they exist, through cooperation or targeted reinforcement of competitive advantage, we have seen destructive unilateralism and the relentless pursuit of costly, diversifying acquisitions. Where competitive advantage is absent, we have seen even more aggressive pursuit of acquisitions and misguided "visionary" strategies where a simple corporate commitment to efficient operations is actually called for.

Although our focus has surely been on these dysfunctional behaviors exhibited by the inhabitants of moguldom, we have not focused on them exclusively. The new regime at Reuters clearly reversed a destructive trend by radically simplifying its corporate structure and operations and targeting those areas where it could successfully reinforce its scale and customer captivity. The shareholders at McGraw-Hill benefited from over a decade of significant outperformance, up until the recent unprecedented credit dislocation, because company managers avoided the orgy of mergers and acquisitions and unremitting portfolio reshuffling pursued by many peers. The management at Dow Jones leveraged the scale of its professional newswire operations and the customer captivity in its consumer franchises to sensibly acquire an asset that would allow it to achieve a leadership position in the adjacent personal finance market in which it had been a minor player. Bloomberg created a multibillion-dollar media franchise almost out of thin air in the face of an entrenched incumbent by capitalizing on an underserved niche. Discovery Communications aggressively repurposed its evergreen content to launch new domestic and international channels while focusing operations to improve margins as it bolstered barriers to entry.

But, to be fair, we have not been particularly kind to the media conglomerates that soak up so much of the public imagination and attention in the sector. This, however, has not been out of spite. These companies have also soaked up far too much of the investing public's hard-earned money as the embarrassing financial returns highlighted at the very beginning of the book demonstrate.

Even among this group of miscreants, there has been a handful of bright spots. The period encompassing the early years of Michael Eisner's reign at Disney and the decade of the 1990s at Rupert Murdoch's News Corporation were happy times for shareholders. Both have been the subject of many fawning articles, books, and even widely read Harvard Business School case studies.[1] In each case, however, the conventional wisdom about what drove these highly unusual examples of superior performance by an old-fashioned media conglomerate is fundamentally misguided. A close examination of the regimes producing these outcomes suggests a complex and fluid mix of good and bad mogul behavior. Understanding how these results were really achieved—and distinguishing between the intertwined positive and negative influences that underpinned that performance—is instructive in considering how they might be achieved again.

THE EISNER MAGIC

Michael Eisner ran Disney for twenty-one years, starting in 1984. The Harvard case ends in 2000, before the angry and expensive litigation involving former executives Jeffrey Katzenberg and Michael Ovitz and the corresponding shareholder unrest that consumed much of Eisner's final years at the helm. An exhibit in the case tracks Disney's stock price from the year before Eisner joined until the end of 2000 and shows it to have grown more than twice as fast as the overall market during that seventeen-year period.

Although Eisner did not do well at managing public perceptions during his last turbulent years at Disney, he has been remarkably successful at mythologizing the source and nature of his earlier achievements. This story line suggests that the moribund Disney which Eisner took over in 1984 had failed to fully leverage its core brands in all potential markets or to exploit the synergistic opportunities available from working across divisions. Eisner instituted a "synergy boot camp" called Disney Dimensions, during which senior executives from across divisions were forced to spend sixteen hours of daily undistracted indoctrination for eight straight days that included cleaning the bathrooms at the parks. There was even a permanent "Synergy Group" that reported directly to Eisner with representatives from each business unit, and it was widely known that the best way to get a big bonus was to demonstrate commitment to synergy. To spur creativity on an ongoing basis, Eisner convened weekly "gong show" meetings at which employees would brainstorm new ideas for further exploiting the franchise.

There is no disputing either that Eisner did these things or that the Disney stock outperformed during the period. There is, however, a very significant question as to whether the two had anything to do with each other. From Table 14.1, it is clear that the only ten-year periods during which Disney outperforms are those which are weighted toward the very earliest years of Eisner's involvement with the company. A close examination of the case data makes it clear that during the first five years of Eisner's leadership, the company dramatically outperformed the market. Starting at around 1989, however, Disney performed roughly in line with the market until it began to substantially underperform at around the time of the announcement of the acquisition of CapCities/ABC in 1995.

What really happened at Disney between 1984 and 1989 that created so much value that the entire 1984–2000 period continues to show such impressive returns despite the unimpressive results of the 1990s? Was it really the impact of the gong shows? Had Disney previously just failed to notice that Mickey Mouse was a great brand that called out to be exploited?

When Eisner took over Disney in 1984, the business certainly had a lot of problems. After the deaths of Walt and Roy Disney in 1965 and 1971, respectively, the company struggled to regain its bearings. It would take

TABLE 14.1   Disney Compound Annual Growth Rates Versus S&P

	Compound Annual Growth Rates			
	'84–'89	'89–'95	'95–'00	'84–'00
DIS	54.8%	11.1%	8.0%	22.2%
S&P	16.6%	9.6%	16.7%	13.9%

Source: Harvard Business School Case 9-701-035

almost twenty years and huge investment for their successors to realize Walt's vision for Orlando with the opening of Epcot in 1982. The last animated megahit had been *The Jungle Book* in 1967 and the live-action division was largely dormant. The focus seemed to be on replicating past successes, with an emphasis on sequels in the film division and licensing a Japanese reproduction of Disneyland in the parks division.

Whatever the faults of the pre-Eisner Disney, it could not, however, be criticized for failing to exploit the Disney brands. After introducing Mickey Mouse in 1928, Walt immediately licensed the image to a pencil tablet and quickly followed with dolls, watches, records, and magazines, both domestically and internationally. The film and television divisions were not far behind with both animated and live-action fare. Then came the theme parks and the live-action touring shows. Throughout, Disney showed remarkable effectiveness in identifying and managing its licensees and determining when a business had reached adequate scale on its own to bring in-house. This was all notably achieved without a single acquisition of size. Even during the dark days in the decade before Eisner joined, Disney managed to launch its home-video distribution division, which would ultimately become a remarkable cash cow for the company, as well as one of the earliest and most successful cable channels.

Eisner and his team did reinvigorate the filmed entertainment division during the 1984–1989 period, but not in the ways generally supposed. The first successful major new animated feature, *The Little Mermaid*, did not hit theaters until late November 1989 and was not released in Europe and Asia until the following year.[2] *Beauty and the Beast*, *Aladdin*, and, most notably, *The Lion King*, would not come until the 1990s. The product that revitalized the TV and movie divisions in fact owed little to the legacy of Walt Disney and the company's supposedly underexploited brands and everything to the legacy of Eisner and his colleagues from earlier days at Paramount, Jeffrey Katzenberg and Rich Frank.

Under the supervision of a tough, hard-nosed operating executive, Frank Wells, the team went about replicating the successful strategy it had pursued at Paramount: producing low-cost story-driven fare that used no-name talent, or those willing to work cheaply for one reason or another. The old joke about the team's doing its casting outside the Betty Ford Clinic reflects both their approach and what a different cultural time it was when publicity surrounding going into rehab was thought to hurt rather than help one's career. Whatever one might think of the R-rated *Down and Out in Beverly Hills*, about a dysfunctional rich family with a variety of sexual, psychological, and eating disorders, or *Splash*, with its partial nudity, it would be hard to argue that their financial success was owed to their ability to leverage the Disney-family franchise. The television production business was built on inexpensive syndicated fare like *Siskel & Ebert at the Movies* and series like *The Golden Girls*, whose connection to the Disney brand and values was as tenuous as that of the company's feature films.

An even cursory look at the numbers during these early Eisner years, however, reveals that the greatest value creation came from the impact of more than doubling the revenues and margins at the theme parks that were already in place when he arrived. The incremental profit generated by the theme parks during this period was more than twice the increment contributed by the filmed entertainment division. How this was achieved had little to do with any synergies extracted from the now booming filmed entertainment division. Although *Pretty Woman* might have been effectively used as the basis for a ride at an adult-oriented theme park, we are not aware of efforts to make significant use of this or any other of the low-budget hits that drove the success of Disney's sister division. Instead, the new Disney management team employed more conventional methods: They charged a lot more and dramatically increased capacity.

When Eisner joined Disney, the company had not significantly raised park admission fees in years. Starting immediately, prices were increased every year at each of the parks, sometimes more than 25 percent. Ticket prices at both Disney World and Disneyland had more than doubled by 1990. Close to half of the incremental revenue in the division during this period came just from the price increases. In addition, the old Disney's preoccupation with the customer experience had led them to limit the number of daily visitors and close for one day a week to ensure proper upkeep of the facilities. These capacity restrictions were eliminated. The team also invested in expanding and updating both the attractions and the associated hotel facilities, but the vast majority of the explosive profit growth came from applying basic revenue management techniques to the existing park franchise.

The purpose of debunking the conventional wisdom related to the most successful aspects of the Eisner regime at Disney is not to belittle them. Rather, our belief is that by properly identifying the source of this success, future generations of executives and investors are more likely to repeat these results. The magnitude of the benefits available to shareholders when talented executives focus intensively on efficiently managing both the cost and revenue side even of businesses that do not have inherently compelling competitive advantages can still be truly breathtaking.

By contrast to the efficient operating initiatives of the early years, Eisner's efforts to launch entirely new businesses to further exploit the brands or to take over operations that once relied on licenses for high-margin revenue have been mixed at best. Retail, fast food, indoor play parks, nightclubs, and book and magazine publishing have all either been shuttered or linger on with marginal profitability owing to their subscale operations. The synergy story is similarly unconvincing. The acquisition of CapCities/ABC seemed to undermine the profitability of both ABC's broadcast network and Disney's filmed entertainment operations. Even apparently "strategic" transactions like the Family Channel came at prices that even the company ultimately conceded were unjustifiable.[3] Much of what has been described as "synergy" sounds an awful lot like efficiently managing the multiple revenue streams of a hit, for which there are plenty of successful examples in companies that achieve comparable results through third-party arrangements.

It is difficult to assess whether Disney's results are better as a result of the gong show, Disney Dimensions, and the Synergy Group. What the numbers make clear, however, is that even if they are, this at best represents a modest part of the story. A more interesting question is why a now former media mogul like Michael Eisner is so committed to a story line that is so at odds with the clear financial and operational evidence. Is it that the culture of media moguls denigrates efficient operations in favor of visionary leadership? Is it that an interpretation that calls attention to efficient operations would highlight the failure of Eisner's later years as the focus of the filmed operations shifted to blockbusters and his legacy became more associated with costly acquisitions and expansions like the Disney Stores and Euro Disney? Or is it just the inevitable curse of the media mogul that successful executives eventually come to believe their achievements flow from an inherent magical power to harness the creative beast?

THE MURDOCH MYTH

Rupert Murdoch is the most complex, creative, and contradictory of the moguls, both personally and in the conglomerate he has built.

The company is by far the most international of the media conglomerates, yet has shown a unique appreciation for the dynamics of local markets, running the business as a multilocal network of franchises rather than a single global operation. Despite this distinctive international sophistication, the company has frequently overpaid or operationally misfired in efforts to translate successes in one market to another without adequate thought or preparation. The company prizes operational excellence and is frequently best in class in profitability while at the same time harboring unprofitable trophy properties that have no serious prospect of performance improvement. Murdoch has demonstrated unparalleled determination and ruthlessness in achieving his business aims but displays surprising sentimentality about certain assets. The same assets that have been the object of inexplicable sentimental attachment have been known to be suddenly abandoned without the least apparent regret. Murdoch has also shown a distinctive ability to combine genuinely brilliant strategic insight with daring and flawless execution to create extraordinary shareholder value. Often, however, much of that value has been eradicated by initiatives that displayed the daring but neither the strategy nor the execution.

Murdoch took over his modest family newspaper business in Australia in the mid-1950s upon completion of his studies at Oxford after the death of his father. He entered the U.K. market in 1968 with the decidedly downmarket tabloid *News of the World,* and crossed the Atlantic through the purchase of three struggling newspapers in San Antonio in 1973. He continued to buy and improve the performance of English-language newspapers on all three continents for the next ten years, dramatically increasing cash flows through a combination of wise investment and aggressive operational rationalization and union negotiations.

While building his global newspaper network, Murdoch made some modest investments in other media: a few magazines in the United States, a television channel in Australia. The modern conglomerate News Corporation, however, was built up between 1983 and 1990 through the acquisitions of 20th Century Fox in film; HarperCollins in consumer books; the Metromedia TV-station group, which became the basis for the Fox network; the Triangle Group, which made News the largest publisher of U.S. consumer magazines; and the money-losing Sky Television and Inter-American Satellite Television, which were acquired to enter the direct-to-home broadcast markets in the U.K. and the United States, respectively.

The periods of greatest outperformance for the modern News Corporation begin in 1990. These results are helped not by how well the company was doing at the time but by how poorly it was doing. The unprecedented acquisition binge—which included the largest and second-largest media deals to that date—was financed with debt, and the company was effectively bankrupt. Negotiations with banks began in October 1990 and their outcome was far from clear.

How did Murdoch escape death and proceed to outperform the market for the ensuing decade? There are two main sources of the superior performance and neither of these is the explanation most often cited—the launch of the fourth broadcast network in the United States. We turn to the two clear successes of the 1990s and examine the uneven legacy of Fox broadcasting.

1. Fly Me to the Moon: The Birth of BSkyB

Most significantly, at the same time that Murdoch was trying to manage his debt load, he was engaged in a costly battle in the U.K. between his fledgling Sky satellite service and British Satellite Broadcasting (BSB), owned by a consortium of blue-chip British media and retail companies that had the backing of the regulatory authorities. The Hollywood studios benefited from the fevered competition for exclusive content by extracting exorbitant fees for the pay-TV rights for their new releases. Murdoch put his foot on the pedal and quickly developed a low-tech alternative to BSB's distribution platform, fought off regulatory challenges, and flooded the market with over a thousand salespeople, some of whom went door-to-door offering attractive introductory offers for the equipment and service. By the time BSB launched its service a year after Sky, Murdoch already had over 1 million households.[4]

Murdoch understood that U.K. satellite television was a market where there was a first-mover advantage and was willing to risk the very survival of his company to secure it. Being first allowed Sky to achieve economies of scale that BSB would never be able to attain.

Other unique aspects of the U.K. broadcasting environment made the value of achieving this position particularly powerful. The dominant provider of entertainment programming was the government-run British Broadcasting Corporation, a venerated but sleepy organization whose objectives were defined in terms of what the public should see rather than what they wanted to see. Although the government had allowed the establishment of two new privately owned terrestrial channels, the variety of available programming was a fraction of what was available elsewhere. Murdoch perceived that although the British television audience thought it was satisfied, providing broad viewing choice for the first time would create an explosion in demand. Furthermore, a variety of geographic and regulatory restrictions made cable competition both modest in total scale and highly fragmented, so the first-mover advantage achieved by Sky over BSB would extend to the entire pay-TV domain.[5]

Although much better capitalized, by late 1990, BSB was losing four times as much as Sky. In November, the two businesses merged, giving Murdoch 50 percent ownership and control of the combination, which together was losing well over 10 million pounds a week. Within nine months Murdoch would eliminate more than half the combined cost base of the businesses by eliminating well over half the staff, rationalizing the channel lineup, and renegotiating the outlandish movie deals that the studios had previously secured.[6]

The studio negotiations also served to cement the renamed BSkyB's competitive advantage for some time to come. The annual output of two to three major studios is required to provide enough film product to support a competitive pay-TV film channel—the arrangements are actually called "output deals" and avoid negotiation over particular film titles. The fact that BSkyB was now the only major outlet in the U.K. market to serve the pay-TV window gave significant incentive to the studios to renegotiate long-term deals. The studios knew that BSkyB could otherwise simply not renew when the current agreements lapsed at little cost to itself and great cost to the studio. Furthermore, BSkyB staggered the termination dates of the renegotiated output deals so that in any given year not enough would come up for renegotiation to allow the immediate creation of a competing channel. As a result, if a cable company in the future succeeded in outbidding BSkyB for movie rights—something that given BSkyB's relative scale would probably be foolhardy to try in any case—it would have nothing it could practically do with the rights for at least a year. It would then need to try to outbid BSkyB again the following year in the hopes of obtaining enough rights to establish its own pay-TV film channel.

Murdoch succeeded in completing his renegotiations with the banks in February 1991 on the back of the Sky-BSB merger and his commitment to essentially undo the largest of his acquisitions to date. In June 1991, Murdoch sold most of the company's magazines from its $3 billion 1998 acquisition of Triangle and some others for a mere $650 million, leaving him with only *TV Guide* and the money-losing *Mirabella*. The losses from Triangle were dwarfed, however, by the benefits from the BSkyB coup. In December 1994, BSkyB would raise $1.4 billion in an IPO, almost a billion of which was used to pay back News for its investments to date. When the smoke cleared after the offering, News would own 40 percent of an independent FTSE 100 company with a total market value of almost $7 billion. By the end of 2000, News Corp.'s share of BSkyB would itself be valued at over $8 billion.

The strategic vision that drove the BSkyB success was grounded in Murdoch's deep insight into the U.K. satellite TV market. No one better understood or could better navigate the local idiosyncrasies related to the structure of the pay-TV business, the regulatory environment, and consumer preferences. Murdoch tried to apply this local success to markets around the world with dramatically different dynamics, even at one point planning to package these businesses into a separate public company on the theory that they could sensibly constitute a single integrated business. His experiences in the United States and Asia reflect just how different these businesses that he proposed to combine were.[7]

In 1993, Murdoch purchased 64 percent of Star TV, a satellite broadcaster that reached across much of Asia, for $525 million and then paid an additional $345 million for the balance in 1995. In 1996, the business was still losing $100 million a year. If BSkyB served a unitary audience and market in a political context that Murdoch understood better than anyone, it could not have had less in common with Star. Although the potential foothold in the vast Chinese market is what attracted News, the service reached dozens of different local markets with distinct industry structures, languages, mores, and rules.

The modest audience for the initial pan-Asian English-language programming attracted little advertising revenue and the service was routinely stolen and redistributed by cable operators around the region, limiting the opportunity for subscriptions. As it turned out, the service had questionable authority to broadcast in mainland China, a critical fact that Murdoch had somehow overlooked.[8] Although the business grew significantly more sophisticated over time, localizing the content and distribution strategies, its target date for anticipated profitability was postponed on an almost annual basis.[9] Indeed, when the business finally did break even in 2005, this was achieved based on the performance of the markets outside of China, most notably in India. To this day, the operations in China are at best break-even.[10]

The U.S. satellite TV market was as unlike the U.K. as Asia but in entirely different ways. Cable was highly developed and there were already two fiercely competitive satellite pay-TV operators who battled each other and the cable operators for customers. Unlike in the U.K., where BSkyB controlled all of the key pay-TV content and could charge their cable competitors high prices for the right to redistribute their channels, in the United States, ESPN, HBO, and Showtime had already secured the most valuable premium movie and sports content. Murdoch embraced and then abandoned a series of expensive but ultimately impractical routes to participate in this difficult market starting in 1983.[11] By the time he achieved his prize over twenty years later in 2003 by obtaining control of DirecTV, it was clear that the lack of a two-way connectivity in an era of high-speed broadband services would forever relegate satellite to competing for rural and low-end customers.

Barely three years after finally gaining control of DirecTV, Murdoch announced he was selling this interest to John Malone as part of a complicated tax-free trade for Malone's large News Corp. stakes.[12] The decision came shortly after CNBC reported that Murdoch had begun to refer to the asset as the "turd bird" and enabled him to eliminate Malone's threats to his control of the overall enterprise.[13] His willingness to jettison his long-held romantic ideal of a global satellite network when the industry dynamics called for it reflects Murdoch's leadership and vision. Despite his ability to book a gain on this last trade in the long-running satellite saga, Murdoch's shareholders could be forgiven for wishing he had experienced this epiphany somewhat sooner.

2. Read All About It: Newspapers

The question of why News Corporation dramatically outperformed its peers for the decade of the 1990s answers itself when one looks at its asset mix. In 1990, News was the only major conglomerate that had any newspapers at all. In fact, fully a third of News's profits were derived from this asset class in the fiscal year ending June 30, 1991. Notably, the second-largest profit contributor at the time was the magazines (18 percent), most of which were sold at a loss that June. We have already shown that shares of pure newspaper companies performed far better than both the conglomerates and the market as a whole until very recently.[14] It should not be surprising then that the sole conglomerate that was predominately a newspaper company should significantly outperform the others.

News was not just any newspaper company. The largest English-language publisher in the world, Murdoch had transformed the structure of the two markets he now dominated—the U.K. and Australia—by rationalizing the cost base and consolidating his leadership position, achieving twice the scale of the next competitor. In Australia, News commanded around 70 percent of the newspaper market. Murdoch largely exited his limited position in the U.S. newspaper market, where he had mostly purchased competitive tabloids in major markets, although he repurchased the *New York Post* in 1993. The impressive results of the overall division come despite the fact that the *Post* reportedly loses around $50 million every year with no serious prospect of substantial improvement.

By 2000, newspapers still composed around a third of News's profits. But in the interim the company had grown substantially, fueled by over $20 billion in new acquisitions after the BSkyB IPO through the end of 2000. Almost none of those acquisitions were of newspapers, and in fact Murdoch was a net seller of papers during the period because of his divestitures in the United States. Despite the historic role of newspapers in the success of News, Murdoch's decision to reenter the newspaper acquisition game with gusto in 2007 with the $5.7 billion purchase of Dow Jones—well after the chronic decline of newspapers had been established, in a market in which News had limited other assets from which the properties could derive cost savings and at values well above those commanded even when newspapers were in robust health—is unlikely to replicate the benefits of his earlier unique exposure to this once indomitable asset class.

3. Broadcasting: Who Outfoxed Whom?

From afar, the biggest growth engine of News Corporation appears to have been the Fox broadcast network, which was still in its infancy in 1990. And this is certainly true. But the growth was driven by an additional $9 billion in station-group acquisitions—$3.5 billion for New World in 1997 and $5.4 billion for Chris-Craft in 2000—on top of the initial $2 billion paid for Metromedia in 1985 and a number of other significant investments explored here. The real question then is whether this investment created superior value for shareholders.

The most significant development at the network after its dramatic launch was Murdoch's daring decision to submit a preemptive bid for NFL rights in 1993, which CBS refused to come close to matching. The conventional wisdom about the Fox network in the 1990s is that this fateful decision "made" the network. The move unambiguously accelerated Fox's ascension among the broadcast networks. It also unambiguously accelerated the decline of the overall attractiveness of the business into which Murdoch so much wanted full acceptance.

Football rights had been subject to the same informal gentlemen's agreement that made all of broadcasting wildly profitable even as ratings declined in the face of cable growth. At the time of Murdoch's gambit, the three networks were poised to potentially renew at lower prices their four-year deals for three different slices of the football pie: ABC had *Monday Night Football* for $225 million a year, NBC had the American Football Conference at just under $200 million a year, and CBS had paid $250 million a year for the NFL. These packages, in total, cost the networks around $2.5 billion over the period.[15]

Murdoch secured the NFL rights by paying $395 million a year, almost 60 percent more than CBS. CBS, which had claimed to lose money on the previous deal, offered to go as high as $295 million in the face of the challenge. ABC and NBC quickly offered slight increases to $230 million and $218 million a year, respectively, to renew their deals, increasing the total amount flowing from the networks to around $3 billion over the next four-year period.

The question of whether News "made money" on the deal is more complicated than it first seems and has been the subject of much debate and speculation. It is not simply a question of adding all the operating costs to those of the rights and subtracting the advertising revenues generated for the network during the broadcasts. The financial impact on the owned stations must be considered as well. More important and more difficult to quantify are the spillover effects on ratings of adjacent programming specifically and on the network generally, which data suggests could be substantial.[16] Nonetheless, in an unguarded moment, Murdoch himself said: "Did we over pay? Of course we did."[17]

But the real strategic justification for News was articulated by David Hill, who ran Fox Sports Television: "This was all about an affiliate play. A lot of Fox affiliates were UHF [and not required to be carried by cable operators under so-called must-carry rules] . . . [I]f we had football, every cable channel in the country would carry us."[18] So, the argument goes, News received significant incremental benefits from apparently overpaying, owing to the potentially sustainable ratings improvement that became available across the entire network. However, two aspects of this reasoning make it seem less than compelling. First, it was obviously not believable to News's accountants, who required the company to write down $350 million of their $1.58 billion deal in 1995.[19] Second, if this fixed the affiliate problem, why did the company need to spend $9 billion over the next several years to buy more of its own stations?

Even if one suspends disbelief and gives News the benefit of the doubt over the positive spillover effects from the decision to overpay, we must give equal time to the negative spillover effects. These are substantial and dwarf even the most generous interpretation of the positive ones. First, in football itself, it is true that Murdoch's decision had only a modest impact on the prices paid overall in 1994 for rights. But the impact at the next renewal in 1998 was dramatic, resulting in eight-year deals together totaling $12.8 billion. This represented a doubling of the annual cost, which now exceeded total ad spending on games by $1 billion.[20] This escalation in bidding set off by News's original "strategic" decision extended to other sports as well, so that in 2002 the company had to write down close to $1 billion across rights contracts for the NFL, Major League Baseball, and NASCAR.[21]

Nor did the negative spillover effects end at the shores of sports rights. Producers smelled the blood in the water and knew the discipline that had been exercised by the networks in years past was at an end. For the first time, when established series came up for renewal, they held an auction, and sure enough, they were not disappointed. In 1998, NBC was forced to increase its price per episode of *ER* from $2 million to $13 million after Fox and ABC each offered close to $20 million an episode.[22]

Other historic profit-maximizing practices fell by the wayside as networks fought openly and often irrationally for affiliates, stars, and programming. Indeed, as suggested by the remarks of Fox's Hill, getting affiliates to switch—which is achievable only by bidding up so-called network comp payments for the privilege—had become central to their strategy. In 1994, Murdoch shocked the broadcasting world by paying Ronald Perelman's New World station group $500 million to switch the affiliation of ten stations. Ironically, none of the projected benefits in performance materialized,[23] although the impact on overall levels of network comp now being sought by affiliates across the industry was real enough. As a final insult, Perelman threatened to switch affiliation again and sell the group to another buyer in order to force Murdoch to pay up once again.[24] "He had me over a barrel" was how Murdoch justified the breathtaking $3.5 billion ultimate price tag for the underperforming station group that already carried his network.[25] The net result of Murdoch's decimation of the prevailing culture of cooperation among networks was billions of dollars in value shifting from their shareholders into the pockets of producers, station owners, film stars, and athletes.

At the time of the initial NFL deal, the Fox network had met its business plan targets through clever programming and distribution choices that enticed the three incumbents to allow the new network an affiliate membership in the established highly profitable club. News could have pursued its sports ambitions in any number of alternative ways. ESPN and TNT had partnered in 1994 to obtain *Sunday Night Football* rights without upsetting the established order and Fox could have established a similar partnership with one of the existing players. As it was, the new environment created by Fox's decision resulted in ESPN's jettisoning its partner and more than doubling what the two had paid together for the right to do it alone. Alternatively, at the time Fox could have bought up all the auto-racing rights it would ultimately target for its FX channel and other sports that did not have well-established pricing and ownership. As it was, News Corp.'s shareholders learned the hard way an important corollary of Groucho Marx's adage about not wanting to join a club that would have him as a member. If full membership requires burning down the club, it is probably not worth the effort.

In contrast to his approach to broadcasting, Murdoch's building of his cable channel franchise was inspired and has created significant shareholder value. Murdoch's creation of Fox News drew on his unique strengths as a creative executive—only his global populist perspective could appreciate the demand for a new news channel with a strong editorial voice (the inside joke of "fair and balanced" notwithstanding) that violated every one of the peculiarly American, and ultimately rather dull, journalistic conventions. FX leveraged Murdoch's low-cost operating expertise to repackage a variety of content that might not otherwise be fully exploited around a themed general interest channel targeting Fox's core demographic. Both required significant investment, but neither entailed expensive acquisitions.

Fox Sports Net, on the other hand, did require investment. News paid in $350 million to equalize ownership in the initial joint venture involving $2 billion worth of combined assets with John Malone in 1995.[26] The venture invested an additional $850 million to secure 40 percent of Rainbow's sports channels and add them to the network, and News eventually bought out Malone for $1.5 billion.[27] But by being first to establish a national footprint of regional sports networks and buying up critical local sports rights before their value—particularly in the context of a national network—was fully appreciated, Murdoch again identified an area where the first-mover advantage did apply.[28] And the combination of his global expertise in sports programming and appreciation for intensely local content enabled him, after some false starts, to develop a remarkably resilient and profitable franchise.[29]

How then to assess the contradictory legacy of Murdoch the mogul? The numbers suggest that among the media conglomerates, News Corp. is the most consistent performer. But it is still not a consistent outperformer of the market as a whole. It seems that for every genuinely brilliant strategic move, there is a genuinely misguided one. For every MySpace, there is an IGN. The appreciation for operating efficiency is consistently undercut by a willingness to participate in or launch self-defeating bidding wars. The genius of the Fox network launch was undermined by the foolhardiness of the NFL assault. The clear-eyed willingness to abandon a twenty-year quest by selling DirecTV was quickly followed by an inexplicably sentimental obsession with owning the *Wall Street Journal* at almost any price.

There will be multiple books and already are countless articles detailing the ins and outs of Murdoch's ultimate realization of his dream of owning Dow Jones.[30] The very short version is that he paid the controlling Bancroft family more than twice what it was worth. The business generated just over $300 million in EBITDA in the last twelve months during which it was public, which is likely more than it has generated since. Murdoch's purchase price of $5.7 billion, a 66 percent premium at the time, represented eighteen times EBITDA. The *New York Times* has consistently traded at six to seven times

EBITDA recently, which is a substantial premium to where other newspapers have traded in recent years. And as far as synergy is concerned, there is no evidence that the combination has enhanced the operating performance of Dow Jones or News Corp.'s other assets. Along with the *Wall Street Journal* franchise, which actually represented a minority of Dow Jones profit, Murdoch got an apparently unsalable collection of community newspapers and a slowly declining collection of business information assets facing significant new competitive pressure from the Thomson Reuters combination.[31]

More concerning from a shareholder perspective is the amount of time the Dow Jones acquisition still commands of the CEO. Although the paper represents well under 10 percent of the value of News, some reports suggest that he was devoting half his time to its design and still spends one to two days a week on the property.[32] Murdoch's unique ability to pull a rabbit out of a hat has led some to give him the benefit of the doubt on Dow Jones even after his accountants forced the company to quickly write down the value of the acquisition. But Murdoch has also shown a unique ability to make wildly optimistic predictions with respect to recently acquired "gems." Star TV, it will be recalled, was meant to break even by 1995 but did not turn a profit for a decade.[33] This pales in comparison to Murdoch's recent contention that the *Wall Street Journal* would add $300 million in online subscriptions each year for the next several.[34] The online *Journal* was already the largest paid-subscription news business on the Web, having grown its subscriber base to 1.1 million since its launch in 1996, but still generated barely $60 million in subscriptions in 2007.

We hope that the Dow Jones purchase is not Murdoch's anticlimactic last hoorah, for he alone possesses all the elements of the perfect mogul. Murdoch values and knows how to achieve operating efficiency in assets that have no meaningful structural barriers to entry. He understands the centrality of industry structure to the possibility of achieving competitive advantage and has shown exceptional creativity in managing competition in ways that reflect that environment. He has shown a willingness both to walk away from businesses that have lost their competitive advantage despite their popular appeal and to stay with more mundane enterprises that generate exceptional returns. He leverages his global sophistication to enhance rather than homogenize nuanced, locally based operating strategies.

It is never too late to let your inner good mogul reemerge.

The Future of Media: The End of the Curse?

We are neither technologists nor futurists. We are probably not the right people to ask about the next hot consumer device or how people will communicate around the globe in twenty years. This book is about how and why large media companies have performed poorly as a group. The answer to these questions has to do with a fundamental and consistent disconnect between the strategies pursued by the moguls and structure of the industries in which they operate.

The form that our media will take in the coming years will be determined, however, by the changing structure of the key media segments that make up the industry mosaic. How the current and next generations of moguls respond to the challenges and opportunities presented by these changes will also have an impact. Despite this general uncertainty, the dire predictions of the "death of media" are both overblown and misguided.[1] There is no evidence of "less" media being made available to consumers or professionals—quite the contrary. The ubiquity of media—its ability to reach us and our ability to access it anytime, anywhere—has resulted in our spending more and more of our waking hours interacting with media of one sort or another.[2]

The growth in media consumption has not translated into growth in media profit. We have spent a great deal of time describing and analyzing a wide range of business segments operating at different points along the media value chain. Although each has had a distinct structure, they overwhelmingly share a single characteristic. The explosion of digital media has had a significant impact on the media business, and not in a good way. The foundation of our approach is the simple insight that barriers to entry are the source of value creation for shareholders. Digital media systematically lowers the cost of entry into most markets—it is far easier to start a local Web site than a local newspaper. This cannot help but color our overall prognosis for the industry.

From the perspective of a media consumer, the ease with which new entrants are able to come to market is a good thing. Even if certain activities are curtailed because they are no longer as profitable, this will be precisely because a variety of alternative competitive media has drawn the attention of a once captive audience. For example, local newspapers have cut their costly original national and international coverage. But the Internet gives individuals real-time access to other local and international news outlets as well as blogs and citizen journalists. Together, these new sources provide a deeper, more textured collection of viewpoints on any given news event than could have been provided by the outlets upon which newshounds once relied exclusively—no matter how much more publishers once invested in coverage. Concerns that the resulting information overload will mean that more is really less underestimate the ability of media entrepreneurs to develop compelling new products to guide consumers through the cacophony of content.

More broadly, content creation has always been the part of media that has the lowest barriers to entry. On the one hand, this has meant that pure content businesses have generally not been very profitable, but on the other, it has ensured that there has never been any real risk that creative genius would have trouble finding expression. The general lowering of barriers in all segments of the media value chain has provided content creators with a broader range of options. They now both have more tools at their disposal to craft creative product without outside help and are in a better position to disintermediate those who once made a living packaging and delivering the fruits of their labor. The end user of media should anticipate an era of unprecedented plenty.

From a shareholder perspective, these developments are not a cause for celebration. Nor, however, are they a cause for despair. The digital revolution predicted by Goldman Sachs's 1992 "Communicopia" report is in full swing and, as they anticipated, any period of such profound change will produce both winners and losers. Where we differ with the "Communicopia" approach is in our conclusion that the structural nature of this change has ensured, and will continue to ensure, that the losers will outnumber the winners.

Within traditional media businesses that enjoyed limited protection to start with, the biggest losers are likely to be the "talent" that has managed to suck out all the "excess" profits from any successful creative ventures. To the extent that the competitive environment—or illegal downloads or whatever—leaves less excess profit to suck out, one would expect the businesses to do about the same but the real-estate market in Malibu to take a hit. In entertainment ventures, the talent includes not just the performers but the writers, the producers, and the creative executives.

More broadly, the winners will be those who focus on efficient operations and the losers will be those who chase high-priced acquisitions—Internet or otherwise—on the theory that the "solution" to their problem is to buy growth in the form of higher-growth businesses with questionable synergies. Efficiency in content businesses has many elements, but effective talent management is critical to the cost side and getting the most out of that content is critical to the revenue side. Both require sustained management attention. Digital media acquisitions and investments have, unfortunately, absorbed a disproportionate amount of management time and attention among conglomerates. Time Warner, Sony, News, Viacom, CBS, NBC Universal, and Disney together have completed over one hundred digital transactions since the Internet bubble burst in 2000. These have ranged from early stage investments of under $1 million to major strategic acquisitions of over $1 billion and represented almost every conceivable business model, subject area, and geographic region.

The Internet has greatly reduced established barriers to entry in media. But the fact that the Internet is disruptive of incumbent businesses with competitive advantages does not mean that every disruptive business has competitive advantages. Indeed, the very environmental factors that allow a new entrant the opportunity to attack an established franchise are those that will make it all the more challenging to establish a new franchise of its own.

But our biggest complaint is not that every one of these deals was necessarily misguided or overpriced—although given the sheer breadth of them, and the feverish competitive environment for many, we would be surprised if most were not both. Rather, the relentless process of identifying and adding and integrating these businesses has become a troubling and prevalent distraction to the senior leadership. Moguls seem to long for anything to divert their attention from the crucial business of just running their companies efficiently. Internet acquisitions have stepped in to fill that void.

Within those businesses that do have competitive advantages but find them increasingly under threat, the winners will be those that cooperate with their similarly situated peers and tailor their strategies to reinforce their positions. There is indeed a long history of cooperation in some media segments like broadcasting. Although the increasing competitive market pressures have made it harder to maintain the integrity of these often informal regimes, they have also made it that much more imperative. The continuing failure of the major film, music, and book companies to agree on common online platforms and approaches to date is indicative of the industry's recent track record in this regard.

The losers will be those who fritter away their advantages. This can happen when a mogul becomes preoccupied by petty rivalries or implements strategies that do not buttress or leverage their barriers. Increasingly, however, the most dangerous tendency is for moguls to refuse to recognize when competitive advantage has disappeared altogether. These moguls continue to foolishly reinvest cash flow that would be better returned to shareholders.

Talent, again, is likely to come up short. Traditional media franchises that once had predictably high profits were happy to share the spoils with the talent. This reflected in part a sensible strategy of cooperating with those inside the organization who contributed to the business's competitive advantage. Often, however, it also represented management indifference to efficient operations in the face of plenty to go around. So, for example, journalists and editors who commanded high salaries disproportionate to their contribution to sustaining the barriers to entry in the newspaper business will now face radical changes in living standards.

The general direction of structural change in the media industries is relatively easy to anticipate. The approach of the moguls to the next wave of transformation is harder to predict, although their track record to date should temper expectations. One cause for optimism, however, is the fact that many of the largest media companies have relatively new leaders. Given the predictability of the actuarial tables, other new leaders will emerge in short order.

Our hope is that the urgency of the new challenges leads the moguls of the future to more closely align their behaviors with the structural imperatives of their industries. We would not have written this book if we did not believe such a change in approach could make a dramatic difference in the performance of these companies. To that end, we propose six principles for the good mogul to live by as a guide to action in the media industry of the coming era.

DARE TO DREAM

A satirical MySpace page set up under the name of Rupert Murdoch lists "world domination" as among his identified general interests.[3] Based on the moguls' relentless track record of acquisitions, the public could be excused for imagining that this is the subject about which they are most likely to dream. Indeed, moguls themselves are forever accusing one another of harboring precisely these kinds of secret aspirations.[4]

Whether moguls do or do not actually dream this way, our admonition relates to a very different kind of reverie. The dreaming we would propose is of how the industries in which they operate could be most effectively organized. Ignore for a moment the actual or imagined obstacles imposed by egos, regulators, unions, and the legacy infrastructure that defines the current organization.

If done right, what will typically emerge is an industry that bears little resemblance to the one currently in operation. Excess capacity will be eliminated from the system and a variety of physical operations will likely be consolidated in sometimes entirely new locations, different players will specialize in different niches, a variety of ways of cooperating will surface all along the value chain from joint procurement to joint marketing efforts, and some functions may not even continue to be undertaken by the industry at all as everyone outsources to the same few efficient large-scale providers.

Hold that image.

This is a lot harder than it seems. In the best of circumstances, undertaking this kind of exercise is made difficult by the relentless daily demands and decisions faced by executives. The constant need to choose short-term tactics often crowds out the ability to reflect in this way. In the case of media moguls, the challenge is magnified by the fact that this vision is completely at odds with their inclinations and aspirations. But the best way to judge the wisdom of a strategy is to consider whether it moves you and the industry closer to this ideal.

The most compelling example of this is in telecommunications infrastructure. An ideal world would consist of local hybrid networks—wireless and fiber—with exclusive territories cooperating across regional boundaries. The resulting structure would minimize costs, maximize potential service quality, and not coincidentally, generate high profits at reasonable prices. The overlapping competitive investments of current cellular, cable, and wire-line companies are moving away from—not toward—this ideal.

KEEP IT LOCAL, KEEP IT FOCUSED

When looking for a media business that might have the prospect of producing superior returns over an extended period of time—whether as a manager, an investor, or just an employee—ignore all the conventional wisdom about the attractiveness of high growth, global footprint, electronic distribution, and the like.

At the end of the day, superior returns are made possible only by barriers to entry, and barriers to entry are easier to defend within tightly defined boundaries. Within media, this typically means either narrow geographic territories or, more likely, product niche. Specialized media have the double benefit of increasing the likelihood that scale can be achieved quickly and decisively and that the nature of the audience—by virtue of whatever shared activity, inclination, or demographic defines the niche—will lend itself to developing customer captivity. And as we have seen time and again, there is no better defense than multiple sources of competitive advantage.

At the corporate level, it is certainly possible to run a diversified conglomerate of specialized media franchises, each with high barriers to entry, all simultaneously defended with equal vigor and intelligence. In practice, however, it is hard to come up with a media company that this describes. Indeed, most companies that have generated truly superior returns over truly extended periods of time—from Coke to Intel to Wal-Mart—generally have in common a relentless focus by top management on a single core business. In media, the decision to enter new unrelated business lines is associated with a growing uncertainty with respect to the continuing vitality of the existing ones. But this is precisely the time when management should intensify its concentration on the business challenges rather than diffuse its focus by entering new businesses in which it is likely to have little expertise.

Almost all of the bad moguls who appear in these pages did not start out that way. Whether it is in the nature of media or just the nature of power, over time these moguls have strayed from the early principles that allowed them to achieve their initial success. And the dark path they have taken is inevitably away from the local and the focused toward the diversified and the global. The good-mogul characteristics Eisner exhibited in his early years at Disney are not recognizable in his later ones. Even Lew Wasserman, in some ways a model of how a mogul should behave, eventually began making foolish diversifying acquisitions in his later years at the helm. The travails in the Redstone family have been caused by a variety of misguided diversifying investments, not just CBS but notably in subscale game software and arcade businesses. It is a bitter irony that the "solution" to this problem may be that they are forced to sell the original business upon which the dynasty was built—National Amusements, one of the most efficiently operated, regionally focused movie theater chains in the world.[5]

As we have said before, a company's most precious asset is the time and attention of senior management. The opportunity cost to a franchise under siege of a diversifying acquisition or investment is likely to be substantial and potentially terminal. At a minimum, it is almost certain to accelerate whatever disturbing trends led management to look elsewhere for a more exciting and less troublesome business to run or build.

EFFICIENCY IS COOL

The challenges faced by even the strongest media franchises are going to make efficiency more rather than less important in the coming years. The cultural objection of media moguls to caring about efficiency in some cases seems potentially insurmountable. Convincing a mogul to focus on efficiency is like selling abstinence-only sex education in high school. Both efforts are well intentioned and well grounded in the facts. And both have almost no prospect of success.

We have no simple solution to this conundrum. We would observe, however, that attracting mogul attention to revenue management is easier than attracting attention to cost management. One possibility is that the mogul simply outsources the cost side to another executive whom he compensates based on achieving success in this area. Something like this seems to be what Rupert Murdoch has done. Murdoch gave a largely free hand to COO Peter Chernin and his lieutenants to run the film studio as profitably as possible until Chernin's resignation in 2009. Murdoch instead preoccupied himself more with how to monetize that output most effectively on a global basis and what new underserved niches—like, say, a populist conservative news voice in the United States—can be economically developed given the changing marketplace and their existing assets on the ground.

In certain media segments, inefficient operations are lionized by employees and segments of the broader community as actually essential to the public interest. Leaders of family-owned newspaper dynasties have long been encouraged to ignore reader and advertiser preferences as well as financial discipline in designing the core product in favor of producing what the reportorial classes believed was best for society (and, maybe not coincidentally, themselves). In an industry with insurmountable entry barriers, this approach had its virtues and in any case was sustainable as long as the barriers held. But all barriers eventually fall, and when they did in this case, what was exposed was a management infrastructure understandably with little sense of its customers' desires or how the business makes money. The values promoted by the professional journalism industry essentially left these businesses unarmed when facing the new more competitive battlefield for ideas and dollars. By persuading these families to ignore efficient operations, however honorable their intentions in doing so, these supposed protectors of journalism unambiguously hastened the decline of these great newspaper franchises, many of which now face bankruptcy.

DON'T BE SUCH A BIG SHOT

Convincing moguls that efficiency is cool is only slightly more challenging than persuading them that cooperating doesn't make you a wimp. Winning a contested auction, stealing a high-priced artist for your own label, getting a local television station to switch affiliation, outbidding everyone else for valuable sports rights—such is the stuff of mogul "victories" about which they love to crow. Although the mogul is inevitably positioned as a strategic genius who returns from the battlefield as the conquering hero, almost without exception the true source of the "success" is rather more pedestrian—he paid too much.

The cash outlay understates the price of such imagined triumphs. We have seen over and over in the case studies presented that the spillover effect of individual decisions to bid irrationally is considerable. Such behavior quickly infects interactions far beyond the domain implicated by any particular overpayment.

But if destructive competition is a communicable disease, cooperation can be similarly contagious. By finding even small areas of collaboration, moguls can begin to build an alternative universe in which mutual benefits replace mutual assured destruction as logical ends of the path followed. Unfortunately, in many of the segments in which moguls operate there are absolutely no barriers to new entrants, so cooperation provides little upside. Even in these instances, however, there will almost certainly be gains to be had elsewhere from having established a basis for future profitable partnership when the opportunity does arise.

WATCH YOUR BACK

Great media businesses don't stay that way. Behind many of the consistently worst-performing media sectors lies a forgotten history during which robust returns were generated. The movie business was once dominated by a few family-controlled studios that carefully avoided expensive intra-industry squabbles. Each had a stable of stars, writers, and directors who operated under long-term arrangements with a particular studio. There was no poaching and cordial relations were maintained under which reciprocal deals to lend talent for particular projects were routinely worked out. Even the music industry managed to produce a decent return in an earlier era. Then, the scale requirements of manufacturing, marketing, and distribution were so overwhelming that only a handful of industry leaders could effectively perform this service and major artists could not move so easily among labels.

Today's apparently impregnable fortresses—whether Google or Moody's or Bloomberg or BSkyB—will eventually be scaled in ways both expected and surprising. The need for unrelenting vigilance is heightened in the current environment. Companies face a variety of potentially disruptive technologies and customers' willingness to respond unsentimentally and opportunistically is unprecedented. A constant reassessment of the strength and reinforcement of the source of competitive advantage is called for.

Launching a suite of adjacent niche cable channels ensures both that relative share of the growing channel capacity is maintained and that the core franchise is protected. Building proprietary software to integrate your data products into customer work flow both enhances customer captivity and helps to dissuade new entrants from attempting to develop their own competing data products. Using your established customer base to launch a social network or establish a specialized marketplace improves results and protects against future competition. Developing customized product extensions and applications in cooperation with users increases switching costs. The possibilities are as multifaceted and nuanced as the challenges that face established franchises.

The accelerating speed of change does not only destabilize established barriers to entry. Where an atmosphere of cooperation and trust prevails among a small group of industry competitors, a volatile external environment can test even the most well-established collaborative regime. Just as even the best marriage requires work to ensure it does not go astray through indifference or miscommunication, the core competitive advantages needed to protect the integrity of even apparently entrenched modes of mutual assistance must be monitored with vigilance. Increased competition with other forms of media may make it more tempting for the established television broadcast networks to break ranks, but in fact continued cooperation is more important than ever. And where there is no history of cooperation, the threat of new common enemies can sometimes serve as an impetus to establish a new kind of relationship. Google's willingness to supply search for AOL—and for AOL to welcome paying for this service—would have seemed incredible just a few years ago. Cooperation among nearby regional newspaper publishers to establish a single shared printing, sales, and distribution infrastructure may once have seemed inconceivable. It isn't anymore.[6]

THERE IS MUCH TO BE SAID FOR DYING WITH DIGNITY

No one likes to admit they have lost it. Many of us look in the mirror and see that same hepcat who wowed the ladies in college more than twenty years ago. A harmless self-deception. But when a franchise has lost its competitive advantage, the resulting self-deception is anything but harmless to the shareholders.

It is not in a mogul's nature to admit defeat, even after the war is long over. So, rather than milking a declining franchise and returning the proceeds to shareholders, moguls often decide to reinvest them in projects that have little prospect of generating an adequate return or paying a "synergistic" value for an unrelated but attractive asset where no synergy exists.

Verizon's decision to invest over $20 billion to build an entirely duplicative broadband infrastructure—with a product called FiOS—to compete more aggressively with cable in selected high-density markets rather than simply increasing the dividend appears to be the starkest example of this. This investment amount is greater than the entire equity capitalization of Time Warner Cable at the end of 2008. Indeed, the capital spending required for Verizon to connect a home is substantially greater than what the market values cable competitors' existing connections. Many independent analysts have accordingly stated that there is no realistic prospect of earning enough to justify this investment but fatalistically conclude that it is unrealistic to expect moguls to act otherwise: "With FiOS Capital spending costs alone in the range of . . . two-and-a-half times the entire enterprise value of its closest competitor, Verizon's FiOS surely faces a dizzying challenge in earning a desirable return for shareholders."[7]

Verizon does not provide enough data to allow anyone to precisely calculate the return on investment from FiOS. But one doesn't require a calculator to know that building a second broadband infrastructure is not the most efficient way to organize the ecosystem. The danger to the overall competitive environment in which Verizon operates is that the introduction of excess capacity—particularly if the folly results in forced change of management and dramatic asset write-downs—will put pressure on the generally disciplined pricing regime that has prevailed between it and the cable operators with whom it competes in providing broadband access and other services.

On the acquisition front, the decision to reseparate CBS from Viacom was justified in part based on the belief that a different shareholder base would be attracted to CBS's high steady cash flow in contrast to the sexy, faster-growing assets that remained with Viacom. CBS management apparently thought differently when it decided to pay $1.8 billion for CNET, a leading Internet content and commerce site focused on the technology segment. The price represented almost a 50 percent premium to the public share price of CNET, which had been available for sale for years.[8]

CBS had strong positions in the TV broadcasting, billboard, and trade book publishing markets. It defies common sense to imagine that CNET would be more "strategic" to it than any other suitor in the sense that we have defined *strategic*. Yet according to the "background to the transaction" section of the public filings in connection with the deal, none of the more obviously strategic Internet-oriented buyers ever expressed serious interest in CNET—much less bid on the asset. CBS claimed the deal to be strategic based on the supposed complementarity of the Web traffic, the ability to cross-promote, and most peculiarly, the supposed assistance it provided in building CBS's overseas presence (the deal moved CBS international exposure from 11 percent to 12 percent). A Gartner analyst wondered aloud what the two companies had to do with each other: "It's a peculiar mix," he said.[9]

In the cases of both Verizon and CBS, it is worth reminding the moguls behind them that there is no shame in giving the money back to the shareholders.

The curse of the mogul is that while their careers invariably begin with a great insight that creates value for shareholders, they somehow lose the thread of what the actual source of that initial value creation was. We started this book with the stark data that show unambiguously just how far from that course they have wandered as a group. In subsequent chapters, we tried to show where they have gone wrong and light the path toward shareholder righteousness. Although it may be fun to dramatize the instances of particularly egregious value destruction, in most cases the moguls in place appear to have the capabilities to generate superior results. The evidence suggests that over time moguls lose their bearings, one way or another. And for this, shareholders are at least partly to blame.

The public has been the great enabler of the most damaging strategies by allowing itself to be seduced by the often incoherent visions spun by the most out-of-control moguls. By permitting the constant mogul misdirection toward engaging topics largely unrelated to corporate performance, shareholders have dug their own financial graves. The principles outlined here are not just for the moguls themselves, but for shareholders to consider in determining whether to call management to account or, more likely, simply to sell. By consistently failing to do either, shareholders encourage the very culture that has produced these anemic returns for generations. In the end, shareholders get the moguls they deserve.

Postscript

Despite its provocative title, *The Curse of the Mogul* stands for a quite benign proposition—that media businesses are subject to the same economic rules as other businesses. What has distinguished media companies over the last generation, we argue, has been their persistently poor performance. This observation, too, is not controversial and is based on stock prices and operating results familiar to anyone with access to an Internet connection.

A book based on an innocuous premise and widely available data would seem unlikely to attract interest, much less stir up controversy. Yet *Curse* has been the subject of dozens of reviews, articles, and essays in general media like *USA Today*, *Time*, and *Star* magazine (a "Hot Pick of the Week" no less); major business press outlets like *The Wall Street Journal* and *Fortune*; and even trade journals serving media and finance professions like *Variety* and *Asset International*—to say nothing of appearances around the blogosphere. If *Curse* has something original to contribute it is the logical connection between these two incontrovertible truths, one conceptual (media is a business like any other) and one empirical (media businesses have underperformed most others). The breadth and depth of the reaction to the book may stem from the very fact that the basis for its central argument had been hiding in plain sight for so long.

The Curse of the Mogul argues that the poor performance of the media industry is the responsibility of media company management's stubborn refusal to accept the economics of basic business strategy. The book demonstrates how the key tenents of media conventional wisdom, which have driven media strategy for decades, appear designed to ensure disastrous results. And it shows how even media companies, when they focus on reinforcing genuine barriers to entry and efficient operations, can yield superior results.

But is there any evidence that all this publicity garnered by *The Curse of the Mogul* has actually changed the way that media companies operate? Or, at the very least, is there any evidence of a more skeptical attitude by the mogul-enablers—the journalists, bankers, research analysts, and, ultimately, investors who have historically served as cheerleaders for a long line of value-destroying strategies and transactions?

Not nearly enough time has passed to definitively answer these questions. The media deals that have been announced since the book went to press nonetheless provide some preliminary clues. The fact that there has been less M&A activity than in previous years is in itself a hopeful sign given how much of media value destruction has been attributable to the sector's overreliance on acquisitions to satisfy its unhealthy growth fetish. This, unfortunately, has more to do with the overall economic environment than media companies having permanently decided to eschew acquisitions. More promising is the continuing trend toward media conglomerates narrowing their range of operations and exiting noncore and subscale businesses. Time Warner's spin off of AOL and Cox's sale of a controlling interest in the Travel Channel are recent examples.

The deals that did happen, however, suggest that old habits die hard. The very same qualities that made the "dirty half dozen" of media mergers and acquisitions highlighted in chapter 12 so unsuccessful are evident in many of these as well.

The 30 percent premium The Walt Disney Company paid in its nearly $4 billion dollar acquisition of Marvel Entertainment is particularly striking in light of the fact that the majority of Marvel's value is tied up in long-term licensing deals to other studios. *Spiderman* resides with Sony, the *X-Men* with Fox, and the *Incredible Hulk* with Universal. Even when Marvel produces films itself, the distribution rights are committed to other studios far in advance. So not only was the recent hit *Iron Man 2* distributed by Paramount (a Viacom company), but *Iron Man 3*, along with the upcoming *Thor*, *Captain America*, and *The Avengers* will be as well.

In theory, once the term of these licenses expire, Disney could take them over rather than bid them out as Marvel always had. But this begs a fundamental question—why was Disney the only major studio that never seemed to win when Marvel auctioned these major film licenses and rights in the past? Could it be that the other studios' skills at exploiting these particular kinds of brands were stronger and so were prepared to pay more for the rights? If so, were Disney to decide later to keep the license rather than agree to be paid by a competitor who valued it more highly, this would constitute a dissynergy not a synergy.

On the conference call announcing the Marvel deal to investors and analysts, Disney's CFO conceded that there would be no significant cost benefit from combination. "This deal is not principally driven by cost savings," he said in response to an analyst's request for detail on the magnitude of potential expense reductions.[1] Yet the company insists that it will be able to generate significantly greater revenue from the Marvel franchise.

Revenue synergies without cost synergies are rare beasts indeed. Revenue synergies are typically the result of overlapping functions in a merger where the stronger performing team is kept in place and its best practices are applied across the firm. How likely is it that an acquirer with no experience in an area will do a better job at producing revenues than the veterans at the acquired company?

Disney is certainly a global leader in brand licensing. But all licensing is not the same. And the primary driver of the Marvel acquisition was Disney's consistent failure at establishing a meaningful presence in the tween boy market. Serving this energetic demographic clearly requires different skills and is reached through different marketing channels than Disney's core franchise. How many tween boys do you think were excited that their favorite action hero is now under the direction of the people who brought you *Cinderella*? Starting with Time Warner's combination with AOL, most of the worst deals happen when an acquirer is frustrated by its inability to successfully enter a market viewed as more attractive than its own. Rather than wisely conclude that it is not a market in which they should operate, they decide to overpay for someone else who already does.

The point is not that entering adjacent markets is necessarily misguided. Indeed, this is often a crucial element of successful strategies to reinforce barriers to entry. But calling something an adjacency and deriving genuine strategic benefit from it are two different things. The benefits from building adjacencies are that it can leverage the existing fixed cost infrastructure and potentially strengthen the captivity of customers. The former would imply precisely the kind of synergies that are absent here and the latter would require a newly discovered commonality in taste between tween girls and tween boys. The bottom line is that no amount of showmanship can change the fact that in the absence of meaningful cost savings, paying a significant acquisition premium is unlikely to be a good deal for investors.

The Marvel acquisition may ultimately turn out well for Disney shareholders. If it does, however, it will more likely be because the still untitled Sony-produced fourth Spiderman movie (without Tobey Maguire) unexpectedly sells $2 billion in tickets—complemented by superheroic results from the rest of its planned slate of Marvel films to be produced or distributed by others—rather than that there were any synergies.

Unlike the Marvel deal, the acquisition of a controlling interest in the Travel Channel by Scripps Networks Interactive (SNI) at a $1 billion valuation made unambiguous strategic sense. Despite its sexy digital sounding name, SNI is overwhelmingly a pure cable channel company owning, most notably, Home and Garden TV, Food Network, and DIY Network. The company was established in 2008 when the E.W. Scripps newspaper company spun its cable channel assets (along with its misguided Internet shopping engine investments) into the new entity. As discussed in chapter 8, as an aggregator rather than primarily a content creator, cable channels are a rare scale business in the traditional media firmament. Cox had no other channels and wisely sought to exit. SNI was a leader in nonfiction programming, although in terms of absolute scale it remained a midsize player that could benefit from increased scale. What's not to like?

The price. Like Comcast's acquisition of AT&T broadband, strategically sound does not guarantee financially sensible. The problem in both instances was that where the same asset is equally strategically sound for multiple players, the seller invariably pockets the value of those strategic benefits as the competing suitors bid up the value. Here, SNI had the advantage that complex tax issues made Cox unwilling to sell to Discovery, who arguably was an even more strategic owner. Discovery, however, was not SNI's only rival for The Travel Channel. News Corp., whose ownership of a controlling interest in the National Geographic Channel made it an equally good buyer, also coveted the asset. And it only takes two enthusiastic strategic buyers to ensure that "successful" buyer's shareholders are unlikely to fare well.

Market reaction and coverage of both these transactions, although not uniform, at least suggests the end of the era when analysts and commentators alike immediately declared the conquering mogul a visionary genius after each new acquisition. To be sure headlines like "Is Disney's Chief Having a Cinderella Moment"[2] and investment banking research reports like "Make

Mine Marvel!"[3] are reminiscent of the free pass moguls have long received to do as they wish with their shareholders' money. But these now seem more likely to be balanced with competing narratives under captions like "Disney-Marvel: A Superhuman Price?"[4] or "Scripps Pays $1B for Travel: Good Price . . . ? Depends How You Figure It."[5]

The most important media deal of recent years by far, however, was Comcast's acquisition of NBC Universal (NBCU) from General Electric for $30 billion. The reaction to early rumors of the potential transaction was skeptical bordering on scathing. Many articles about the combination cited *Curse* specifically and suggested that the deal epitomized precisely the kind of mogul bad behavior criticized by the book. As such, the deal was characterized as not strategic and extraordinarily expensive. Although we are not big fans of the transaction, we think both of these charges are unfair.

From a strategic perspective, the NBCU transaction results in significant cable channel consolidation. Comcast is contributing its own cable channels and cash to gain 51 percent of the combined entity, which will generate over 80 percent of its cash flow from the cable channels. In the same way that the SNI/Travel Channel is strategic, this one is as well. Although most of the public focus has been on how Comcast's cable system business will be able to strategically leverage these channels, the film studio, and the TV network in the context of the broader competitive environment, the real strategic story is in the rationalization of the cable channel infrastructure. Even if there are no regulatory restrictions placed on what Comcast can do to secure eventual approval of an overall transaction, we are skeptical that this content/distribution combination will help either the content or distribution side of the equation.

From a cost perspective, $30 billion does indeed seem extraordinarily expensive given the performance and prospects of NBCU. But Comcast is not writing a check for $30 billion. More than half of what Comcast contributed to gain control was its own subscale collection of less-than-premium cable channels. The actual value of Comcast's channels is a fraction of the over $8 billion attributed to them in the deal. So both sides are both a buyer and seller in this transaction and the effective premium being paid *to* Comcast by GE is probably greater than that being paid *by* Comcast.

That said, the media assets being contributed by NBCU are much larger than those contributed by Comcast, so this is still no bargain. In other words, even though Comcast's cable channels are being overvalued by a bigger *percentage* in the deal than the NBCU assets are, the fact that

NBCU is four times larger swamps this benefit to Comcast shareholders. Furthermore, history has shown that the practical challenges associated with effectively managing such a diverse set of largely unconnected media assets is more likely to be underestimated than overestimated. Our point is simply that, particularly when the value of the cost savings in combining the channel businesses is taken into account, the transaction is not nearly as expensive as portrayed.

One might ask why, if the Comcast acquisition is not a good deal, even if less bad than some have suggested, Comcast's stock went up when the deal was announced. Comcast's share price performance generally is actually as positive a sign that investors have begun to internalize the fundamental principals of *Curse*. The stock popped when the details of the transaction were revealed simply because the terms were better than expected. In addition to the attributes already discussed, a number of creative structural mechanisms were used both to ensure that the cost of the remaining 49 percent of the venture would not be prohibitive and to assuage concerns that there would be any further significant diversifying investments.

Ever since Comcast's unsuccessful unsolicited bid for Disney in 2004, shareholders have assumed that the company was committed to broadening its horizons well beyond its core cable business. When Time Warner spun off its cable business in 2009, shareholders had an opportunity to compare the value attributed to largely comparable companies with a single big difference—one, Time Warner Cable, was broadly held by the public and led by a CEO who vociferously insisted he would never buy media content assets while the other is controlled by a family that has made clear its desire to diversify in precisely that way.

The verdict of shareholders could not be clearer. Time Warner Cable has consistently traded at a significant premium to Comcast. This is despite that fact that Comcast has maintained higher margins in its core cable business and is arguably a superior operator. The NBC Universal acquisition has reduced the size of the discount that Comcast trades at both because it was less expensive than expected and it eliminated the uncertainty regarding how the company's mogul ambitions would be manifested. But the discount is still there and is likely to remain, suggesting that for the first time in media, the market has imposed a mogul discount.

Execution and pricing issues aside, the real verdict of the Comcast-NBC Universal transaction will hinge on the future of the cable channel business on which they have made an enormous bet. These businesses still trade at a huge premium to cable systems, reflecting their continued growth and astonishing free-cash flow margins. As we detailed in chapter 8, the strength of the structural competitive advantages of these packages can be easily underestimated. They are not insurmountable, however. The digitization of media has made the question of the unbundling of content one of how and when not whether. In a world where individual shows, events, and movies are available when and where a consumer wants it will be no better for cable channels than the ability to avoid having to buy all twelve tracks on a CD has been for music companies. How this inevitable unbundling plays out for video will involve complex and extended negotiations among numerous players in the media ecosystem, including regulators. It will be interesting to see whether the ownership of cable systems will help or complicate Comcast's efforts to maximize the long-term value of the channels it owns.

Ironically, the incumbent media companies best positioned to respond to the potential threat of so-called over-the-top digital distribution of all manner of content over the Internet are those, like Comcast, with a pipe into the home. "Over-the-top" distribution refers to the transmission of entertainment content in a way that can be viewed on any device with an Internet connection—without the need for a cable box at all. As televisions themselves increasingly have Internet connections and more and more content is made available "over the top," the speculation is that progressively more homes will "cut the cord" and stop paying for cable service.

But cord-cutting is not necessarily bad for cable companies. Evidence to date is that "in home" consumption of bandwidth-needy content will continue to increase—whether over the top or via cable. And with only two pipe providers likely to be in a position to provide that bandwidth capacity—the historic local telephone and cable monopolies—their future could be bright regardless of how this all plays out. This would be true at least as long as the two incumbents in each market behave intelligently on pricing, the regulators allow them flexibility in charging for their capacity and no radical new technology allows others to deliver comparable video streaming to the home. Indeed, an argument can be made that the cable companies actually do better in a pure "over the top" world because they can avoid the significant incremental capital expenditure requirements of the existing cable box based system.[6]

The scenario under which the cable and telcos are the only survivors of the digital media wars who maintain their current profitability has been called "The Dumb Pipe Paradox."[7] Readers of this book should find nothing paradoxical about it. Media shareholders seem to have a deep psychological need to believe that they will be rewarded for backing the right creative visionaries rather than dumb pipes. But about the only sure thing in the creativity business is that the visionaries are smart enough to keep as much of the value of what they create for themselves as the market will bear, leaving little for the shareholders. The retail end of the media business where the dumb pipe sits has always been the most resilient in the face of changes in technology and consumer demand. In between the content creation and the local distribution remain the aggregators who must continue to up their game if they are to stay ahead of the digital onslaught.

Digitization does create opportunities for new businesses and new models to serve consumers increasingly overwhelmed by the modern era of unprecedented media plenty. But it creates those opportunities more democratically than ever, making both establishing and maintaining competitive advantages more challenging than ever. The successful mogul of this era will need to exhibit a rare combination of operating excellence, relentless vigilance, and profound humility.

Notes

Introduction: The Curse of the Mogul

1. See Jonathan A. Knee, "Who's Afraid of Media Cross Ownership," *Regulation*, Summer 2003.

2. Stephen Labaton, "FCC Plan to Ease Curbs on Big Media Hits Senate Snag," *New York Times*, September 17, 2003, p. A1. When the FCC did finally put into place a modest liberalization of the rules in late 2007, Chairman Martin described the change as a "relatively minor loosening" of the previous restrictions: http://www.fcc.gov/kjm121807-ownership.pdf. Unsurprisingly, this did not placate those opposing any easing of the rules. See John Eggerton, "FCC Loosens Newspaper-Broadcast Cross-Ownership Limits," *Broadcasting & Cable*, December 18, 2007.

3. See Rakesh Khurana, "The Curse of the Superstar CEO," *Harvard Business Review*, September 2002.

4. Quoted by Neal Gabler, *An Empire of Their Own: How the Jews Invented Hollywood* (New York: Crown, 1988), p. 187.

5. With respect to a small portion of the overall studio's output (i.e., certain animated fare), Disney and its Pixar subsidiary may be the exceptions to this rule.

6. When *Advertising Age* collected this data just a few years ago, it apparently did not consider a company like Google to be a media business despite the fact that Google's revenue by that time would have earned it a place on the list.

7. Sharon Waxman and Laura M. Holson, "The Split Between Disney and Miramax Gets a Little Wider," *New York Times*, June 7, 2004, p. C1.

8. Peter Biskind, *Down and Dirty Pictures: Miramax, Sundance, and the Rise of Independent Film* (New York: Simon & Schuster, 2004).

9. Some investors and journalists have begun to look in recent years. See, e.g., David Lieberman, "Aging Media Giants' Glamour Fades," *USA Today*, September 13, 2004; Geraldine Fabrikant, "Growth or Value? Media Stocks Seem to Be Neither," *New York Times*, August 1, 2005. The authors of these articles are both alumni of our Columbia Business School class.

Chapter 1: The Media Landscape

1. Jean-Marie Messier, Group Overview and Strategy, Analysts' Presentation, November 11, 2000.
2. Jean-Marie Messier, *J6M.com: Faut-il avoir peur de la nouvelle économie?* (Paris: Hachette Littératures, 2000), was followed up with an unapologetic defense of his vision and an angry attack on those who facilitated his ultimate downfall: Jean-Marie Messier avec Yves Messarovitch, *Mon Vrai Journal* (Paris: Éditions Ballard, 2002).
3. Exhibits to an instructive Harvard case on Messier provide a partial list of the acquisitions and divestitures. Rakesh Khurana, Vincent Dessain, and Daniela Beyersdorfer, *Messier's Reign at Vivendi Universal*, Harvard Business School Case 9-405-063, July 21, 2005, Exhibits 2 and 4.
4. Interview with senior Houghton executive.
5. See Bruce Wasserstein, *Big Deal: Mergers and Acquisitions in the Digital Age* (New York: Warner, 2000), pp. 262–290, for a discussion of the buildup of conglomerates in the 1960s and their deconsolidation in the 1980s and 1990s.
6. Matthew Karnitschnig, "That's All Folks: After Years of Pushing Synergy, Time Warner Inc. Says Enough," *Wall Street Journal*, June 2, 2006, p. A1.
7. We deal separately with business and professional media conglomerates later in Chapter 1 and in Chapter 8.
8. Chris Anderson, *The Long Tail: Why the Future of Business Is Selling Less of More* (New York: Hyperion, 2006). Anderson argues that the Internet has shifted the mix of content consumed away from mass toward niche media. In a recent *Harvard Business Review* article, Professor Anita Elberse looks at data from the music and home video industries and concludes usage has become more concentrated among fewer hits so that the size of the collective tail may have diminished. Anita Elberse, "Should You Invest in the Long Tail?," *Harvard Business Review*, July–August 2008.
9. See Joseph Weber, "BULL'S-EYE IN THE HEARTLAND: Iowa's Meredith Rides the Home-and-Hearth Wave," *BusinessWeek*, June 23, 2003, p. 54; North Carolina History Project, http://www.northcarolinahistory.org/encyclopedia/82/entry.

10. The other major category of institutional sales is TV Programming, representing the wholesale arm of consumer media companies that sell their product through institutional distribution channels which pay them fees. This would cover everything from sales to airlines for their in-flight entertainment systems to license fees received from cable, satellite, and phone companies.

11. Jason Singer, "For VNU, a Shareholder Revolt May Lead to Its Sale or Breakup," *Wall Street Journal*, October 25, 2005, p. A3.

12. VNU's stock at the time the World Directories deal closed in February 1998 was almost identical to the 29.50 euro price paid by the consortium in 2006. In the interim the stock had peaked at 76.70 euros during the height of the Internet boom in March 2000.

13. These complaints began even before McGraw, who was named president and COO in 1993 and given the CEO role in 1998, beame a top executive. Johnnie L. Roberts, "Short Circuit: McGraw-Hill's Push into Electronic Data Fails to Bolster Profits: Critics Contend the Publisher Suffers from Nepotism and Weak Acquisitions," *Wall Street Journal*, February 6, 1990, p. A1. They continued throughout the decades of outperformance that followed. Sandra Ward, "Brave New World," *Barron's*, October 21, 1996, p. 21; Andrew Bary, "Free S&P," *Barron's*, January 30, 2006, p. 24.

Chapter 2: The Landscape of Competitive Advantage

1. See, e.g., Warren Buffett, 1986 Chairman's Letter to the Shareholders of Berkshire Hathaway Inc.

2. WIPO Patent Report, 2007 edition.

3. See Harold L. Vogel, *Entertainment Industry Economics: A Guide for Financial Analysis* (New York: Cambridge University Press, 2007), pp. 110–111.

4. Qualcomm owns patents on a number of key mobile communications technologies and the license revenue it gets from these is an important part of its overall business.

5. See note 21 in Chapter 4.

6. The huge price ultimately paid by Sony for Columbia compensated Coke for many of its travails during its period of ownership. The experience, nonetheless, had a lasting impact on Coke board member Warren Buffett. Prior to selling CapCities/ABC to Disney, Buffett had considered combining the business with Turner Communications. Buffett scratched the deal after he became convinced that Turner would later buy a movie studio. Ted Turner, *Call Me Ted* (New York: Grand Central, 2008), p. 307.

7. Scott D. Pierce, "Strange Reign of Jamie Tarses at ABC Comes to a Sudden End," *Deseret News*, August 31, 1999, p. C9.

8. Warren Buffett, 1980 Chairman's Letter to the Shareholders of Berkshire Hathaway Inc.
9. See, e.g., R. Mork, A. Schleifer, and R. W. Vishny, "Management Ownership and Market Valuation: An Empirical Analysis," *Journal of Financial Economics* 20 (1988), pp. 293–315.
10. In its conclusion to a seven-part series on "The Downsizing of America," the *New York Times* pointed to United employee ownership as a potential blueprint for balancing employee concerns and competitive realities. "Eighteen months ago, many doubted United's buyout would assure its survival. Today, while the airline still has plenty of problems, the signs are encouraging. In the last year, the company's stock price has doubled, easily outpacing the industry's average . . . [T]he unions, with a greater stake in corporate profits, are suddenly far more flexible about work rules." David E. Sanger and Steve Lohr, "A Search for Answers to Avoid the Layoffs," *New York Times*, March 9, 1996, p. 1. The well-documented debacle that followed belied this optimism.
11. Michael Bloomberg, *Bloomberg by Bloomberg* (New York: John Wiley, 1997; 2001 paperback edition), p. 46.
12. See, e.g., David Lieberman, "Time Warner May Unplug Cable Systems," *USA Today*, October 4, 1996; Raymond Snoddy, "Time Warner to End Interactive TV Trial," *Financial Times*, May 2, 1997.
13. Kate Maddox, "Full Service Network Concerns—Costs May Rain on FSN Parade," *Interactive Age*, January 16, 1995, p. 29.

Chapter 3: The Structure of Media Industries

1. Ted Turner, *Call Me Ted* (New York: Grand Central, 2008), p. 12.
2. Ibid., pp. 237–247.
3. Ibid., p. 390.
4. Ibid., p. 241.
5. Ibid., p. 53.
6. Ibid., p. 111.

Chapter 4: Debunking Media Myths

1. Connie Bruck, "Bronfman's Big Deals," *New Yorker*, May 11, 1998.
2. Return on Invested Capital or ROIC is calculated by the total return (net interest paid plus net income) earned on capital after tax divided by capital employed (equity plus net debt). Weighted Average Cost of Capital or WACC is what must be paid to investors in order to attract the funds invested voluntarily—that is, not through forced reinvestment of retained earnings. This cost per dollar

invested is the fraction of debt invested times the interest paid on that debt (after corporate income tax) plus the fraction of equity invested times an estimate of the returns available to equity investors in comparably risky alternatives.

3. Roger Smith, "Do Movies Make Money?," *Global Media Intelligence*, October 24, 2007. Analyzes 2004–2006 period during which it is estimated that revenues actually fell 5 percent, primarily because of slowing home video sales, while costs increased 13 percent. The report observes that even as revenues recovered in 2007, costs grew faster.

4. "News Corp. to Acquire Intermix Media, Inc.," News Corp. Press Release, July 18, 2005.

5. Saul Hansell, "Google Deal Will Give News Corp. Huge Payoff," *New York Times*, August 8, 2006.

6. In the prepared comments on its disappointing Q4 2007 results, Google CFO George Reyes pointed to the "performance of a few AdSense partner sites, for which we are required to make guaranteed payments. We have found that social networking inventory is not monetizing as well as expected." Cofounder and president Sergey Brin provided more color: "[W]e have had a challenge in Q4 with social networking inventory as a whole and some of the monetization work we were doing there didn't pan out as well as we had hoped . . . I don't think we have the killer best way to advertise and monetize the social networks yet." Q4 2007 Google Earnings Conference Call, Voxant FD Wire, January 31, 2008.

7. Tim Bradshaw and Matthew Garrahan, "Rival Forecast to Catch YouTube as Push for Advertising Founders," *Financial Times*, November 17, 2008.

8. Julia Angwin and Dennis K. Berman, "News Corp. to Pay $650 Million for Operator of Web Game Sites," *Wall Street Journal*, September 8, 2005, p. B6.

9. Richard Siklos, "News Corp. with IGN in Its Stable, Backs Up Promise to Be Bigger Web Player," *New York Times*, September 9, 2005, p. 6.

10. "Two Sides of Space Race: Redstone Blames Freston for Blowing Deal for Site," *Daily Variety*, October 8, 2006.

11. Adam Lashinsky, "Look Who's Online Now," *Fortune*, October 31, 2005, p. 56.

12. Brian Deagon, "Murdoch and MySpace: Crazy Like a Fox," *Investor's Business Daily*, September 4, 2007. The following fiscal year FIM generated around $80 million in profit, but when News announced an $8.4 billion asset write-down in February 2009, it described $821 million in "other" write-downs as "principally IGN." Tim Arango, "News Corp. Loss Shows Trouble at Dow Jones," *New York Times*, February 6, 2009, p. B1.

13. See, e.g., "NBC Uni Beefing Up International," *Television Business International*, October 1, 2006, p. 71.

14. Bruce Greenwald and Judd Kahn, "All Strategy Is Local," *Harvard Business Review*, September 2005.

15. Frank Rose, "Think Globally, Script Locally: American Pop Culture Was Going to Conquer the World, but Now Local Content Is Becoming King," *Fortune*, November 8, 1999.

16. John Wiseman, *Global Nation: Australia and the Politics of Globalization* (New York: Cambridge University Press, 1998), p. 75.

17. Kerry Capell, "MTV's World Mando-Pop," *BusinessWeek*, February 18, 2002, p. 40. Viacom has about half the international exposure of News and this is still more than the other major media conglomerates.

18. Sumner Redstone interview with Kai Ryssdal, *Marketplace Morning Report*, American Public Media, May 15, 2006.

19. Barry Layne, "Levin: No Seat for Seagram," *Hollywood Reporter*, January 26, 1994, p. 1.

20. "Michael Eisner Launches Internet Video Studio," NewsMax.com Wires, March 12, 2007.

21. Sony followed its purchase of CBS Records in 1987 with the acquisition of Columbia Pictures in 1989. The latter resulted in an over $3 billion write-down and has been described as the "most public screwing in the history of the business." Nancy Griffin and Kim Masters, *Hit & Run: How Jon Peters and Peter Guber Took Sony for a Ride in Hollywood* (New York: Touchstone, 1997), p. 10. Matsushita reversed its embarrassing purchase of MCA in 1990 through the sale of 80 percent of its stake to Seagram in 1995 for exactly what it paid originally. Andrew Pollock, "Matsushita Tells Why It Decided to Abandon Hollywood," *New York Times*, April 12, 1995, p. D10. Another Japanese hardware company, Pioneer Electronic, invested in Carolco Pictures and Live Entertainment in 1990, also only to be forced to write these down several years later. "Pioneer to Take Write-Off for Film Unit," *New York Times*, April 14, 1995, p. D3.

22. Brent Schlender, "Sony Plays to Win," *Fortune*, May 1, 2000, p. 142 (quoting former CEO and chairman Norio Ohga).

23. B. A. Kaplan, et al., "Communicopia: A Digital Communication Bounty," Investment Research Report, Goldman Sachs, 1992.

24. Kenneth N. Gilpin, "Business & Investing: Buying in to 'Communicopia,' a Rich New Data Landscape," *New York Times*, January 10, 1999, p. 4, sec. 3.

25. Kaplan, et al., "Communicopia: A Digital Communication Bounty," p. 4.

26. Ibid., p. 78.

27. Ibid.

Chapter 5: The Internet Is Not Your Friend

1. Speaking at Deutsche Bank Securities Inc. Media Conference, June 7, 2005.

2. The Monster board was founded as part of a human resources company called Adion owned by Jeff Taylor. Initially the site simply listed job descriptions from its other customers. In 1995, a yellow pages advertising agency founded by Andrew McKelvey in 1967 called TMP (for Telephone Marketing Programs) bought Adion for less than $1 million along with Online Career Center (OCC), a larger Web site started in 1992. TMP went public in 1996 and the two Web sites were merged and rebranded as Monster.com in 1999. After purchasing and divesting a number of other businesses, TMP became a pure online recruitment business and changed its name to Monster Worldwide in 2003. Saul Hansell, "The Monster That's Feasting on Newspapers," *New York Times*, March 24, 2002, p. 1.

3. Bruce Greenwald and Judd Kahn, *Competition Demystified* (New York: Portfolio, 2005), p. 6.

4. Johnnie L. Roberts, "Murdoch's New Groove; A Conversation with the News Corp. Chairman, Who's Emerged as a Leader in Digital Media After Some Smart Bets," *Newsweek*, February 13, 2006.

5. John Consoli, "Disney's Iger: No AOL Bid; CEO Says Search Engines Are His Company's Allies," *Adweek*, March 12, 2008.

6. Jefferson Graham and Michelle Kessler, "Question: What Are These? Answer: They're All Media Players; Video Leads the Parade as Old Media and New Media Hook Up," *USA Today*, January 8, 2007, p. B1.

7. Roberts, "Murdoch's New Groove."

8. See Paul Verna, "User Generated Content: Will Web 2.0 Pay Its Way?," *eMarketer*, June 2007. Projects worldwide user-generated content advertising to grow from $1.6 billion in 2007 to $8.2 billion in 2011.

9. Kevin Delaney, "Google Push to Sell Ads on YouTube Hits Snag," *Wall Street Journal*, July 9, 2008, p. A1.

10. August 2007 Comscore data shows 118 million unique visitors to social networking sites out of a total of 181 million total U.S. unique visitors, which is representative of recent trends.

11. Delaney, "Google Push to Sell Ads on YouTube Hits Snag."

12. Daisy Whitney, "Perez Hilton Pulls Videos from YouTube," TVWeek.com, December 20, 2007.

13. Ronald Grover, "CBS: Outside the Hulu Huddle," BusinessWeek.com, May 4, 2009.

14. A possible exception to this is the billboard industry discussed in chapter 7.

15. Michael Schrage, "Arthur Ochs Sulzberger Jr.," *Adweek*, June 28, 1999.

16. The Newspaper Association of America Web site has most of the key historical data at www.naa.org.

17. Jonathan A. Knee, "Should We Fear Newspaper Cross Ownership?," *Regulation,* Summer 2003, p. 16.

18. *2006 Pew Research Center for the People & the Press News Consumption and Believability Study,* p. 28.

19. Interview with senior national newspaper executive. According to the Pew Center study, "people ages 50–64 are just as likely as the youngest cohort to read online newspapers." *2006 Pew Research Center for the People & the Press News Consumption and Believability Study,* p. 20. The issue is that only 29 percent of those eighteen to twenty-nine years old read a newspaper in any medium and this percentage has not changed for a decade—although the Internet may have helped stem the decline.

20. One of the oldest newspapers in the world in Sweden suspended publication in 2007. "World's Oldest Newspaper Goes Purely Digital," Associated Press, February 5, 2007. In the United States, some titles have become online only, as the *Christian Science Monitor* has announced it intends to do in April 2009, while others have closed down entirely. A number of hybrid strategies have also emerged, like limiting home delivery to subscribers to selected days of the week and providing electronic access otherwise. "Bold Transformation of Detroit Free Press and the Detroit News Lead Nation and Industry with Expanded Digital Offerings," PR Newswire, December 16, 2008.

21. http://newslink.org/nynews.html.

22. http://www.naa.org/info/facts04/dailynewspapers.html.

23. Transcontinental, the Canadian printer under contract to Hearst, announced the establishment of a separate U.S. newspaper division in February 2007; http://www.transcontinental-gtc.com/en/5-news-centre/07-02-21.html.

24. Henry Blodget, "Huffington Post Deal: $25 Million at $100 Million Valuation," *Silicon Alley Insider,* December 1, 2008. At the time, newspaper industry stalwarts like A. H. Belo and Lee Enterprises had public market values well under $100 million.

25. Janet Whitman, "Declining Failure Rate Suggests a Modest Dot-Com Comeback," *Wall Street Journal,* October 16, 2002, p. B3E; Amy E. Knaup, "Survival and Longevity in the Business Employment Dynamics Data," *Monthly Labor Review,* May 2005, p. 50.

26. CNET Press Release, January 20, 2000.

27. CNET 2007 10-K.

28. E. W. Scripps Company Press Release, June 6, 2005.

29. "USA Interactive to Change Name to InterActiveCorp.," Business Wire, June 19, 2003. In renaming the company, Diller articulated his goal "to be the world's largest and most profitable interactive commerce company by pursuing a multi-brand strategy."

30. Ronald Grover, "From Media Mogul to Web Warlord: Will Barry Diller's Cherrypicking Succeed on the Net?," *BusinessWeek*, May 19, 2003.

31. Diller did articulate a number of criteria for buying Internet businesses. But some of these, like market fragmentation, were probably reflective of the lack of competitive advantage. Julia Angwin, "Boss Talk: Faith in Online Magic—Though Many Others Failed, Barry Diller Sees a Big Future in Internet Shopping, Services," *Wall Street Journal*, May 6, 2003, p. B1.

32. Andrew Edgecliffe-Johnson, "End of an Era for IAC/InterActive," *Financial Times*, July 31, 2008. Ironically, even after spinning off four separate companies, the remaining IAC will still have over thirty different brands without any central theme. In the press release, the new streamlined IAC has an even more amorphous vision—"a truly integrated Internet conglomerate"—than the original IAC did at its creation almost five years earlier. "IAC Announces Plan to Spin Off HSN, Ticketmaster, Interval and LendingTree as Four Publicly Traded Companies," PR Newswire, November 5, 2007.

33. Bala Iyer and Thomas H. Davenport, "Reverse Engineering Google's Innovation Machine, *Harvard Business Review*, April 2008, p. 59

34. In a blog on the company's official site, Google's chief economist, Hal Varian, rejects a number of explanations proffered by others and offers up "learning" as the sole distinguishing feature of the franchise. A close reading of the posting suggests that Varian does not really believe that this single quality explains Google's success and a cynic might be forgiven for thinking that he is intentionally playing semantic games to further Google's well-known penchant for secrecy about the underlying nature of its strategy and strength. Hal Varian, "Our Secret Sauce," The Official Google Blog, February 25, 2008.

35. Chris Gaither, "The One Bit of Info Google Withholds: How It Works," *Los Angeles Times*, May 22, 2006; Chris Ayres, "Shrouded in Secrecy: An Awe Inspiring Fount of Information," *The* (London) *Times*, June 15, 2006.

36. Adam Lashinsky, "Who's The Boss," *Fortune*, October 2, 2006.

37. "The 70 Percent Solution: Google CEO Eric Schmidt Gives Us His Golden Rules for Managing Innovation," *Business 2.0*, November 28, 2005.

38. Most recently, Google abandoned its expensive efforts to sell ads on radio. Jessica Vascellavo, "Radio Tunes Out Google in Rare Miss for Web Titan," *Wall Street Journal*, May 12, 2009.

Chapter 6: Content Is Not King

1. *The Charlie Rose Show*, Interview with Jeff Zucker, president and CEO of NBC Universal, May 21, 2008.

2. The March 2004 $2.6 billion LBO of Warner Music did initially generate substantial returns for Edgar Bronfman and his private equity partners—Thomas

H. Lee, Bain, and Providence. After the acquisition, costs were quickly cut and the unprecedented availability of debt was exploited to quickly pull out much of the initial investment that same year. Josh Friedman and Chuck Philips, "At Warner Music Cuts Go Deep," *Los Angeles Times*, March 12, 2005. The company then went public at seventeen dollars a share in May 2005 and saw its shares soar to almost thirty dollars the following year. Devin Leonard, "Warner Music: A Big Hit for Bronfman," *Fortune*, May 15, 2006. At the end of 2008, the stock stood at little more than two dollars a share, with the private equity triumvirate still owning most of the equity.

3. This is consistent with the production filmography of the major production companies available on imdb.com and the anecdotal views of many studio executives. See Michael Eisner, *Work in Progress: Risking Failure, Surviving Success* (New York: Hyperion, 1999; paperback edition), p. 168. (Eisner quotes Frank Wells approvingly as having said: "I do not believe that the true head of production . . . can manage more than 15 pictures per year and give each one the individual attention it requires.") Also, author interview with Ron Meyer, president and COO, Universal Studios.

4. The 2005 LBO of MGM initially envisaged limited new production besides franchises like James Bond, but the availability of cheap financing led the company to revive the United Artists label with the help of Tom Cruise and aggressively pursue new production. Tatiana Siegel, "MGM's Sloan Signs Three-Year Deal; Exec Will Continue as Chairman, CEO," *Daily Variety*, August 4, 2008. As the continued availability of that financing has become more questionable, so has the strategy, leading some to suggest that the company's debt burden will require a sale. Amanda Andrews, "MGM Orders Review but Insists It Is Not for Sale," the (London) *Times*, August 27, 2008.

5. Sigmund Freud, *The Future of an Illusion* (New York: W. W. Norton, 1989), p. 40.

6. Thomas Simonet, *Regression Analysis of Prior Experiences of Key Production Personnel as Predictors of Revenues from High-Grossing Motion Pictures in America* (New York: Arno Press, 1980), and Bruce C. Greenwald and Rebecca Dragiff, *Maximus Films*, Harvard Business School Case, 1982. See also Thomas H. Davenport and Jeanne G. Harris, "What People Want (and How to Predict It)," *MIT Sloan Management Review*, Winter 2009.

7. Ian Ayres, *Super Crunchers: Why Thinking-by-Numbers Is the New Way to Be Smart* (New York: Bantam Dell, 2007), p. 143.

8. Malcolm Gladwell, "The Formula," *New Yorker*, October 16, 2006.

9. Sore Eyes Blog, quote from Copaken October 24, 2006. http://soreeyes.org/archive/2006/10/20/calling-bullshit-on-epagogix/.

10. Company Web sites, uplaya.com, and platinumblue.com.

11. RIAA Year-End Shipment Statistics.

12. IFPI 2008 Digital Music Report.
13. Soundscan.
14. Company Web site.
15. "Madonna Announces Huge Live Nation Deal: Changes in Music Business Entice Singer to Jump from Warner Bros.," Associated Press, October 16, 2007.
16. Cortney Harding, "Merlin Indie Label Membership Tops 12,000," Billboard .biz, June 10, 2008.
17. Source: 1988, 1999 Studio Market Share: Michael G. Rukstad and David Collis, *The Walt Disney Company: the Entertainment King*, Harvard Business School Case 9-701-035, July 25, 2001; 2006 Studio Market Share: Boxofficemojo.com.
18. Figures are taken from annual reports. Some of the variations in margin could be a function of different corporate allocation policies. For ROC estimates, we have assumed industry approximate average of 75 percent capital/assets.
19. Book Industry Trends 2008, and Statistical Abstract of the U.S. 2008, Table 1119.
20. Data available on Magazine Publishers of America Web site at www.magazine.org.

Chapter 7: Efficient Operations in Media

1. Connie Bruck, *When Hollywood Had a King: The Reign of Lew Wasserman, Who Leveraged Talent into Power and Influence* (New York: Random House Trade Paperback, 2004), p. 77.
2. Ibid., p. 210.
3. Ibid., p. 250.
4. Ibid., p. 397.
5. Company Annual Reports.
6. Returns on capital are calculated by assuming capital is 75 percent of assets and inferring returns on assets in the earlier period (1971–1984) from the return on sales and the ratio of assets to sales in the later period.
7. Geraldine Fabrikant, "MCA Turns Hand to Acquisitions," *New York Times*, February 9, 1987, p. D1.
8. Richard Turner, "MCA Agrees to Sell Its LJN Toy Unit for Cash and Stock— Acclaim Entertainment Inc.'s Purchase Cost Is Said to Be About $30 Million," *Wall Street Journal*, March 13, 1990, p. B6.
9. David J. Jefferson, "MCA Net Falls," *Wall Street Journal*, July 22, 1900.
10. Company reports.
11. James B. Stewart, *Disney War* (New York: Simon & Schuster, 2006; paperback edition), p. 117.

12. Bernard Weinraub, "The Talk of Hollywood: Though a Year Old, Disney Memo Still Provokes Gossip," *New York Times*, February 11, 1992, p. C11.

13. William Goldman, *Adventures in the Screen Trade* (New York: Warner Books, 1983; paperback edition), p. 39.

14. Claudia Eller, "Marketing Costs Scale the Heights," *Los Angeles Times*, October 20, 2002, p. C1.

15. David Teather, "Fade to Red," *Guardian*, November 30, 2007. The disturbing trends in marketing costs are available on the MPAA Web site. See Motion Picture Association of America, *Theatrical Market Statistics 2007*, p. 6.

16. James Bates, "For Your Consideration: Ads a Mere Ego Massage," *Los Angeles Times*, December 12, 2005, p. E6.

17. "Digest: Vivendi Launches Campaign," Hollywood Reporter Online, November 28, 2006.

18. Peter Kafka, "EMI's $400,000 Coke and Hookers Budget," *Silicon Alley Insider*, January 12, 2008.

19. "OC Register to Outsource Some Editing to India," Associated Press, June 24, 2008.

20. Ryan Nakashima, "Hollywood Has Busiest On-Location Filming Quarter," Associated Press, July 17, 2008.

21. Erik Siemers, "Execs Excited to See Albuquerque Studios Working at Capacity," *Albuquerque Tribune*, August 16, 2007.

22. Geoffrey A. Fowler and Karen Mazurkewich, "Leaping Tiger: How Mr. Kong Helped Turn China into a Film Power," *Wall Street Journal*, September 14, 2005, p. A1.

23. A number of old studio lots have been sold for development over the years, but the core lots of all the major studios remain in place.

24. Professor John Roberts suggests that the failure of Sony's high-definition television, digital audiotape, and Minidisk initiatives and the failure to adequately invest in R&D for the core consumer electronics business can be tied to these acquisitions. *The Modern Firm: Organizational Design for Performance and Growth* (New York: Oxford University Press, 2007; paperback edition), p. 221.

25. Gabriel Snyder, "Yes, They Do Windows," *Daily Variety*, August 21, 2005. Then Time Warner CEO Richard Parsons provided some support for Disney's otherwise lonely position. George Szalai, "Parsons: Release Windows Will 'Live Together,'" *Hollywood Reporter*, December 9, 2005.

26. Disney sold over three hundred of its stores to Children's Place after searching for a buyer for a year and a half. Merissa Marr, "Disney Agrees to Sell Its Stores to Children's Place," *Wall Street Journal*, October 21, 2004. When Children's Place filed for bankruptcy in 2008, Disney agreed to take back the stores but immediately announced its intention to close a third of them. Martine Geller, "Disney Buys Back North American Disney Store Chain," Reuters, May 1, 2008.

27. Ronald Grover and Cliff Edwards, "Game Wars," *BusinessWeek*, February 25, 2005; Laura M. Holsom, "Blockbuster with a Joystick," *New York Times*, February 7, 2005.

28. Louise Story, "Digital Billboard Up Ahead: New-Wave Sign or Hazard," *New York Times*, January 11, 2007 (citing a Citigroup analyst as saying that digital signs can have 70 percent profit margins as compared to 45 percent margins for static signs).

29. John Roberts, *The Modern Firm*, pp. 164–76.

30. Stephen Galloway, "Paramount Takes a Bold New Step," *Hollywood Reporter*, January 16, 2007. This costly move was justified on the basis of the firms' increasing commitment to international growth. Ironically, the original 1981 venture raised antitrust concerns, which the partners fought vigorously, and only achieved final clearance in 1999. Jonathan Annells, "EC Won't Revisit UIP Decision," *Hollywood Reporter*, September 21, 1999.

31. Interviews with former Universal executives.

Chapter 8: Putting It All Together

1. Economics of Basic Cable Networks, SNL Kagan, 2008.

2. Bruce Greenwald, *USA Cable Networks*, Columbia Business School Case, 10#080326, December 16, 2008.

3. Kim Masters, "Small Screen Mastermind," NPR interview on *Morning Edition*, August 18, 2008; available at http://www.npr.org/templates/story/story.php?storyId=93357966.

4. These profit margins, as elsewhere, reflect EBIT rather than EBITDA and so are not directly comparable to the USA Network's margins. Discovery Communications EBITDA margins are approximately 5 percent higher than their EBIT margins.

5. Bruce Greenwald, *Reuters PLC*, Columbia Business School Case 080318, May 14, 2008.

6. Telerate was launched in the late 1960s and sold to Dow Jones in a series of transactions in the late 1980s for $1.6 billion. Dow Jones sold what was left of Telerate to Bridge for $510 million in 1998. Bridge was another attempted Reuters competitor, backed in 1994 by LBO firm Welsh, Carson, Anderson, & Stowe, which had previously purchased a number of other smaller competitors, including Knight Ridder Financial. Bridge filed for bankruptcy protection in 2001 and was sold off in pieces, some of which, including Telerate, ended up back with Reuters.

7. Michael Bloomberg, *Bloomberg by Bloomberg* (New York: John Wiley, 1997; 2001 paperback edition), p. 42.

8. Ibid., p. 53.

9. Ibid., p. 46.

10. Ibid., p. 44.

11. Ibid., p. 68.

12. Bank for International Settlements.

13. World Federation of Exchanges.

14. Bloomberg, *Bloomberg by Bloomberg.*

15. September 2008 Structured Ratings Transistions, Moody's Credit Policy, October 2008, Exhibit 1A.

16. Ibid., p. 75.

17. Reuters 2000 Half-Year Report, July 2000.

18. Thomson Reuters Investor Relations.

19. Reuters annual reports.

20. Reuters Annual Report and Form 20-F 2004. See also Kenneth Klee, "Dispatch from Reuters," *The Deal,* May 23, 2005.

Chapter 9: Managing Competition in Media

1. Robert Axelrod, *The Evolution of Cooperation* (New York: Basic Books, 1984), p. 126. Although Axelrod focuses his discussion on military rather than commercial settings, his conclusions are equally applicable.

2. Warren St. John, "So Why Did Newhouse Sell Random House to Bertelsmann Boys," *New York Observer,* March 29, 1998.

3. One widely publicized example occurred when Reprise Records bought out the contract of alternative-country idols Wilco and as part of the buyout deal gave them the rights to the recent album they had deemed unacceptable. Wilco then sold the album to Nonesuch Records. Both labels are owned by Warner Music, which actually paid twice for the same album. Brian Steinberg, "A CD Spins Full Circle at AOL—a Hard-to-Peg Band Named Wilco Was Out—Then Back In," Dow Jones Newswires, May 8, 2002.

4. Sony's missed opportunity to cooperate is recounted in James Lardner, *Fast Forward: Hollywood, the Japanese, and the Onslaught of the VCR* (New York: Norton, 1987).

5. Toshiba reported losing 160 billion yen, or around $1.5 billion, by the time it threw in the towel on HD-DVD. AFX Asia, "Japan's Toshiba to Post 1st Profit Fall in 3 Yrs on Lower Chip Prices, DVD Loss," April 28, 2008.

6. Johnnie L. Roberts and Jennifer Ordonez, "Selling CDs for a Song," *Newsweek,* September 15, 2003. The failure of the strategy ultimately forced Universal to scale back the initiative. Ethan Smith, "Harsh Feedback: Why a Grand Plan to Cut CD Prices Went off the Track," *Wall Street Journal,* June 4, 2004, p. A1.

7. Edward Jay Epstein, "The Iger Fatwa," *Slate,* September 6, 2005.

8. Rebecca Dana, "Post-Strike, Networks Revamp Pilot Season—Staggered Scheduling, Cheaper Debuts Pondered; a Challenge for Ad Buyers," *Wall Street Journal,* March 31, 2008, p. B1.

9. Until recently, the network actually paid the affiliates an annual lump sum in return for their agreement to affiliate. This so-called network compensation is in the process of being phased out.

10. Some programming costs can develop a variable element, as when a show becomes a hit and the producers and stars hold out for better terms in subsequent seasons. The overall cost structure is still largely fixed.

11. Bill Gorman, "Looking Back at the Eras of Network Television"; http://tvbythenumbers.com/2008/06/14/looking-back-at-the-eras-of-network-television/4110#more-4110 Nielsen TV Ratings Data, 2008.

12. Michael Bloomberg, *Bloomberg by Bloomberg* (New York: John Wiley, 1997; 2001 paperback edition), pp. 64–65.

Chapter 10: All (Profitable) Media Is Local

1. See Chapter 5 for discussion of newspapers and Chapter 9 for discussion of broadcasting.

2. Individual theater chain counts are as of May 1995, from Geoffrey Verter and Anita M. McGahan, *Coming Soon: A Theatre Near You*, Harvard Business School Case 9-797-011, September 24, 1998, Exhibit 8. Industry totals are from 1995 year-end numbers at natoonline.org.

3. Financial data summarized from Exhibit 9 in ibid.

4. Josh Wolk, "Movie Per-plex," *Entertainment Weekly*, September 1, 2000.

5. Industry data is available at natoonline.org.

6. Brent Shearer, "A Slow Fading to Red Ink Blurs the Outlook for Movie Theatre Chains," *Mergers & Acquisitions*, November 1, 2000.

7. In June 2005, AMC sold five Japanese theaters previously acquired; in June 2006, it converted Hong Kong theaters from an owner situation to a licensed arrangement; in May 2006, it sold Spanish theaters. In FY 2007, its remaining major international holding was in Mexico, with forty-four theaters and 488 screens. Source: Company 10-K, April 2008.

8. Company 10-Ks.

9. See Kathleen Pender, "Hollywood on the Rocks," *San Francisco Chronicle*, November 26, 2000. All screens are not equal, however. The average number of screens per location has continued to rise as the actual number of theaters has slowly declined and the proportion of multiplexes has risen. Among the efficiencies of multiplex operations is that a portion of increased screen capacity can be used to provide multiple start times for the same popular film. This still does not economically justify the increase in the absolute number of screens.

10. Analysis of company reports of Verizon, SBC, BellSouth, and GTE.

11. Analysis of company reports of Time Warner, Comcast, and Cablevision.

12. Analysis of company annual reports.

13. Company annual reports and international market share information.

14. Where an international player has established a leading position outside of its home country, more often than not, this has been achieved through acquisition of an already leading local site.

Chapter 11: Reinforcing Competitive Advantage in Media

1. John Gaudiosi, "How the Wii Is Creaming the Competition," *Business 2.0*, April 25, 2007.

2. Ibid. The Wii uses a chip similar to the one that powered the GameCube, an earlier Nintendo machine that was not a bestseller.

3. Frederic Descamps, *Electronic Arts in 2002*, Stanford Business School Case SM-24C, September 23, 2002.

4. Top twenty movies by domestic grosses from boxofficemojo.com. Top-twenty video games by domestic units from Entertainment Software Association. Author judgment of what constitutes a sequel.

5. The other critical factor is whether the underlying franchise is licensed under terms requiring each successive version to be bid or is owned by the studio or game developer. Although there are a wide variety of arrangements in place in both industries, the mix toward owned content favors the game industry relative to the movie business.

6. Electronic Arts 2002 Annual Report.

7. Laurie J. Flynn, "Red Ink at Electronic Arts Despite a Rise in Revenue," *New York Times*, February 4, 2009, p. B7.

8. Entertainment Software Association 2008 Consumer Survey.

9. The next two most popular subscription MMOG game franchises in mid-2008, Runescape and Lineage, are owned by Jagex Ltd. (a private U.K. company that received an investment from Insight Venture Partners in 2005) and NCsoft (a South Korean online computer-game company), respectively.

10. When Activision, despite having double the game-publishing market share of Vivendi, could not convince Vivendi to sell it the Blizzard subsidiary, which published World of Warcraft, it agreed to sell itself to Vivendi. Ben Fritz, "Activision Tried to Buy Blizzard Before Merging with Vivendi Games," Variety.com, July 10, 2008.

11. Descamps, *Electronic Arts in 2002*. At the time of the quote, Riccitiello was president and COO. He subsequently left the company briefly before returning as CEO.

12. EA's justification for the decision from its 2004 10-K: "We now consider online capability and gameplay to be integral to our existing and future products. Accordingly, beginning April 1, 2003, we no longer manage our online products and services as a separate business segment, and we have consolidated the reporting related to our online products and services into reporting

for the overall development and publication of our core products for all reporting periods ending after that date. We believe that this will better reflect the way in which our Chief Executive Officer (our chief operating decision maker) reviews and manages our business and reflects the importance of our online products and services relative to the rest of our business."

13. David B. Yoffie and Michael Slind, *Apple Inc.*, 2008, Harvard Business School Case 9-708-480, September 8, 2008. Apple finally relented in 2009 and allowed multiple price points in exchange for removal of DRM restrictions. Ed Christman, "NameYour Price: iTunes," *Billboard*, January 17, 2009.

14. John Markoff, "New Economy: Apple's Success with iPod May Presage the Ascendance of Hardware over Software," *New York Times*, January 19, 2004, p. C4. Although the iPod initially could sync only with Macs, in 2002 iPod for Windows was introduced.

15. Jim Carlton, *Apple: The Inside Story of Intrigue, Egomania, and Business Blunders* (New York: Times Business/Random House, 1997).

16. John Markoff and Steve Lohr, "Apple Plans to Switch From I.B.M. to Intel Chips," *New York Times*, June 6, 2005.

17. John Markoff, "Microsoft Comes to the Aid of a Struggling Apple," *New York Times*, August 7, 1997, p. A1.

18. Vikas Bajaj, "Apple Allows Windows on Its Machines," *New York Times*, April 5, 2006.

19. iPhone sales were not yet material.

20. Maynard J. Um et al, "More Than Just a 'Halo' Effect," UBS Investment Research Report, August 4, 2008.

Chapter 12: Bad Mogul

1. A good review of the ins and outs of the literature is Gregor Andrade, Mark Mitchell, and Erik Stafford, "New Evidence and Perspectives on Mergers," *Journal of Economic Perspectives* 15:2 (Spring 2001), pp. 103–120.

2. See also Mark Grinblatt and Sheridan Titman, *Financial Markets and Corporate Strategy* (Boston: McGraw-Hill Irwin, 2002), pp. 707–713.

3. Patrick Viguerie, Sven Smit, and Mehrdad Baghai, *The Granularity of Growth* (New York: John Wiley, 2008). Although the book is not an "official" McKinsey publication, two of its three authors were formally affiliated with the company and it is widely used by consultants there. The book is a sequel of sorts to *The Alchemy of Growth* (London: Orion Business, 1999) by an overlapping cadre of authors—Mehrdad Baghai, Stephen Coley, and David White.

4. Ibid., p. x.

5. Ibid., p. 34.

6. Ibid., pp. 93–96

7. Ibid., p. 96.

8. This point was made using relatively simple calculations by the Citigroup European Equity Strategy Team in a 2006 research report. Brooks et al., "How Do They Do That?," Citigroup Global Markets, November 16, 2006. More recent academic research similarly concludes that "private equity investments actually substantially underperform the market on average"; Josh Lerner, "Performance: The Enigma of Private Equity," *Financial Times*, April 24, 2007.

9. Douglas S. Shapiro, "Hey Big Media: The Jig Is Up on Big Media Mergers," Bank of America Securities, July 7, 2004.

10. Disney rebranded the channel to ABC Family in November 2001. Average twenty-four-hour ratings for Fox Family had been .49, .52, and .53 for the years 1999, 2000, and 2001, respectively. The corresponding ratings for ABC Family fell to .51 in 2002 and .46 in 2003. Nielsen Media.

11. Sanford Bernstein analysts estimate that the media conglomerates' return on invested capital on average was around 6.5 percent in 2007 and notes that only the very top-performing conglomerates in the sector ever achieve even an ROIC of 9 percent. See Michael Nathanson, Drew Borst, and Brian Nowak, "News Corp.: A Good Company, but No Catalyst for Revaluation," Bernstein Research, April 14, 2008.

12. Public Disney filings.

13. Nielsen Media Research.

14. Thomson Reuters SDC, public filings.

15. The others were Charter and Cox, which were slightly larger than Comcast, and MediaOne, Adelphia, and Cablevision, which were smaller.

16. AT&T Broadband revenue was $9.6 billion in 2001. Although the company's EBITDA margin had been in the teens until recently, it was at 25 percent by the time of the transaction. This still represented a 17-percentage-point margin disparity with Comcast's 42 percent EBITDA margin.

17. Comcast's investor presentation at the time gave a range of between $1.25 and $1.95 billion for potential synergies.

18. Jonathan A. Knee, "An Object Lesson Ignored: Media-Merger Mania Unmasked," *New York Observer*, January 26, 2004; review of Kara Swisher with Lisa Dickey, *There Must Be a Pony in Here Somewhere: The AOL Time Warner Debacle and the Quest for the Digital Future* (New York: Crown Business, 2003), and Nina Munk, *Fools Rush In: Steve Case, Jerry Levin, and the Unmaking of AOL Time Warner* (New York: HarperBusiness, 2004).

19. Munk, *Fools Rush In: Steve Case, Jerry Levin, and the Unmaking of AOL Time Warner*, p. 142.

20. Henry Blodget, *"You've Got Upside": America Online/Time Warner*, Merrill Lynch Capital Markets, February 23, 2000.

21. Even after AOL Time Warner acquired Bebo for $850 million in 2008, Advertising.com for $425 million in 2004, and over a dozen smaller acquisitions in between, most analysts seem to think achieving more than a few billion for what remains of AOL would be aggressive. Michael Nathanson et al., "Time Warner: Our Long National Nightmare Is Over," BernsteinResearch, March 30, 2009. Google has already signaled its intention to write down the 5 percent stake it bought for $1 billion in 2006. Eric Auchard, "Google Admits Its AOL Investment May Be Impaired," Reuters, August 7, 2008.

22. Rakesh Khurana, Vincent Dessain, and Daniela Beyersdorfer, *Messier's Reign at Vivendi Universal*, Harvard Business School Case 9-405-063, July 21, 2005, p. 6.

23. Bernhard Warner, "Vodaphone Buys Out Vizzavi for $141 Million," Reuters, August 30, 2002.

24. Stephannie Larocque et al., *The Seagram Company*, UBS Warburg Global Equity Research, June 15, 2000.

25. Lex Column, "Even Messier," *Financial Times*, June 21, 2000.

26. Merissa Marr, "Vivendi—Bonjour Hollywood, G'day Murdoch?," Reuters, June 20, 2000.

27. Geraldine Fabrikant, "French Media Conglomerate Is Reported Negotiating to Buy Seagram," *New York Times*, June 14, 2000, p. C1.

28. In the United States, Vivendi's settlement with the SEC entailed Messier's agreement to pay a $1 million penalty and give up claims to a $26 million severance package to which he would otherwise have been entitled. He is also subject to a ten-year prohibition on serving as an officer or director of a public company. Jennifer Bayot, "Vivendi Pays $50 Million in Settlement with SEC," *New York Times*, December 24, 2003, p. C1. In France, the financial market watchdog imposed a€1 millon fine for deliberately making statements that were "abusively optimistic." Digby Larner and Simon Clow, "France's AMF Lacks Muscle Despite Vivendi Ruling," Dow Jones News Service, December 10, 2004. At one point, magistrates investigating financial irregularities at Vivendi actually ordered Messier's arrest. Martine Orange, "La Garde à vue de M. Messier intervient après la mise en examen de plusieurs responsables du groupe," *Le Monde*, June 23, 2004. Police had earlier raided Messier's homes looking for evidence. Jo Johnson, "Police Raid Vivendi HQ and Messier homes," *Financial Times*, December 13, 2002.

29. William Emmanuel, *Le Maître des illusions: l'ascension et la chute de Jean-Marie Messier* (Paris: Economica, 2002).

30. Victoria Chang, *Ron Meyer: Universal Studios President and COO, Stanford Graduate School of Business Case EM-4*, February 8, 2008.

31. Messier's failure to inform the board of the extent of these buybacks became the subject of controversy. John Carreyrou and Martin Peers, "Damage Control: How Messier Kept Cash Crisis at Vivendi Hidden for Months," *Wall Street Journal*, October 31, 2002, p. A1.

32. Company filings, Thomson SDC, Capital IQ.

Chapter 13: Media M&A That Works

1. Geraldine Fabrikant, "Hearst to Buy 20% ESPN Stake from RJR," *New York Times*, November 9, 1990, p. D17.

2. Sally Bedell Smith, "An ABC Strategy Goes Wrong," *New York Times*, December 9, 1984.

3. Felicity Barringer, "The Media Business: Dow Jones Says Its President Plans to Retire," *New York Times*, October 22, 1998, p. C1.

4. Holly Rosenkrantz, "Marketwatch.com set to kick off '99 IPO Market," Reuters, January 14, 1999.

5. Aaron Lucchetti, "Heard on the Street: MarketWatch.com IPO Continues Web-Stock Boom," *Dow Jones Business News*, January 18, 1999.

6. "Now Legal Snags Hit Marketwatch," *Sunday Business*, June 3, 2001.

7. Interview with the authors.

8. SEC filings by Microsoft.

9. Ibid.

10. Ibid.

11. Seattle Tech Report, the Microsoft Blog, "Even Internally, Microsoft Mum on Yahoo 'Synergies,'" http://blog.seattlepi.nwsource.com/microsoft/archives/131206.asp.

12. Jack Flack, "Business Spin: Parsing Yahoo's Response to Icahn," Portfolio.com, May 15, 2008.

13. John Gapper, "The Perils of a Passionate Helmsman," *Financial Times*, November 20, 2008.

Chapter 14: Good Mogul

1. Michael G. Rukstad and David Collis, *The Walt Disney Company: The Entertainment King*, Harvard Business School Case 9-701-035, revised July 25, 2001; Bharat Anand and Kate Attea, *News Corporation*, Harvard Business School Case 9-702-425, revised June 27, 2003.

2. *Who Framed Roger Rabbit*, a successful mixed animated/live-action feature, was released in 1988.

3. Meg James and Sallie Hofmeister, "The Family Was Really Messed Up," *Los Angeles Times*, June 15, 2004. Dissident directors Stanley Gold and Roy Disney cited an internal analysis suggesting the channel was possibly worth as little as $1.2 billion—or $4 billion less than the company had paid. Richard Verrier, "Eisner Foes Say Disney Hid Fallen Value of ABC Family," *Los Angeles Times*, May 8, 2004.

4. Details of the launch of BSkyB can be found in Mathew Horsman, *Sky High: The Amazing Story of BSkyB—and the Egos, Deals and Ambitions That Revolutionised TV Broadcasting* (London: Orion, 1997); Pankaj Ghemawat, *British Satellite Broadcasting versus Sky Television*, Harvard Business School Case 9-794-031, January 8, 2007; Debra Spar and Paula Zakaria, *BSkyB*, Harvard Business School Case 9-798-077, August 7, 1988.

5. BSB was literally the first mover, but the advantage accrued to the player, Sky, that was first to achieve scale.

6. News Corporation 1991 Annual Report.

7. See Elizabeth Lesley, "Murdoch's 'Cosmic Armada': Pie in the Sky?," *Business-Week*, May 26, 1997.

8. Bruce Dover, *Rupert Murdoch's China Adventure: How the World's Most Powerful Media Mogul Lost a Fortune and Found a Wife* (Tokyo: Tuttle, 2008). This short book by Murdoch's former general manager for China provides an entertaining diary of the ups and downs of News's ultimately unsuccessful efforts to crack the market.

9. "News Extends Star Break-Even Date," *Reuters News*, February 10, 1999.

10. Dover, *Rupert Murdoch's China Adventure*, p. 242.

11. Murdoch's 1983 launch of Skyband entailed an initial $75 million investment in Inter-American Satellite and closed in under a year after losing $20 million. In 1995, he tried to build a company called American Sky Broadcasting, or ASkyB, in connection with MCI, and agreed to invest $682.5 million, half the cost of an orbital slot that covered the market. That relationship soon fell apart. Murdoch's February 1997 $1 billion acquisition of 49 percent of EchoStar and associated ASkyB partnership ended with the May 1997 $5 billion breach-of-contract lawsuit by EchoStar. In October 2001, News ended a twenty-month campaign to gain control of DirecTV after the board of General Motors postponed its decision. See Special Report, "Murdoch's 21-Year Quest: That's How Long It Took News Corp. Titan to Gain Control of a DBS Operation," *Broadcasting & Cable*, November 24, 2004.

12. Richard Siklos, "Murdoch and Malone Find a Way to Make Up," *New York Times*, December 6, 2007, p. C1.

13. Murdoch denied the remark, declaring "I love it," in response to a direct question on the matter. Richard Morgan, "Murdoch Opens the Bird Cage," The Deal.com, September 20, 2006.

14. See Chapter 10.

15. Bharat Anand and Catherine Conneely, *Fox Bids for the NFL—1993*, Harvard Business School Case 9-704-443, December 11, 2003; Victoria Chang and George Foster, *Fox Sports and News Corp's Sports Empire*, Stanford Graduate School of Business Case SPM-10, September 3, 2003.

16. In his teaching note to the Fox Sports cases, Professor Bharat Anand also points to the cross-promotional benefits and research he has done showing that a single ad exposure for a TV show significantly increases the probability that an individual will watch it. This line of argument seems to fall prey to the fallacy of most cross-promotional "synergy" arguments. With limited inventory for ads of any kind, the shows that would benefit most should buy ad time on the football broadcasts. If the rights holder instead uses this time only to promote its own shows regardless, this is a dis-synergy. Ron Shachar and Bharat Anand, "The Effectiveness and Targeting of Television Advertising," *Journal of Economics and Management Strategy*, August 1988.

17. Richard Sandomir, "The Man Carrying the Ball for Murdoch," *New York Times*, September 4, 1994, p. 1, sec. 3.

18. Chang and Foster, *Fox Sports and News Corp's Sports Empire*, p. 6.

19. Richard Sandomir, "The Seemingly Never-Ending Inflation in the Cost of Sports Contracts May Be Near an End," *New York Times*, February 14, 2002, p. C10.

20. Sallie Hofmeister, "Losses Predicted on NFL Deals," *Los Angeles Times*, January 15, 1998.

21. Sandomir, "The Seemingly Never-Ending Inflation in the Cost of Sports Contracts May Be Near an End."

22. Bharat Anand and Catherine Conneely, *Fox and the NFL—1998*, Harvard Business School Case 9-704-444, December 11, 2003.

23. Jenny Hontz, "Fox Affiliate Switch Predictions Fail to Materialize," *Electronic Media*, February 26, 1996. The trade magazine obtained confidential earlier Fox projections of the anticipated impact of the switch.

24. Kathryn Harris, "Perelman's Tinseltown Swan Song: What They're Talking About in Hollywood," *Fortune*, August, 19, 1996.

25. Geraldine Fabrikant, "Despite the Risks, News Corp. Pursues an Aggressive Expansion," *New York Times*, July 29, 1996, p. D1.

26. John Lafayette, "News Corp., TCI in Deal to Buy Sports," *Electronic Media*, November 6, 1995.

27. See Johnnie L. Roberts, "Rupert's Team," *Newsweek*, July 7, 1997; "News Corp. Will Acquire Liberty Media's Stake in Sports-TV Venture," *Dow Jones Business News*, April 6, 1999.

28. The lack of segment data and the complexity of the multiple transactions that resulted in the shape of the current Fox Sports Net make it impossible to calculate return on investment with precision. For instance, the 2006 DirecTV transaction with Malone entailed Murdoch's returning three of the regional networks to Liberty in order to equalize that transaction. The structure of these industries and these deals—along with the failure of subsequent well-capitalized attempted market entrants like Time Warner with its vast cable operations and *Sports Illustrated* brands—suggests that News's shareholders did very well.

29. It could be argued that another positive spillover effect of the Fox network is that it could be leveraged to allow the sports network to more effectively acquire local sports rights. We believe that any benefit from this was more than counterbalanced by the dramatic price increases all sports rights have since experienced by virtue of the decision to launch the 1993 bidding war for NFL rights.

30. The first book to press is Michael Wolff, *The Man Who Owns the News: Inside the Secret World of Rupert Murdoch* (New York: Broadway Books, 2008), which will apparently be followed shortly by one from *Journal* reporter Sarah Ellison. See Keith Kelly, "Dueling Journal-ists," *New York Post*, December 12, 2007.

31. Michael Wolff claims that all the senior executives at News were well aware that the company was paying far more than Dow Jones was worth and anticipated that their share price would plunge on the announcement. Wolff attributes their lack of opposition to the deal nonetheless to "the extrabusiness-like characteristics of News Corp. itself." Argues Wolff: "In a world in which corporations have long been conditioned to respond to shareholders' short-term needs, News Corp. has always been more interested in expanding its power than in getting a high return on capital. It isn't about what shareholders want; it's about what Murdoch wants." *The Man Who Owns the News*, p. 289. If this observation is true, it makes the fact that News still manages generally to be the best performer among conglomerate media stocks all the more extraordinary.

32. Johnnie L. Roberts, "Murdoch, Ink.," *Newsweek*, April 28, 2008.

33. Fionnula Halligan and Sheel Kohli, "Murdoch Waves No Magic Wand to Transform Star Losses," *South China Morning Post*, October 11, 1995.

34. Nat Worden, "Rupert Murdoch: WSJ Online Subscription Revenue to Increase," Dow Jones Newswires, September 17, 2008.

Epilogue: The Future of Media

1. See, e.g., Danny Schechter, *The Death of Media: And the Fight to Save Democracy* (New York: Melville House, 2005).

2. Bob Dart, "Media Occupies Half of Americans' Lives, Data Book Shows," Cox News Service, December 15, 2006.

3. Sallie Hofmeister, "Amid a Plethora of Parodies, MySpace Has Become His," *Los Angeles Times,* July 21, 2005.

4. "Rupert wants to rule the world, and he seems to be doing it," according to fellow mogul Sumner Redstone. Geraldine Fabrikant, "Despite the Risks, News Corp. Pursues an Aggressive Expansion," *New York Times,* July 29, 1996, p. D1.

5. Sakthi Prasad, "Redstone Agrees Partial Sale of Theatre Chain," Reuters, December 4, 2008.

6. Even cooperating on writing stories is now on the table. Richard Perez-Peña, "Washington Post and Baltimore Sun Will Share News Content," *New York Times,* December 23, 2008, p. B2.

7. Sanford Bernstein's cable and satellite analyst Craig Moffett quoted in Mike Farrell, "Disconnect on Cost: Economics of FiOS Rollout Make Little Sense for Verizon," *Multichannel News,* January 21, 2008.

8. CNET's inconsistent financial performance in recent times led activist share-holders to launch a proxy battle for board seats and press for a prompt transaction. See Alasdair Barr, "Jana Wins Big as CBS Agrees to Buy CNET for 45% Premium," Dow Jones News Service, May 15, 2008; Andrew Ross Sorkin, "A Loophole Lets a Foot in the Door," *New York Times,* January 15, 2008.

9. Quoted in Merissa Marr and Kevin J. Delaney, "CBS to Acquire CNET for $1.8 Billion—Deal Is Bid to Diversify from TV and Radio and Expand on the Web," *Wall Street Journal,* May 16, 2008, p. B7.

Postscript

1. Transcript of August 31, 2009, Disney analyst call.

2. Brooks Barnes, *New York Times,* April 9, 2010, p. BU1

3. Spencer Wang et al., Credit Suisse Equity Research, November 12, 2009.

4. Michael Corkery, *WSJ Deal Journal,* August 31, 2009.

5. Mike Farrell, *Multichannel News,* November 9, 2009, p. 5.

6. Craig Moffett et al., *Web Video: Friend or Foe . . . And to Whom,* Bernstein Research, October 7, 2009.

7. Ibid., p. 47.

Index